MW00834321

Jesus the Jew in Christian Memory

Jesus the Jew is the primary signifier of Christianity's indebtedness to Judaism. This connection is both historical and ongoing. In this book, Barbara Meyer shows how Christian memory, as largely intertwined with Jewish memory, provides a framework to examine the theological dimensions of Historical Jesus research. She explores the topics that are central to the Jewishness of Jesus, such as the Christian relationship to law and otherness as a Christological category. Through the lenses of the otherness of the Jewish Jesus for contemporary Christians, she discusses such topics as circumcision, natality, vulnerability, and suffering in dialogue with thinkers seldom drawn into Jewish–Christian discourse, notably Hannah Arendt, Julia Kristeva, Martha Nussbaum, and Adi Ophir. Meyer demonstrates how the memory of Jesus' Jewishness is a key to reconfiguring contemporary challenges to Christian thought, such as particularity and otherness, law and ethics after the Shoah, human responsibility, and divine vulnerability.

Barbara U. Meyer is Associate Professor of Religious Studies at Tel Aviv University. She is the author of *Christology in the Shadow of the Shoah: In the Light of Israel* and numerous articles on contemporary interreligious dynamics and changing Christian approaches to law.

Jesus the Jew in Christian Memory

Theological and Philosophical Explorations

BARBARA U. MEYER

Tel Aviv University

 CAMBRIDGE
UNIVERSITY PRESS

CAMBRIDGE
UNIVERSITY PRESS

University Printing House, Cambridge CB2 8BS, United Kingdom

One Liberty Plaza, 20th Floor, New York, NY 10006, USA

477 Williamstown Road, Port Melbourne, VIC 3207, Australia

314–321, 3rd Floor, Plot 3, Splendor Forum, Jasola District Centre,
New Delhi – 110025, India

79 Anson Road, #06–04/06, Singapore 079906

Cambridge University Press is part of the University of Cambridge.

It furthers the University's mission by disseminating knowledge in the pursuit of
education, learning, and research at the highest international levels of excellence.

www.cambridge.org
Information on this title: www.cambridge.org/9781108498890
DOI: 10.1017/9781108689755

First published 2020

Printed in the United Kingdom by TJ International, Padstow Cornwall

A catalogue record for this publication is available from the British Library.

Library of Congress Cataloging-in-Publication Data
NAMES: Meyer, Barbara U., 1968– author.
TITLE: Jesus the Jew Christian memory : theological and philosophical explorations /
Barbara Meyer, Tel Aviv University.
DESCRIPTION: Cambridge, United Kingdom ; New York, NY, USA :
Cambridge University Press, 2019. | Includes bibliographical references.
IDENTIFIERS: LCCN 2019035711 (print) | LCCN 2019035712 (ebook) |
ISBN 9781108498890 (hardback) | ISBN 9781108712835 (paperback) |
ISBN 9781108689755 (epub)
SUBJECTS: LCSH: Jesus Christ–Jewishness. | Christianity and other religions–Judaism. |
Judaism–Relations–Judaism.
CLASSIFICATION: LCC BT590.J8 M49 2019 (print) | LCC BT590.J8 (ebook) |
DDC 232.9/06–dc23
LC record available at https://lccn.loc.gov/2019035711
LC ebook record available at https://lccn.loc.gov/2019035712

ISBN 978-1-108-49889-0 Hardback

For Jon

Contents

Acknowledgments

As an anti-missionary Christian theologian at an Israeli university, I typically do not initiate conversations about Jesus with my colleagues. But we do talk about topics important to Christology, such as difference, uniqueness and belonging, the migration of knowledge, translation, how to avoid essentialism, or how to affirm cultural continuity. For this atmosphere of openness and methodological critique, I thank my colleagues in Interreligious Studies, first and foremost Menachem Fisch, who initiated and built CRIS (The Center for Religious and Interreligious Studies at Tel Aviv University), as well as Adam Afterman, Yossi Schwartz, Lena Salayme, and Ahmad Ighbariyye. Our seminars in Cambridge, together with Simon Goldhill and Christian Wiese, also gave me opportunities to speak with David Ford, whose theological work I greatly admire. Menachem Fisch's confident advice and appreciative mentorship have been extraordinary – blessed is the academic who has such a senior colleague to consult with.

Teaching Christian Thought in a Religious Studies program in a predominantly Jewish context sharpens the question of what precisely can be called Christian. I thank my colleagues of our small but intellectually intriguing Religious Studies program: Hami Verbin, Ron Margolin, Gidi Bohak, Uriya Shavit, and especially Shlomo Biderman, who founded the program and welcomed me there as a theologian. Tel Aviv University has become my academic base, and I thank many colleagues from other departments for making me feel at home here, especially Galia Patt-Shamir, Arye Edrei, Dalit Rom-Shiloni, Ishai Rosen-Zvi, Hagi Kenaan, Zohar Shavit, Aviad Kleinberg, Scott Ury, Yifat Monnickendam, Rivka

Feldhay, Jose Brunner, Eyal Zisser, our previous, and Leo Corry, our current dean.

While I have only recently begun using the word "Christology" in the titles of my seminars, my teaching about Jesus in Israeli academia goes back a long time, beginning at the Hebrew Union College in Jerusalem and then, for many years, at the Interdisciplinary Center Herzliya (IDC). These teaching experiences, and the many fresh insights offered by both rabbinical and secular Israeli students there, have helped shape my theory of Jesus the Jew in Jewish memory. I thank Yehoyada Amir, who established "Introduction to Christianity" as a mandatory course for all rabbinical students at Hebrew Union College. And I thank my colleagues from IDC for their ongoing support and friendship, especially Lior Barshack, Uriel Procaccia, Marina Arbiv, and Haya and Yoram Shachar. I would also like to thank Uri Reichman and Amnon Rubinstein for their outstanding support in the early stages of my career.

I am grateful for an international circle of scholars serious about the Christological questions arising from the new Jewish-Christian encounter. We have convened in Rome, Istanbul, Chicago, and San Antonio, and I hope we will continue this and further conversations. Thanks to Tamara Eshkenazi, Hans Hermann Henrix, Jasper Svartvik, Phil Cunningham, Norbert Hofmann, John Pawlikowski, Joseph Sievers, Michael McGarry, Peter Pettit, and especially Mary Boys for her inspiring thoughts, and also for making me aware of Elisabeth Johnson's work. I thank Ruth Langer for her remarkable scholarly guidance and Katharina von Kellenbach for her amazing cross-cultural insights. Many thanks to Ulrike Link-Wieczorek, Martin Hailer, Manfred Oeming, Randall Zachman, Ursula Rudnick, Wolfgang Raupach Rudnick, Christian Staffa, and Gabi Zander for their support and sharing of theological questions.

As for my local interreligious community, I am indebted to my friends from the Jerusalem Rainbow club who have discussed various memories of Jesus the Jew with me. This Jerusalem study group is engaged in a lifelong conversation among Jewish and Christian academics. I especially thank Zev Harvey for his interest in my work, for our many conversations, and for sharing his wide erudition; Debbie Weissman, whose decisive religious self-criticism feels close in spirit; my teacher Michael Krupp, the Christian expert for Mishna manuscripts, who first introduced me to Honi the Circle-Drawer as a Talmud student at Hebrew University; as well as Raphi Jospe, Yehuda Gellman, Eugene Korn, David Neuhaus, Jamal Khader, and all the other members whose commitment I greatly value. I am grateful to Menachem Lorberbaum, Moshe Halbertal, Steven

Kepnes, and Yael Fisch for discussing theological aspects of Halakhah with me, and I am inspired by Hanoch Ben-Pazi's, Avraham Elkayam's, and Roberto Arbiv's true love for religious otherness. The ups and downs of writing this book were shared by my friends Astrid, Naama, Sheli, Ethan, and Smadar – so glad you are always there! Three summers of intense writing and a sabbatical were intellectually elevated by friends at Binghamton University: Allan Arkush, Randy Friedman, Gina Glasman, Jacqueline and Isaac Karp, Orly and Shalom Shoer, Steven Englund, and especially Bat-Ami Bar On who invited me to spend a semester at the Institute of the Advanced Studies in the Humanities (IASH).

My friend Astrid Schmetterling has broadened my horizon with her expertise in intercultural memory. I thank Adam Sutcliffe for reading an early version of the book and sharing important suggestions on how to improve its readability, and I thank the anonymous readers of the manuscript for their engaged comments, one of which I even quoted!

I thank my Cambridge editor Beatrice Rehl for her interest in my book and her immediate understanding of its unusual interdisciplinary crossroads. And I thank everyone involved in the production of this book, especially Eilidh Burrett. Heartfelt thanks go to Juan José Garcia for allowing me to use the artwork "sham/shem" by Moshe Gershuni, his late life partner, as the cover image of this book. I thank Amitai Mendelsohn, the curator of Israeli Art at the Israel Museum, and Rahel Laufer for helping to make this happen.

I thank all my family: my mother Ute Meyer; my father Christian Meyer, who helped with proofreading the index; and especially my aunt and Godmother Edelgard Meyer who refers to Levinas, Marquardt, van Buren, Alice Eckardt, and Adi Ophir as "old friends" – dear Edelgard, many new friends too to meet in this book! Dietrich Ritschl, my dear *Doktorvater*, passed away this spring. In this book, his spirit is very much present.

Discussing my thoughts on Christological dogma with the historian Jon Karp, who is the love of my life, is probably as good as it gets. Jon Karp has edited this book. He has taken out all the colons and exclamation marks: at least, all the ones he could catch! Jon: I love you!

While I was writing this book, our daughter Julie Miriam grew up to be the most loving and creative second grader, consoling her mother who can hardly fold an envelope, let alone a paper plane: "Never mind, you are creative in your writing!"

Introduction

The Jewishness of Jesus as a Theological Challenge

What is theologically important about Jesus being a Jew? This book is about the theological implications of Jesus' Jewish identity as well as philosophical questions raised by the ongoing presence of Jewishness within Christian ethical and dogmatic discourse. Unlike many of the historical accounts of Jesus the Jew, which focus on Jesus' Judean context, this book is an inquiry into the meaning and theological consequences of Jesus' Jewish belonging.[1] Specifically, this study explores the theological and philosophical questions raised by his Jewishness as understood in terms of memory. Memory is not usually included among the core theological categories. But precisely with the intersection of revelation and history in the human life of Jesus, memory becomes a helpful term for the theological assessment of the historical Jesus. The Jewishness of Jesus is well described as a memory precisely because it is a historical fact that has never been completely forgotten but has often been neglected or suppressed in Christian tradition and self-understanding.

So why should the historical fact of Jesus' Jewishness be any more important than the other basic biographical facts of him being a man, of Galilean upbringing, with Mediterranean culture, and a carpenter by trade? I intend to show that Jesus' being a Jew is not just a historical detail informing Christology, but a significant factor for Christian theology as such. Both terms, "theology" and "Christology," will be used respectively for discourse and questions about God and Christ rather than

---

[1] I deliberately use the word "belonging" instead of "origin" so as to refer not just to the past. My wording seeks to allow inquiry into various features, memories, narratives, and practices that express and detail how a person belongs to a certain group or tradition.

as systems of answers. Thus, theology and Christology provide frameworks for the discussion of teachings about God and Christ. Theology is
not a discipline limited to Christianity, but a discipline shared with
thinkers of Islam and Judaism. David Ford's deliberately expansive definition of theology as "thinking about questions raised by and about
the religions" stakes out a wide field.[2] I add to this broad theological
discourse philosophical horizons as well, since I will show that Jesus'
being Jewish bears not just historical but also philosophical – as well as
interreligious – meaning.

While Jesus the Jew is at the center of my inquiry, I assume that the
Jewishness of Jesus does not in itself solve theological problems nor does
it automatically lead to a new closeness between Christianity and Judaism. Since the second half of the twentieth century, Christians throughout
the world have proclaimed and confessed Jesus' Jewishness in numerous
Church declarations.[3] Even when the statement "Jesus was a Jew" is
formulated in the past tense, it is usually not intended as a historical
statement but as a Church confession and a theological pronouncement,
although this has not always been made explicit. The Jewishness of Jesus
is indeed not a new discovery and does not at all reflect a change in
Christian belief. This is why I find "memory" a helpful category to
explain the Christian awareness of Jesus' Jewishness. This memory, this
knowledge, has been present but dormant throughout Church history,
like a well-hidden treasure, though without a conscious understanding of
its true worth. Christians have always known that Jesus was a Jew. The
fact was never explicitly denied (the exception being the so-called Aryan
Christianity of Walter Grundmann and other Nazis),[4] but was often
suppressed, neglected, and overlooked. Correspondingly, the intention
to remember Jesus' Jewishness actively and explicitly is usually connected
to repairing Jewish–Christian relations. Since the end of World War II,
theologians and engaged lay people have been reminding others and

---

[2] David F. Ford, *Theology: A Very Short Introduction*, second edition (Oxford: Oxford
University Press, 2013).
[3] For an overview, see the website of the International Council of Christians and Jews
(ICCJ): www.jcrelations.net/Statements.65.0.html.
[4] The Nazi Walter Grundmann came to the conclusion that Jesus was not a Jew but an
"Aryan." This perspective was not based on scholarly research but on the ideology of
German National Socialism. It should be noted that this view is not within the spectrum of
the Christian creed. Walter Grundmann, *Jesus der Galiläer und das Judentum* (Leipzig:
Georg Wigand, 1940). See also Susannah Heschel, *The Aryan Jesus: Christian
Theologians and the Bible* (Princeton, NJ: Princeton University Press, 2008).

themselves of Jesus' Jewishness in order to bring Judaism and Christianity into closer communication with one another. At the same time, today closeness is no longer an unquestioned priority in the Jewish–Christian conversation; rather, the current prevailing objective in interreligious relations may be best described as respect for difference.[5]

Historically, the Jewishness of Jesus has been pointed out in order to counteract antisemitism, and to this day there remains a prevailing expectation that the consciousness of his Jewish belonging would have an immediate effect on elevating Christian respect for Judaism. But it is important to recognize that an emphasis on Jesus' Jewishness does not automatically preclude a Christian attitude of spiritual superiority vis-a-vis Judaism. In fact, a missionary approach toward Jews can even emphasize and exploit Jesus' Jewishness, the classical example of which is Luther's early non-antisemitic writing *"That Jesus Christ was born a Jew."*[6] Supersessionism, that is, thought patterns that suggest or imply that Christianity has superseded Judaism, is not necessarily diminished by means of the general notion of Jesus' Jewishness.

Still, I am convinced that the traces and implications of Jesus being a Jew can help us discover a Christianity that is not based on a de-evaluation of Judaism. More than that, I hope to show how an in-depth study of Jesus being a "non-Christian" opens the Christian mind to deeper insights into Christian belief and a closer awareness of its original, or, perhaps, its potential truths. In the early stages of post-Shoah Jewish-Christian dialogue, emphasizing Jesus' Jewish identity may have had the flavor of reductionist Christology, that is, of reducing the notion of Christ's divinity. Instead, I seek here to examine the significance of Jesus Christ being Jewish in terms of the complexity of dogmatic discourse. For example, I ask whether and how Jesus's Jewishness is reflected in twentieth-century interpretations of the early church creeds.

The acclamation of Jesus' Jewishness has been central to most of the Church declarations on the revised Christian approach to Judaism promulgated at least since the late 1960s. But that the Jewish Jesus entails an affirmation of today's Judaism has mainly been implied rather than

---

[5] Jonathan Sacks, *The Dignity of Difference: How to Avoid the Clash of Civilizations* (New York: Continuum, 2002).

[6] Martin Luther, "Daß Jesus Christus ein geborner Jude sei (1523)" in *D. Martin Luthers Werke: Kritische Gesamtausgabe* (Weimarer Ausgabe) vol 11, 314–336. See also the recent critical commentary of Matthias Morgenstern, *Dass Jesus Christus ein geborener Jude sei: und andere Judenschriften. Bearbeitet und kommentiert von Matthias Morgenstern* (Berlin: Berlin University Press, 2019).

explained in recent Christian theology. Only a few systematic theologians have thus far built their Christologies on affirming *both* Jesus' Jewishness *and* present-day Judaism. The Anglican-rooted Paul van Buren is the most important American theologian to be mentioned in this regard; he pioneered the topic with a Christology embedded in a three-volume systematic theology.[7] In Europe, the Lutheran-based German theologian Friedrich Wilhelm Marquardt produced a Christology of Jesus the Jew that is at the heart of a comprehensive theology, a seven-volume dogmatics.[8] More recently, Catholic theologians have taken the lead in the theological exploration of Jesus' Jewishness, among them Mary Boys, Philipp Cunningham, and Hans Hermann Henrix.[9] Karl Barth has pointed out that the historical truth of Jesus being a Jew is not accidental but necessary.[10] Although Jesus' being a Jew was not explicitly regarded as a necessary truth until the mid-twentieth century, all Christian theologies that are based on the ecumenical creeds and scripture are bound to this verity.

I intend to look at the encounter of history and reason embedded in the Jewishness of Jesus Christ. I will explore the theological meaning of his Jewishness in rites of passage to which little attention has been paid, such as birth and circumcision. The interpretations of his death and their shadowing legacy for Jewish–Christian relations have been comprehensively analyzed by Mary Boys.[11] Consonant with the title of her major study, *Redeeming Our Sacred Story*, Boys has done serious work on the Christian narrative in greatest need of redemption. Yet, beyond Luther's reminder that Jesus was born a Jew and the more recent critical emphasis that he also died a Jew, my focus is rather on his living as a Jew. This leads

---

[7] Paul M. van Buren, *A Theology of the Jewish-Christian Reality: Part I: Discerning the Way* (1980), *Part II: A Christian Theology of the People Israel* (1983), *Part III: Christ in Context* (1988) (San Francisco: Harper&Row).

[8] Friedrich-Wilhelm Marquardt, *Von Elend und Heimsuchung der Theologie: Prolegomena zur Dogmatik*, 1988; second revised and expanded edition (1992); *Das christliche Bekenntnis zu Jesus, dem Juden: Eine Christologie* (1990 and 1991). *Was dürfen wir hoffen, wenn wir hoffen dürften? Eine Eschatologie* (1993, 1994, and 1996). *Eia, wärn wir da – eine theologische Utopie* (1997) (Munich: Kaiser).

[9] Philip A. Cunningham, Joseph Sievers, Mary C. Boys, Hans Hermann Henrix, and Jesper Svartvik, eds., *Christ Jesus and the Jewish People Today: New Explorations of Theological Interrelationships* (Grand Rapids, MI; Cambridge: William B. Eerdmans, 2011).

[10] Karl Barth, *Dogmatics in Outline* (New York: Harper & Row, 1959), 76.

[11] Mary C. Boys, *Redeeming Our Sacred Story: The Death of Jesus and Relations between Jews and Christians* (Mahwah, NJ: Paulist Press, 2013).

to the historical question of what Jewish life meant in the Second Temple period, a question that has garnered much attention in recent years. Even more difficult is the inquiry into first-century Torah observance and discussions of Jewish law before their canonization, beginning only at the end of the second century.

The Jewishness of Jesus has so far been mainly an issue to look back to: a topic for historical investigation and a question of the Church's memory. But Christology is not just an intellectual discipline reflecting on the past. Rather, it is an inquiry into Jesus as the Christ in present understandings and interpretations. Jesus was a Jew, and it is correct for Christians to say that Jesus Christ is Jewish and will always remain Jewish. Yet historical Jesus research and Christology remain at odds. My intention here is not to harmonize them artificially but rather to show how historical reference to early church dogmatic discourse can reveal their fundamental connectedness. The historical fact of Jesus' life became part of the Christian creed – first and foremost in Nicaea (325) and in a highly sophisticated way again in Chalcedon (454). Thus, drawing on historical research to advance dogmatic discourse should not be mistaken for reductionist theology. In late twentieth-century theologies committed to a revised Christian approach to Judaism, Jesus' Jewishness has often been understood as a critique of dogma. In this book, I argue for the Jewishness of Jesus as a key corrective of Christology, as a means of conversing with historical research and underscoring the critical capacities of the early Church's dogmatic discourse.

Christologies developed in the context of the Jewish–Christian dialogue in the 1980s show an inverse relationship between the humanity and the Jewishness of Jesus Christ. Instead of perceiving his humanity as the more inclusive category, as was traditionally the case, the Lutheran theologian Friedrich-Wilhelm Marquardt began to understand his true humanity precisely as true Jewishness: "The true Human is the true Jew."[12] While it has been common until recently to discuss Jesus' Jewishness as a topic connected mainly to his humanity, since the 1990s we have also seen attempts to relate Jewishness to Christ's divinity. Paul van Buren deliberately writes about "Christ in his Jewish context" instead of the

---

[12] Friedrich-Wilhelm Marquardt, *Das christliche Bekenntnis zu Jesus, dem Juden: Eine Christologie I* (Munich: Kaiser, 1990), 138f. Compare Marquardt here with the famous 1781 statement by the champion of Jewish civic emancipation Christian Wilhelm von Dohm, that "the Jew is more man than Jew." See Paul Mendes-Flohr and Jehuda Reinharz, eds., *The Jew in the Modern World: A Documentary History*, third edition (Oxford: Oxford University Press, 2011), 28.

more common "the Jew Jesus."[13] But it is only from the start of the twenty-first century that we find explicit discussion of how Jesus' Jewishness is expressed in terms of his divinity. While the dogmatic Church tradition has been typically regarded by critics as silencing Jesus' Jewish belonging, the Catholic theologian Hans Hermann Henrix has recently pointed to the traces of Jesus' Jewishness in the ecumenical creed of Chalcedon.[14] The theological interest in Jesus the Jew is ecumenical also in the contemporary use of the term; that is to say, Catholic, Anglican, Lutheran, and other Protestant theologians alike contemplate his Jewishness as key to a self-critical Christology. I would even propose the thesis that the re-discovery of Jesus' Jewishness constitutes the greatest ecumenical commonality of late twentieth-century Christology.[15] The American Methodist Roy Eckardt, the German Protestant Friedrich-Wilhelm Marquardt, the American Anglican Paul van Buren, the Dutch Reform Simon Schoon, the American Catholic John Pawlikowski, and the German Catholic Hans Hermann Henrix – all of these theologians share an emphasis on the Jewishness of Jesus in their Christological works.[16] There is also no difference in the main line of argumentation: for all of them, the Jewishness of Jesus is not a new discovery, due to interreligious encounter or reconciliation, but a fundamental historical and religious truth.

Christian and Jewish scholars alike have regarded the Jewishness of Jesus as a link between Judaism and Christianity. Jewish scholars have typically stated that the "belief in Jesus" divides Jews and Christians. Both statements belong to the early phase of Jewish–Christian dialogue, when the Christian side's foremost aspiration was to establish a sense of closeness to Jews and Judaism. But since the 1990s, some Christian scholars have begun to value difference as a desirable component of the interreligious situation. This is due largely to the influence of the great French Jewish philosopher Emmanuel Levinas, who created a language for an

---

[13] Paul van Buren, *Christ in Context.*

[14] Hans Hermann Henrix, "The Son of God Became Human as a Jew: Implications of the Jewishness of Jesus for Christology," in Philip A. Cunningham, Joseph Sievers, Mary C. Boys, Hans Hermann Henrix, and Jesper Svartvik, eds., *Christ Jesus and the Jewish People Today: New Explorations of Theological Interrelationships* (Grand Rapids, MI and Cambridge: William B. Eerdmans Publishing Company, 2011), 114–143.

[15] Karl Barth famously described Jewish–Christian relations as the "great ecumenical question" of the twentieth century. See Michael Weinrich, *Karl Barth. Leben-Werk-Wirkung* (Göttingen: Vandenhoeck & Ruprecht 2019), 278.

[16] See for example A. Roy Eckardt, *Reclaiming the Jesus of History. Christology Today* (Minneapolis, MN: Fortress Press, 1992) and John T. Pawlikowski, *Christ in the Light of the Jewish-Christian Dialogue* (New York: Paulist Press, 1982).

ethics of otherness.[17] While the Jewish tradition carries a deep knowledge of difference as a generally positive value, Christian theologians have usually seen commonalities as key to interfaith understanding. Also here we can see how both Protestant and Catholic theologians have similarly begun using the language of otherness that was made famous by Levinas.[18] The Talmud scholar Daniel Boyarin has gone so far as to identify the notion of difference with Judaism and the striving for closeness with Christianity.[19] Yet this view of Boyarin depicts the traditional missionary attitude as essentially Christian but does not take into account the recent Catholic withdrawal from missionary activity toward Jews since the Second Vatican Council. Indeed, Boyarin and others have overlooked the fact that "difference" is a major component at the very heart of the Christian faith. To Christians of Gentile descent, Jesus is and remains different. This interruption of identification does not need to estrange Christians from the Jesus they feel committed to. Rather, this experience of difference needs to be further explored interreligiously – both in its theological and spiritual dimensions.

Although the acclamation that Jesus was a Jew is central to most of the recent Church declarations that aim to revise the Christian approach to Judaism, his Jewishness has been more declared than elaborated on or explained. A lack of in-depth reflection on Jewish identity is also characteristic of many academic presentations of these shifts in interpreting Christian text traditions and doctrine. Even in contemporary Christologies, the Jewish context of Jesus has been dealt with more in a descriptive than a discursive, analytical, and constructive manner. What has usually been missing is an effort to show how the Jewishness of Jesus interacts with Christian dogmatic discourse. Only a very few systematic theologians, such as Paul van Buren, Roy Eckardt, and Friedrich-Wilhelm Marquardt, have built their Christologies on affirming Jesus' Jewishness along with the ongoing legitimacy and vitality of Judaism. At first sight,

[17] Among his many books, see especially Emmanuel Levinas, *Otherwise than Being or Beyond Essence* (Pittsburgh: Duquesne University Press, 1998).

[18] Phil Cunningham describes the learning within Jewish–Christian encounters as the "sacrament of otherness"; compare Philipp A. Cunningham, "Celebrating Judaism as a 'Sacrament od Every Otherness'," in Kristen Colberg and Robert Krieg, eds., *The Theology of Cardinal Walter Kasper: Speaking Truth in Love* (St. Johns, MN: Liturgical Press, 2014), 223–240. Friedrich-Wilhelm Marquardt has described God as protector of otherness. See Friedrich-Wilhelm Marquardt, *Was dürfen wir hoffen, wenn wir hoffen dürften? Eine Eschatologie*, 1993, 191ff.

[19] Daniel Boyarin, *A Radical Jew: Paul and the Politics of Identity* (Berkeley: University of California Press, 1994), 232–236.

the notion of Jesus' Jewishness seems primarily to be an issue of history and memory. Christology, though, prioritizes the present, as the Christian faith refers to an ongoing connectedness of Christ with the world. Moreover, post-Shoah theologies present not the past but the future as the main field of Christian reinterpretation. Along these lines, several of this book's chapters refer specifically to the constitutive Christological temporal modes of Jesus's Jewishness, past, present, and future. Another chapter, "Between Jesus, the Jew and the Other," opens up an interreligious perspective, one which entails looking for Jesus "between the times and the intellectual spaces." Here I listen not only to Jewish but also to Muslim interlocutors and suggest taking interreligious discourse seriously as a mode of theological introspection.

I begin my study by outlining a Christian theory of memory that serves as an intellectual framework to explore the historical and theological crossing of Jesus' Jewishness. Jesus the Jew is a key example of the interreligious quality of Christian memory. I develop my concept of Christian memory in conversation with Yosef Yerushalmi's and Avishai Margalit's respective theories of Jewish memory and historiography, their discussions of the imperative to remember and the concept of communities of memory. I will show that Christian memory – in the broad sense of comprising not just basic narratives but also legal, social, and theological reflections of those stories – is, to a large extent, textually shared with Jews. The discipline of memory will provide a framework to look at different ways of remembering and transmitting the same texts. Memory in a narrower sense will serve as the prism for an intellectual discourse highlighting, enacting, reviving, and criticizing stories and thought traditions in the present. In the second chapter, I explore the theological implications of the more recent historical research on the Jewish Jesus. In the Historical Jesus research of the last few decades, two new phenomena have come to the fore: first, the cooperation between Jewish and Christian historians and New Testament scholars in academic research, and second, the so-called Third Quest for the Historical Jesus, emphasizing "context" and focusing on Jesus's integration into Second Temple Judaism. Historical research has come a long way since World War II; interpreting Jesus within his Judaic context has now become mainstream in academia.[20] Building on this research I examine the specifically

---

[20] The most comprehensive work has been done by Wolfgang Stegemann, who combines historical accuracy with theological reflection. Wolfgang Stegemann, *Jesus und seine Zeit* (Stuttgart: Kohlhammer, 2010).

theological implications of Jesus' observance of contemporaneous Jewish law. I develop a theory that presents Jesus' Jewishness in opposition to Docetism (the heresy that Jesus was not a real human being) as well as to Marcionism (the proposition of a previously unknown God – rather than the God of Israel – having sent Jesus). I thus show Jesus's Jewishness as constitutive of key early church dogmatic decisions.

While this assessment of the theological implications of Jesus as a Second Temple Jew principally reflects historical research, the third chapter opens a conversation with an entirely different genre of intellectual literature. I discuss Jesus' present-day Jewishness in conversation with the African American theologian James Cone's remarkable formulation that while Jesus *was* Jewish, he *is* black.[21] It is not the tension but rather the connection between Jewish and black identity that catches my attention here. In tandem with the notion of a Jewish/black Jesus, I also look at understandings of Jesus the Jew among Palestinian Christians. What does it mean for Palestinian Christians to confront the Judaic roots of the Christian faith amid day-to-day political struggle? This juxtaposition, at the same time, begs the question of ancient and modern Jewish continuity. Hence, my subsequent exploration of the allusive category "Jewishness" leads to a conversation with Jewish philosophers about aspects of Jewishness that connect the first with the twenty-first century. I agree with contemporary Jewish scholars that there is no simply defined and eternal "essence of Judaism," but I dare to sketch out what I regard as Judaism's continuous "textual frame of reference." I argue that characteristics of Torah and prophetic texts, such as collective self-criticism embedded in narrative and an ethics considerate of the socially disadvantaged, are constitutive for Jesus' as well as today's Judaism. It is more the polyphony than the actual content of these texts that I regard as a consistently shaping feature of Jewish hermeneutics.

After discussing the ongoing relevance of Jesus' Jewishness for Christological languages that typically prioritize the present tense, in the fourth chapter I look toward the future. Interestingly, the future has emerged as the main context for post-Shoah thought – manifest, for example, in the title of a major conference project of the end of the twentieth century, "Remembering for the Future." Rosemary Radford Ruether has powerfully criticized Christianity's tendency toward "realized eschatology," the idea that the promised future of reconciliation has already been

---

[21] James Cone, *God of the Oppressed* (Maryknoll, NY: Orbis Books, 1975), 123.

accomplished with Christ. Responding to the post-Shoah philosopher Emil Fackenheim's question "Has Good Friday overwhelmed Easter?," I focus here on what might be called the future of the human spark after the Shoah, engaging in the process with the writings of both Primo Levi and Hannah Arendt. Fackenheim's questions to Christian theologians and Ruether's Christian self-criticism converge in the task of delaying or questioning the Christian tradition's idea of Christ's past victory over "sin." What we see instead is that Christian theologians have begun to emphasize the mode of promise and make its fulfillment conditional on human ethical responsibility. Fackenheim's painstaking questions about the physical vulnerability of Jesus as being fully human remain a challenge to a contemporary Christological thinking committed to post-Shoah responsibility as well as to dogmatic discourse. In this vein, I examine the meaning of Jewishness for a Two-Natures Christology in discussion with the latest publication on this question by the theologian Kayko Driedger Hesslein, who, like me, considers Jewishness as meaningful regarding Christ's divinity as well as his humanity.

Both notions of "humanity" and "divinity" are challenged by thinking of Jesus' suffering as Jewish suffering. Despite a strong tradition of connecting positively the notions of suffering and salvation, remembering the Jewishness of Jesus effectively challenges Christian talk of agony and pain. I discuss this central Christian topic in the fifth chapter in conversation with some contemporary Israeli philosophical (Adi Ophir) and radically revised Christian (Alice Eckardt and Johann Baptist Metz) approaches. Since Levinas' powerful essay "Useless Suffering" (1982), philosophers have been rethinking the distinction between unavoidable suffering and the forms of pain and misery that can actually be reduced or prevented. Christian theologians have only just begun to revise understandings of suffering that have long been paralyzed by fixed Christological thought traditions. When Jesus' suffering is discussed in connection with other Jews' suffering, as represented for instance by Paul van Buren, traditional Christian thought is most seriously challenged. I show how the Israeli philosopher Adi Ophir's moral philosophy provides a language for Christians to move from explaining ("Christsplaining") suffering to instead prioritizing the search for resisting human-caused suffering. Levinas' major statement of explaining the Other's pain as source of all immorality leads to my in-depth reflection on the language of otherness for contemporary Christological thinking.

In the sixth and final chapter I trace the roots and the changing meaning of the term "otherness" within twentieth-century philosophical and theological thought and discuss its appropriateness for Christology. The Jewishness of Jesus and his otherness in Christian perspective meet in Jesus' observance of Torah. This was initially reflected in the writings of Paul, which are currently being re-interpreted and discussed under the signature of "new perspectives."[22] I contribute to this contemporary hermeneutical discourse by asking what Paul's Jewishness actually means for the question of the Torah–Christ connection. Unexpectedly, it was precisely the Torah-committed Jesus that was presented to Christians in the document "A Common Word" published in 2007 by the Jordanian Institute for Islamic Thought. Following David Ford, who was the first systematic theologian to address this interfaith document within the framework of Christian theology, I explore its challenge to Christological reflections on Jesus.[23]

I have chosen the division into history, past, present, a future because it helps to shed light on some specific Christological questions concerning Jesus the Jew. Of course, the subject matter's affiliation is most obvious with regard to memory. Hundreds of books have been written about the "Historical Jesus" and quite a few about Jesus the Jew in history. Christologies focusing on Jesus the Jew that use the present tense are fewer, while post-Shoah theologies that challenge the notion that sin has been overcome in principle, and that therefore turn toward the future, are fewer still. Throughout this book, I explore the philosophical dimensions of the difference that still remains between the Jewish Jesus and his contemporary Christian followers. Far from Daniel Boyarin's identification of Christianity with a striving for sameness (in contrast to his identification of Judaism with difference), my key argument is that the Jewishness of Jesus Christ engenders an otherness that opens up new intellectual, spiritual, and ethical horizons for the non-Jewish Christian.

Finally, inspired by the surprisingly Jewish Jesus presented in the recent Muslim document "A Common Word" and by the philosopher Martha Nussbaum's notion of fragility, I foster a new Christian approach to "interreligious theory." I find Nussbaum's thoughts on vulnerability helpful to creating a language for interreligious thinking that is based on critical conversation, encompassing the principle of dignity as well as encouraging creative disturbances. I develop an interreligious hermeneutics of vulnerability in thought, searching for truths in the spaces and times between the different thought traditions. My conclusion is

---

[22] John G. Gager, *Reinventing Paul* (Oxford: Oxford University Press, 2002).

[23] David Ford, *The Future of Christian Theology* (Malden, MA: Wiley-Blackwell, 2011).

presented as "Interreligious Christology," arguing that the opening of intra-Christian discourse to extra-Christian discussants is a proper option of critical, especially self-critical, theological thought. With Jesus the Jew at its heart, thinking about Christ takes on an inherently interreligious dimension. Accordingly, listening to non-Christians when reasoning and questioning the meanings and memories of Jesus Christ seems a most appropriate Christological undertaking. As we will see, the Jewishness of Jesus facilitates rethinking the complex phenomenon of the Christian faith and helps to formulate anew Christian identity in an interreligious context.

This book focuses on the very contemporary encounter of Jewish philosophy and Christian theology. My theological hermeneutics is committed to post-supersessionist and anti-missionary post-Shoah Christian thought. My opposition to the ideas of the replacement or reduction of the other are connected to the Levinasian notion of responsibility for the otherness of the other. In a turn still unusual for theologies focusing on Jesus' Jewishness, I do not hold Christologies that exclusively stress Jesus' humanity as automatically conveying more respect toward Judaism than Christologies committed to dogmatic discourse that includes discussions of both divinity and humanity. In an additional and perhaps still more unusual step, I show how even the most specifically Christian theories can profit from interruptions by contemporary Jewish as well as Muslim interlocutors.

In *Jesus the Jew in Christian Memory*, I show that taking the Jewishness of Jesus seriously helps to express the particular inner grammar of Christian thought. Beyond the binaries of particularism and universalism, Christian thinking describes a plural way of being related and relating to a specific Other, which is Judaism. Understanding the Jewishness of Jesus as a memory in need of being revitalized presents a critical approach toward a Christian theology that developed as an intellectual island, presenting itself as a self-sustained faith. Abraham Joshua Heschel's famous statement that no religion is an island is especially true for the intellectual Christian tradition. My analysis and exploration of Jesus' Jewishness as corrective memory shows that interconnectedness is not just an objective of a pluralist twenty-first-century Christianity but has been a key feature of the Christian narrative and identity from its beginnings, although a suppressed one. Continuing Karl Barth's line of thought that Jesus was not coincidentally, but necessarily, a Jew, I claim that if not for Jesus the Jew, Christians would not worship the biblical God of creation.

THE NAME OF JESUS: A TERMINOLOGICAL NOTE

The Jesus of memory is not contrasting but complementary to the Historical Jesus. Memory – not just here, but especially in the case of Jesus – is not "history lite." The history of early twentieth-century research shows that Protestant scholars committed to the historical-critical method of studying the Bible questioned not just the historicity of every single saying attributed to Jesus, but his historical existence itself. In contrast, Jewish scholars acquainted with rabbinic literature saw no reason to question the fact that a Jew named Jesus lived, spoke, and acted more or less as recorded in the Gospel narratives.

Although Jewish and Christian scholarly positions have overlapped and, in some cases, flipped, several general tendencies of the two groups remain distinct. Christian New Testament scholars would still tend to be more likely to mention that they talk about the Jesus as presented in the Gospels rather than presupposing a historical person.[24] The prominent New Testament scholar E. P. Sanders would limit his grand claims as statements about the "synoptic" Jesus alone, that is, the Jesus according to the gospels of Mark, Matthew, and Luke. As Sanders writes, "The synoptic Jesus lived as a law-abiding Jew."[25] In the German tradition of New Testament scholarship, the commitment to historical skepticism remains strong. Most recently, the New Testament scholar Klaus Wengst, though himself contextualizing Jesus in the framework of Second Temple Judaism, published a small book arguing against confidence in Historical Jesus research as a whole, even its most recent phase.[26] Remarkably, this highly skeptical treatise was followed by a voluminous work analyzing Jesus' words and deeds according to the gospels.[27]

---

[24] The Jewish scholar Michael Cook has endorsed this precision and suggested it to his Jewish colleagues; see Michael J. Cook, "How Credible Is Jewish Scholarship on Jesus?" in Zev Garber, ed., *The Jewish Jesus: Revelation, Reflection, Reclamation* (West Lafayette, IN: Purdue University Press, 2011), 251–270.

[25] E. P. Sanders, *Jewish Law from Jesus to the Mishnah* (Minneapolis, MN: Fortress Press, 2016), 125.

[26] Klaus Wengst, *Der wirkliche Jesus? Eine Streitschrift über die historisch wenig ergiebige und theologisch sinnlose Suche nach dem 'historischen' Jesus* (Stuttgart: Kohlhammer, 2013). Compare my critique, Barbara U. Meyer, "Wahrhaft historisch, wahrhaft jüdisch – Ein Plädoyer für die fortgesetzte wissenschaftliche Suche nach Jesus, 'in den letzten Tagen geboren aus Miriam'." *Begegnungen: Zeitschrift für Kirche und Judentum* (2015):1: 32–41.

[27] Klaus Wengst, *Mirjams Sohn – Gottes Gesalbter: Mit den vier Evangelisten Jesus entdecken* (Munich: Gütersloh, 2016).

Amy Jill Levine, on the other hand, builds her arguments on the convincing logic of textual transmission. Her assessment of Jesus' parables presents an excellent example of these interpretational insights, displaying a confidence in judgment Christian scholars often lack. To cite a single example, she identifies the literary genre of parables as characteristic for Jesus: A good "reason to think that he spoke the parables is that we see the evangelists wrestling with an attempt to control their meaning."[28] Levine also presents the memory of Jesus' Jewish context as a criterion for judging anti-Jewish interpretational traditions: "If the interpretation of a story told by a Jew to other Jews is based on or yields a negative stereotype of Judaism, then the interpretation has gotten more lost than the sheep, coin, or sons, and it cannot and should not be recovered."[29]

While Christian scholars tend to make a sharp distinction between the "synoptic" (Sanders), the "historical" (Theissen), the "remembered," or "historic" (Tilley) Jesus, Jewish scholars mainly prefer to speak of "Jesus of Nazareth" (Vermes). In modern Hebrew, this has a confusing effect when Jesus' name is translated as "*Yeshu ha-notzri*" – literally, Jesus the Nazarene or Jesus of Nazareth.[30] "*Notzri*" is also the general modern Hebrew term for "Christian," so that "*Yeshu ha-notzri*" can be anachronistically misunderstood as "the Christian Jesus!"[31] In contemporary Israel, my own academic context, any talk about Jesus begins with a decision about how to say his name. It can sometimes tell you a lot about the speaker – but the various interest groups have also mixed in curious ways. Someone saying "*Yeshua*" may be an evangelical or messianic Jew, but could also belong to the Hebrew-speaking Catholic community with its dialogical approach to Judaism going back to pre-Vatican II times.[32] There is another recently-emergent group that feels strongly about saying "*Yeshua*," a small group of Jewish orthodox scholars who engage in

---

[28] Amy-Jill Levine, *Short Stories by Jesus: The Enigmatic Parables of a Controversial Rabbi* (New York: Harper Collins, 2014), 15.

[29] Amy-Jill Levine, *Short Stories by Jesus*, 301.

[30] Joseph Klausner's famous book about Jesus of Nazareth had that title in the Hebrew original from 1922. For the English translation see Klausner, *Jesus of Nazareth: His Life, Times and Teaching* (London: Allen and Unwin, 1925).

[31] To identify Jesus with his home town Nazareth, one could also say "*Yeshu mi-Natzeret*" in modern Hebrew.

[32] About the Hebrew-speaking Catholic community in Israel see my article "*Sfat ben*" ("Son Language"), in Avital Wohlman and Yossef Schwartz, eds., *The Christian Poet of Zion: In Memory of Marcel-Jaques Dubois (1920–2007)* (Jerusalem: Van Leer Institute and Hakibbutz Hameuchad Publishing House, 2012), 61–68.

Jewish–Christian dialogue and distance themselves from using the name "*Yeshu*" that they believe is pejorative.[33] Most Israelis, however, do say "*Yeshu*," which is also the word used by the many Jewish writers and other artists who mostly include a distinctly Jewish memory of him – though with widely varying Jewish content. It seems to me that the name "*Yeshu*" for Hebrew speakers conveys a sense of Jewish belonging. In contrast, adding "*ha-notzri*" has a distancing function. Interestingly, the simple "*Yeshu*" in contemporary Israeli art and literature – where the name carries a wide range of contradictory connotations including reformer, Zionist, anti-Zionist, or simply critic of religion and establishment – is usually expressed in a sympathetic vein.[34]

In this book I explore the memories and repercussions of Jesus remembered as a Jew in early dogmatic discourse, Jewish and Christian historical research, and post-Shoah thought. For the most part, I will simply speak of "Jesus" and consider critical, textual, and even dogmatic memories presented as memories of him as memories of the same person, a Jew of the Second Temple period.

---

[33] According to David Flusser, "Yeshu" is not pejorative at all, but simply the Galilean way of pronouncing "Yehoshua" or "Yeshua." The form Yeshu is attested in rabbinic literature with reference to various rabbis. See David Flusser, *Jewish Sources in Early Christianity* (New York: Adama Books, 1987), 89.

[34] Neta Stahl, *Other and Brother: Jesus in the 20th Century Jewish Literary Landscape* (Oxford: Oxford University Press, 2013).

I

What Is Christian Memory?

This study is about the extraordinary capacity afforded by the Christian memory of Jesus the Jew to transform not just Christianity's relationship to Jews today but also its self-understanding. Jesus' Jewishness had never been completely forgotten within the Church, but it was certainly neglected, overshadowed, and suppressed. This inquiry details the direct and long-term consequences of this neglect, but its main focus is to show how much interreligious and philosophical horizons can be widened for a Christianity that seeks to remember Jesus as Jew.

For this exploration of the Jewish Jesus I do not rely on a specific theory of memory, but use intercultural, philosophical, and interreligious discourses on memory as my key frames of reference.[1] Memory has become a central category in contemporary interreligious academic discussions, including Historical Jesus research, discussions of the "parting of the ways" (or, as some would argue, "the ways that never parted"), and scriptural hermeneutics. The concept of memory proves helpful for developing an understanding of the actual and potential impact of remembering Jesus' Jewishness, since it connects the research of the historical past with thinking about the theoretical future. Although not a traditional Christian theological category, memory is a deeply rooted biblical and liturgical concept. It is impossible to overstate the significance of memory for shaping Jewish tradition, culture, and identity through the ages. But while the scope of remembering differs greatly in Judaism and Christianity, memory in all its variations provides the most

---

[1] Remarkably, there is little reference to theology in the broad interdisciplinary memory discourse at the end of the twentieth century. See Aleida Assmann, *Erinnerungsräume. Formen und Wandlungen des kulturellen Gedächtnisses* (Munich: Beck, 1999).

fitting frame of reference for describing Jewish and Christian languages of the past and their relevance for the present. Neither diffused commonality nor pure difference are adequate parameters for characterizing the intercommunal relationship between Christianity and Judaism. The language of memory proves helpful in developing a grammar, syntax, and extended vocabulary for decoding the historical and theological dimensions of Jewish–Christian relations, especially when based on their unique scriptural interconnections.

Searching for the memory of Jesus the Jew is no less a scholarly undertaking than researching his own history. In fact, leading scholars of Historical Jesus research have adopted "memory" as a crucial category for bridging discussions about the historical, the earthly, and the synoptic Jesus (as we will see in Chapter 2). Contemporary memory studies understand the category of memory not simply as complementary to history but as an activity of the present. At the same time, in post-Shoah thought, memory has been especially linked to the future. Thus, my framing of the discourse on Jesus' Jewishness with a theoretical account of memory will help to connect theological reflections on historical research (Chapter 2) with philosophical discussion of Jewish continuities up to the present (Chapter 3). Meanwhile, the analysis of "future" interreligious post-Shoah ethics (Chapter 4) is based on the notion of memory of suffering (Chapter 5), a memory that holds its own unique set of challenges when Jesus is remembered as a Jew.

THE INTERRELIGIOUS DIMENSION
OF CHRISTIAN MEMORY

I begin by situating the memory of Jesus' Jewishness within a discussion of Jewish and Christian concepts of memory. While in the last third of the twentieth century, literature on Jewish memory-culture has proliferated, few Christian theologians have developed theories of Christian memory. There is one very good reason for this asymmetry: Christian textual memories are deeply intertwined with Jewish narrated memories. A text-based concept of Christian memory underscores the fact that almost all constitutive texts of the Christian canon are either shared with or indebted to Judaism.[2] As Christian memory always overlaps with and contains Jewish memories, it is well described as in itself interreligious.

---

[2] Michael Signer, "Searching the Scriptures: Jews, Christians, and the Book," in Tikva Frymer-Kensky, David Novak, Peter Ochs, David Fox Sandmel, and Michael A. Signer, eds., *Christianity in Jewish Terms* (Boulder, CO: Westview Press, 2000), 85–98.

The memory of Jesus' Jewishness provides a key insight into the inter-religious quality of Christian memory. Memory has still to be established as a category in the study of Christian thought, yet it has played a significant role in recent works on the Historical Jesus as well as in Christologies after the Shoah.[3] Since the start of the twenty-first century, memory studies have focused on describing complex processes of memories crossing national and cultural borders, and the discourse once dominated by the study of collective memory has shifted to the exploration of "multidirectional" and "transcultural" memory.[4] "Trans-religious" is yet another term that can appropriately describe the specific connectedness of Christian to Jewish memory. Alternatively, Friedrich-Wilhelm Marquardt, the outstanding German theologian reformulating Jewish–Christian relations in the last third of the twentieth century, has depicted Christianity as inherently "intercultural." He describes the social and political situation of early as well as contemporary Christians without Jewish family background as structured by relationships and connectedness:

Being born a heathen one cannot become Christian in an intra-religious way, through the simple exchange of one's religious relation from one God to another. And socially becoming Christian does not happen intra-culturally, by joining one's country's church, but only inter-culturally, in the readiness to transfer one's own life interest to an existence out of Israel and for Israel.[5]

This finding of a fundamentally "inter-cultural" quality in Christianity echoes contemporary terms in memory studies, more often using the prefix "trans." One of the leading scholars of contemporary memory studies, Astrid Erll, has described transcultural memory as "a certain *research perspective*, a focus of attention, which is directed towards

---

[3] Wolfgang Stegemann, *Jesus und seine Zeit* (Tübingen: Kohlhammer, 2009).

[4] Michael Rothberg, *Multidirectional Memory: Remembering the Holocaust in the Age of Decolonization* (Stanford, CA: Stanford University Press, 2009).

[5] Friedrich-Wilhelm Marquardt, *Von Elend und Heimsuchung der Theologie: Prolegomena zur Dogmatik*, second edition (Munich: Kaiser, 1992), 454: "Man kann als geborener Heide nicht intern-religiös Christ werden, durch einfachen Tausch des religiösen Verhältnisses von einem Gott zum andern. Und sozial läßt sich Christwerdung nicht innerkulturell – durch Zutritt zur Kirche des eigenen Landes -, sondern nur interkulturell bewältigen: in der Bereitschaft, sein Lebensinteresse auf ein Dasein aus Israel und für Israel zu verlagern." Translation here by Kathrin Wolff; compare the forthcoming English translation of Barbara U. Meyer, *Christologie im Schatten der Shoah – im Lichte Israels* (Zürich: TVZ, 2004).

mnemonic processes unfolding *across* and *beyond* cultures."[6] This processual depiction nicely fits the historical complexity of Christian memory, with its many shared, partially shared, and complementary layers. Erll's choice of the present tense to describe "mnemonic processes" as "unfolding" suits the active memory work seen in Christianity in the last third of the twentieth century.

Christianity has never been a religion independent and disconnected from the Jewish community of memory. Whenever and however the "parting of the ways" occurred – and historical research is continuously postponing the completion of this process – it eventually led to two distinct communities of memory. But the Christian community always remained deeply interconnected to Jewish memory.[7] As broadly agreed today by Christian as well as Jewish historians, this interconnection of theological motifs and intellectual ideas has never been fully reciprocal. Although significant research has more recently explored Jewish receptiveness to motifs viewed as "Christian,"[8] the main flow of ideas from Judaism to Christianity has hardly been contested historically.[9]

Especially in the late twentieth century, Jewish memory has been intensely researched among scholars of intellectual history, with Yosef Yerushalmi's *Zakhor* ("Remember") marking the high point of reflection on the relationship of memory and Jewish historiography.[10] Christian theologians,

---

[6] Astrid Erll, "Travelling Memory," in Rick Crownshaw, ed., *Transcultural Memory* (London and New York: Routledge, 2014), 9–23, 14.

[7] Adam H. Becker and Annette Yoshiko Reed, eds., *The Ways That Never Parted: Jews and Christians in Late Antiquity and the Early Middle Ages* (Minneapolis, MN: Fortress Press, 2007).

[8] Michal Bar-Asher Siegal, *Early Christian Monastic Literature and the Babylonian Talmud* (Cambridge: Cambridge University Press, 2013); for the quite different context of medieval Ashkenaz, see Elisheva Baumgarten, *Practicing Piety in Medieval Ashkenaz: Men, Women, and Everyday Religious Observance* (Philadelphia: University of Pennsylvania Press, 2016). For Christian influences on Hasidism, see Shaul Magid, *Hasidism Incarnate: Hasidism, Christianity and the Construction of Modern Judaism* (Stanford, CA: Stanford University Press, 2014).

[9] Unless the beginning of "Judaism" is dated as following the emergence of Christianity, as Boyarin suggests. See Daniel Boyarin, "Semantic Differences; or, 'Judaism'/ 'Christianity'," in Adam Becker and Annette Yoshiko Reed, eds., *The Ways That Never Parted: Jews and Christians in Late Antiquity and the Early Middle Ages* (Tübingen: Mohr Siebeck, 2003), 65–85. But this historical view eventually leads to disconnecting the rabbinical tradition from the community of memory responsible for compiling the canon of the Hebrew Bible and would thus contradict rabbinical self-understanding as a community of interpretation built on interpreting precisely this text.

[10] Yosef Hayim Yerushalmi, *Zakhor: Jewish History and Jewish Memory* (New York: Schocken Books, 1989).

especially Johann Baptist Metz and many of his students, have also shown
great interest in the topic but have not yet developed any comprehensive
theory equivalently thematizing Christian memory.[11] As can be seen in the
work of John Pawlikowski, the term "memory" is typically used to signify a
critical parameter rather than a comprehensive religious approach.[12] There
is a general tendency in Religious Studies to differentiate between a comprehensive memory held by a religious community, one comprising texts and
narratives, legal and liturgical traditions, on the one hand, and a specific
memory that is reinforced on particular occasions, on the other hand.
Particular memories can gain importance when certain acts of remembering
lead to new formulations reflected in liturgy, law, or the interpretation of
narrative. A certain memory may have a renewed, multidimensional impact
and function as a reorganizing concept within the larger corpus of memories
in narrative and text. For example, the Exodus memory as a summary of the
larger narrative of the Exodus story functions as a directive for formulating
the commandment to respect the stranger.

There are very good reasons for the lack of a distinctive concept of
Christian memory. The main textual reason for Christian memory being
intertwined with Jewish memory is the composition of the Christian canon,
specifically the Hebrew Bible component, referred to by Christians as
the Old Testament, the first part of Holy Scripture.[13] The historical background of Christian canonization is extremely important for any theory
of Christian memory, as it shows that this entwinement was a deliberate
theological choice against the "arch-heretic" Marcion, who shook up
the early Christian community in second-century Rome.[14] His intent was

---

[11] Paul Petzel and Norbert Reck, eds., *Erinnern: Erkundungen zu einer theologischen Basiskategorie* (Darmstadt: Wissenschaftliche Buchgesellschaft, 2003).

[12] John T. Pawlikowski, "Historical Memory and Christian-Jewish Relations," in Philip A. Cunningham, Joseph Sievers, Mary Boys, Hans Hermann Henrix, and Jesper Svartvik, eds., *Christ Jesus and the Jewish People Today: New Explorations of Theological Interrelationships* (Grand Rapids, MI: Eerdmans, 2011), 14–26.

[13] The term "Old Testament" has been problematized in Jewish–Christian dialogue of the late twentieth century and was temporarily replaced by "First Testament." More recently, not the term "old" but its understanding as "obsolete" has become the focus of criticism. While theologians committed to the affirmation of Judaism called for the term "Hebrew Bible" to be used also by Christians, further reflection has led systematic theologians to clarify that the term "Tanakh" describes a specifically Jewish way and the term "Old Testament" a specifically Christian way of reading the same books – which are composed in a slightly different order, as the prophets mark the end of the Old Testament arrangement of books.

[14] Marcion was a successful businessman who had gained considerable influence in Rome's Christian community and began to experiment with scriptural and theological opinions

essentially to disengage the Church from Israel's scriptures and God. He suggested that the God who had sent Jesus had been previously unknown, was not (like the biblical God) responsible for creation, and was not committed to any particular group of people, such as Israel. This God was presented as solely good – parallel to gnostic views in that responsibility for creation was here assessed negatively. The sending of Jesus represents, according to Marcion, this God's only revelation thus far. Yet Marcion's proposal to disentangle Jesus from Israel's scriptures and God was decisively and emphatically rejected by the early Church.[15] Indeed, the challenge of this heresy led to the Church's explicit identification of the one God in both parts of the canon.[16] Now the canon was defined as encompassing both the Hebrew Bible and the Apostolic Writings, composed as "Old" and "New" Testaments.[17]

based on Gnostic views of creation. For a comprehensive study of Marcion's life and thoughts, see Sebastian Moll, *The Arch-Heretic Marcion* (Tübingen: Mohr Siebeck, 2010).

[15] The classic study of Marcion was published by the Church historian and liberal theologian Adolf von Harnack (1851–1930), who was strikingly sympathetic to Marcion's approach. Adolf von Harnack, *Marcion: Das Evangelium vom unbekannten Gott* (Leipzig: Hinrichs, 1921).

[16] The Marcion episode has usually been depicted as constitutive for the process of the canonization of the Christian Bible. In more recent research, assessments are more hesitant and describe Marcion as instead having accelerated the process of canonization.

[17] The terms "old" and "new" have been comprehensively criticized and clarified in the path-breaking Church document of the German Protestant Church Rhineland in 1980: "Throughout centuries the word 'new' has been used in biblical exegesis against the Jewish people: the new covenant was understood in contrast to the old covenant, the new people of God as replacement of the old people of God. This disrespect to the permanent election of the Jewish people and its condemnation to non-existence marked Christian theology, the preaching and work of the church again and again, right to the present day. Thereby we have made ourselves guilty also of the physical elimination of the Jewish people. Therefore, we want to perceive the unbreakable connection of the New Testament with the Old Testament in a new way and learn to understand the relationship of the 'old' and 'new' from the standpoint of the promise: in the framework of the given promise, the fulfilled promise and the confirmed promise. 'New' means therefore no replacement of the 'old'. Hence, we deny that the people Israel has been rejected by God or that it has been superseded by the church." See *Zur Erneuerung des Verhältnisses von Christen und Juden. Handreichung der Evangelischen Kirche im Rheinland* (Düsseldorf: Evangelische Kirche im Rheinland, 1980). An English translation by Franklin Littell (revised by R. Rendtorff) is available online. See "Towards Renovation of the Relationship of Christians and Jews," www.jcrelations.net/Towards_Renovation_of_the_Relationship_of_Christians_and_Jews.2388.0.html?id=720&L=3&searchText=Erneuerung&searchFilter=%2A.

The early Latin Father Tertullian (c.155–c.240 CE) explained Marcion's separation of both parts of the Bible as a deliberate unlinking of Jesus Christ from God: "... that he may establish a diversity between the Old and the New Testaments, so that his own Christ may be separate from the Creator, as belonging to this rival god, *and* as alien from the law and the prophets."[18] Thus from Tertullian we first learn that Jesus Christ cannot be separated from the God of creation, "from the law and the prophets." The word "Jewish" does not appear here, nor the word "Israel." But the only Christ Tertullian knows is not an "alien" vis-à-vis Israel's texts.

Due to his contemptuous language about the biblical God of Israel, Marcion has often been seen as an early example of anti-Judaism. Recent research, however, has taken into account that Marcion's call for separation also contained a certain implicit respect for the specific text-tradition of the Jewish People.[19] The Israeli philosopher Yeshayahu Leibowitz went so far as to praise Marcionism as far less inherently anti-Jewish than Christianity. The assumption that the Jewish people would have suffered less under Marcionism than under Christianity has a certain plausibility. Insofar as Christian hostility to Judaism was a function of its proximity, likeness, dependence, and consequently negative differentiation, a non-Jewish Christianity might indeed have lacked the same aggressive impulse to denigrate rabbinic Judaism and rabbinic Jews. At the same time, one must measure this against the Church's historical treatment of other faiths that came under its power; the absolute refusal to tolerate these faiths stands in contrast to the Church's accordance to Jews of limited, inferior but protected space, in theory if often not in practice, within Christendom.

Yet such counterfactual speculations do not appear terribly useful in themselves. More important is that regarding Jewish–Christian relations, Leibowitz' statement remains a prophetic reminder of the dangers entailed in closeness and overlapping memories. Leibowitz has not gone unheeded on this matter. The late New Testament scholar and Lutheran bishop Krister Stendahl called for disentanglement after decades of intense engagement in Jewish–Christian dialogue.[20] Friedrich-Wilhelm

---

[18] Tertullian, *Ante Nizene Fathers*, Vol. III. Quoted in Harnack, *Marcion: The Gospel of the Alien God* (Eugene, OR: Wipf and Stock, 2007), 151, n. 4.

[19] Joseph B. Tyson, "Anti-Judaism in Marcion and His Opponents," in *Studies in Christian-Jewish Relations* (SCJR) 1 (2005–2006): 196–208 and online at http://escholarship.bc.edu/scjr/vol1/iss1/art21.

[20] Krister Stendahl, "Die nächste Generation in den jüdisch-christlichen Beziehungen," in *Kirche und Israel* 1 (1986): 11–15.

Marquardt differentiated between the Christian obligation to relationship and the Jewish right to distance.[21] But even with the vulnerability of Israel and its historical wounds in mind, a Marcionic "Jesus-community" completely disentangled from Israel would not be Christianity. This is because of the memory of Jesus the Jew.

The language of memory facilitates a more theological perspective on the matter. It was an insistence on the memory of God as creator, the God of Abraham and the God of the Exodus, that led early Christians to refute Marcionism. This God, no other, had sent Jesus. From the perspective of the majority of early Christians, these latest memories of the God of Israel were quite recent; they had been transmitted for only a few generations. One might even put it this way: The memories of the creator God who took Israel out of Egypt were, for the early Church majority of Christians with no Jewish family background, precisely the memories of the Jesus whom they joined. Thus, joining in Jesus' memory, his Jewish memory of God and God's history with Israel, can be described as the most fundamental move of Christian remembering.

Looking at the sharing of scripture through the lens of memory highlights the complexity of what one may call Christian memory. Some Old Testament texts are completely owned by Christians, who may even forget about initially sharing them, such as the narratives of creation and the flood, the Ten Commandments, and the Book of Psalms. Other texts are well remembered and have a rich reception history, such as the binding of Isaac (*akeda*). Here signs of a complex, multi-layered reception process can be discerned. The binding of Isaac is a story well known in Christian cultures, with manifold expressions in art and literature that do not attest to its reception as a text perceived as also belonging to Jews. The motif has certainly shaped the New Testament narrative, but statements like "in Judaism the son was saved, only in Christianity sacrifice was completed" belong to a certain kind of polemics that miss the point of Genesis 22 being an integral part of the Christian Bible.[22]

Perhaps most challenging to Christian memory is the biblical narrative of the Exodus, a narrative that already inner-biblically includes various commandments to remember. In this case, both the constitutive memory

---

[21] Marquardt, *Eschatologie* II, 164.

[22] For a fascinating discussion of the medieval Jewish midrashic exegesis on the *Akedah*, at times with strong parallels in Christology, see Shalom Spiegel, *The Last Trial: On the Legends and Lore of the Command to Abraham to Offer Isaac as a Sacrifice* (New York: Pantheon, 1967).

of the Exodus story and the commandment to remember it are part of the text Christians share as holy. In some Christian traditions, the Exodus narrative is transmitted as Israel's story, without Christians identifying directly with the people fleeing Egypt. Other Christian communities, notably within the African American gospel tradition, quote Israel as the people saved from Egypt but generally self-identify with the Exodus as a people seeking to leave (or having left) slavery behind. In Latin American liberation theologies of the 1960s the Exodus tradition serves as a central motif as well as a structuring element for criticizing poverty and exploitation.[23] There is not one fixed Christian adoption of the Exodus narrative. But clearly the story of God freeing Israel from Egypt has a special presence in "general" Christian memory, however speculative any assessment of such a comprehensive Christian memory would be. The fascinating feature about Christian Exodus memory is that it can be remembered in different perspectives simultaneously. Christians remember the Exodus as Israel's specific liberation as well as their own – the paradigmatic Exodus in general but echoed in the liberation experiences and aspirations of particular Christian communities.[24]

At the end of the twentieth century, theologies engaged in the criticism of supersessionism – the idea that Christianity took Israel's place in a history of salvation – often criticized liberation theologians for their evidently seamless appropriation of the Exodus narrative. But there is no necessity to interpret a direct Christian identification with the liberation from Egypt as invariably supersessionist. Christians can see themselves as liberated from slavery without expropriating the Exodus memory from the Jewish people. Critics of Christians celebrating the Seder evening as a Christian feast have pointed out that remembering Egypt by reading the Passover Haggadah needs to be respected as a specifically Jewish tradition. The case is particularly complicated, as Jesus himself, at least according to the Gospel of Luke, did celebrate the Seder.[25] But while the Passover Haggadah is built on remembering the Exodus, it presents a liturgical text that also weaves together multiple memories of medieval persecution. In these memories, Christians are not

---

[23] Leonardo Boff, *Introducing Liberation Theology* (Maryknoll, NY: Orbis Books, 1987).

[24] See Michael Walzer, *Exodus and Revolution* (New York: Basic Books, 1985); Eric Nelson, *The Hebrew Republic: Jewish Sources and the Transformation of European Political Thought* (Cambridge, MA: Harvard University Press, 2010).

[25] The exegetical discussion over whether the so-called last supper actually was a Seder is ongoing. Yet the historical probability that Jesus the Jew observed the Seder is high when Jesus is situated in the context of Second Temple Judaism.

refugees but persecutors. Thus, when some Christians today celebrate the Seder with reading the Haggadah as their own, this has a taste of forget-fulness and distortion. Only the biblical Exodus story is also part of Christian memory. Since the last decades of the twentieth century, the Christian approach to the Exodus has functioned as a microcosm of a non-supersessionist hermeneutics of the Old Testament, one that has aligned with the directive of reading scripture in a context of interreligious respect.[26]

Apart from direct identification and the remembering of Israel being taken out of Egypt, the Exodus-memory has also had a third impact on Christian faith, indeed one that is traditionally understood as marking its deepest imprint. The Christ-story is told as a story of liberation from sin. In this domain of impact, memory shapes the structure of religious remembrance more than its content. And "Exodus" is also understood here as exiting and being liberated from any situation that limits freedom – such as exploitation and inequality. But Christian memory should not be reduced to either appropriating the biblical narrative of Israel liberated from Egypt or seeking to transform the Exodus story into various con-ceptual patterns of liberation. Rather, Christian memory comprises these converging dimensions of approaching and appropriating the biblical narrative and its inner-biblical echoes. It is the very congruence of these different dimensions that produces the specific scope of Christian memory. It is unique precisely in its multi-layered and interwoven frame-work. Its inherently interreligious structure highlights the methodological problem of calling a memory tradition "Christian" in implied juxtapos-ition to Jewish memory. In such attempts to contrast Christian and Jewish memory traditions in a binary fashion the unique membrane of Christian memory is likely to be distorted.

The complexity of Christian memory goes far beyond the formulation of non-supersessionist hermeneutics of Old Testament narratives. Many recent approaches to Jewish–Christian relations have emphasized the intellectual gap between the rabbinic construction of a Jewish memory culture and the early Christian practices of remembrance, as for example in the sacrament of the Eucharist, as we will see. But even in the post-biblical framework, Christian memory is not disconnected from Jewish understandings of history. The Church historian and post-Shoah theolo-gian Franklin Littell gave expression to this continued historical

---

[26] Philip Cunningham, *Seeking Shalom: The Journey to Right Relationship between Catholics and Jews* (Grand Rapids, MI: Erdmans, 2015), especially 15ff.

interconnectedness when he published an atlas of Church history that includes crucial dates of diasporic Jewish history.[27] I agree with Littell that not only are scripturally shared narratives relevant to Christianity but post-biblical Jewish memories ought to direct Christians' attention to the full span of Jewish history. Nevertheless, the axiomatic case for Jewish memory's ongoing relevance for Christian identity remains, of course, the Jewish historiography of the Second Temple period. In Chapter 2, where I deal with the history of Jesus in research and dogmatic discourse, I will discuss the connections and disconnects between how Christian and Jewish historians examine this period. But insofar as assessing the implications of Jesus' Jewishness still poses a challenge to both theology and history, looking at the Historical Jesus research through the lens of memory offers not just a legitimate but arguably the most appropriate perspective for contemporary systematic theologians as well as many New Testament scholars.

New Testament texts have traditionally been viewed as reflections of early Christian memory. But with the considerably later dating of the emergence of Christians and Jews as distinct groups, reading the Gospels simply as "Christian" texts has turned out to be anachronistic. One need not go as far as Boyarin in this regard, who now describes the Gospels as Jewish texts, attributed not just to Jewish authors but also to Jewish redactors. Even as text compositions eventually adopted only by the Christian community of memory, the Gospels contain numerous mnemonic layers. The most fundamental expression of their interreligious dimension is, of course, their intertextuality. The Gospels tell the story of Jesus through the lens of biblical (Hebrew Bible) memories and expectations. In addition, sayings attributed to Jesus have direct parallels in quotes that are attributed to Hillel, as reflected in early rabbinic texts such as the Mishnah tractate *Pirke Avot*. Thus, the interreligious dimension of the New Testament is not just a historical-textual fact but represents the ongoing connectedness of its interpretational discourse. What might be called "interreligious *Wirkungsgeschichte*"(impact history) can shed light on sayings that are remembered as stemming from both Jesus and Hillel. To the contested discussion surrounding Jesus' authentic sayings, a debate that was largely abandoned by Protestants at the beginning of the twentieth century, interreligious memory might add another hermeneutical perspective. A saying remembered as Hillel's, and ascribed to him in

---

[27] Franklin H. Littell, *Historical Atlas of Christianity* (New York and London: Continuum, 2001).

rabbinic literature, raises the historical probability of being adequately remembered by the authors of the Gospels as stated by Jesus.[28]

Even topics of seeming historical interest only, such as research on the competing groups of Sadducees and Pharisees, profit from adding the perspective of memory. A striking example is the reception history of "Pharisaism" in Christian tradition and exegesis. If the terms "Judaism" and "Jewish" apply to the Second Temple period, then all these contemporaneous groups are equally "Jewish." If "Judaism" is dated as beginning only with the rabbinic period, as Boyarin suggests, and is thus more closely identified with halakhic discourse than with Temple practice, it makes sense to see the Pharisees as standing for Jewish tradition per se.[29] On the other hand, with regard to Jesus, the identification of Pharisaism with Judaism has led to gross distortions, as when generations of Christians learned to perceive the Pharisees as representing Judaism *tout court* in contradistinction to Jesus, who was consequentially perceived as "less Jewish."[30] Here, historical research has made a considerable difference. Since the reception history of Pharisees plays an important role in the study of antisemitism, I will examine the most recent discussions about Jesus' Jewish proximity to versus his distance from this group in Chapter 2.

The interreligious dimension of Christian memory reaches into the present when Jewish historians discuss Jewish continuity. In order for

---

[28] There is a large and growing literature on rabbinic and New Testament parallels. See Amy-Jill Levine and Marc Zvi Brettler, eds., *The Jewish Annotated New Testament: New Revised Standard Version Bible Translation*, second edition (Oxford: Oxford University Press, 2017); and Brad H. Young, *Meet the Rabbis: Rabbinic Thought and the Teachings of Jesus* (Peabody, MA: Hendrickson, 2007).

[29] Although the Tana'im sometimes distanced themselves from the Pharisees. See Boyarin, "Two Powers in Heaven, or the Making of a Heresy," in Hindy Najman and Judith H. Newman, eds., *The Idea of Biblical Interpretation: Essays in Honor of James L. Kugel* (Leiden: Brill, 2004), 331–370, 365.

[30] A similar phenomenon is found in the distorted memory of Judas as a prototype of a Jew, that has played a notable role in the history of antisemitism. Here too the mechanism of anti-Jewish memory works only when the Jewishness of Jesus and the other disciples is forgotten. Amos Oz' novel *Judas* alludes to that distorted memory, while at the same time presenting the Jewish memory of Jesus' Jewishness as well established. The protagonist of the story, which takes place in Jerusalem in the winter of 1959, tries to write his thesis on Jewish views of Jesus. An often overlooked detail of the novel is the protagonist's frustration that Jewish approaches to Jesus have already been well researched. Amos Oz, born Amos Klausner, certainly alluded in this evaluation to his uncle Joseph Klausner, whose impressive book on Jesus was the first of its kind and appeared in Hebrew in Jerusalem in 1922. See Amos Oz, *Judas* (New York: Houghton Mifflin Harcourt, 2016).

the assertion of the ongoing relevance of Jesus' Jewishness to make any sense, the category "Jewish" must be identifiable in a way that reasonably connects the first and the twenty-first centuries, despite all the inevitable risks and qualifications that must accompany such a claim (this continuity is discussed at length in Chapter 3). Being intertwined with Jewish memory is a basic feature of Christian memory up through the present. The memory of the Jewishness of Jesus belongs to the mnemonic genre of recollection, and also serves as a corrective memory, in Yerushalmi's sense of "anamnesis." But even with this corrective available, there is no automatism of trans-religious and interreligious memory leading to inter-religious respect and dignity. Memory in itself does not guarantee a tradition's ethical course, an insight we owe to the philosopher Avishai Margalit.

ETHICS OF MEMORY BETWEEN JEWS AND CHRISTIANS

Toward the end of the twentieth century, intellectual theories discussing cultural memory proliferated. This multi-faceted and interdisciplinary memory discourse was related both to an intensifying awareness of living in a post-Shoah world and to the flourishing of studies on Jewish cul-ture.[31] The Shoah has functioned through the present as an exemplary case of intellectual discourse about memory, as a rich body of literature demonstrates.[32] In the European milieu of Jewish–Christian dialogue, memory was often cited as key to fighting antisemitism. Advocates of memory culture believed it could serve to combat such evils as the loss of democracy, fascism, dictatorship and terror.[33] Even today, decades later, we sometimes find a certain over-estimation of the political powers of memory culture.

---

[31] See Zohar Shavit and Yaakov Shavit, "Jewish Culture, What Is It? In Search of Jewish Culture," in Mitchel B. Hart and Tony Michels, eds., *The Cambridge History of Judaism*, vol. 8: *The Modern Period, 1815–Present* (New York: Cambridge University Press, 2017), 677–698; Kirsten Lise Fermaglich, *American Dreams and Nazi Nightmares: Early Holocaust Consciousness and Liberal America, 1957–1965* (Waltham, MA: Brandeis University Press, 2006).

[32] See Dan Diner, *Gegenläufige Gedächtnisse. Über Geltung und Wirkung des Holocaust* (Göttingen: Vandenhoeck & Ruprecht, 2007); Dan Diner, *Cataclysms: A History of the Twentieth Century from Europe's Edge* (Madison: University of Wisconsin Press, 2007).

[33] Wulf Kansteiner, *In Pursuit of German Memory: History, Television, and Politics after Auschwitz* (Athens, OH: Ohio University Press, 2006).

But while the efficacy of acts of remembrance in preventing the repetition of atrocities can be overstated, skeptical questions about memory have also been posed by scholars and philosophers. This skepticism has been strikingly on display in Israeli society, where the commitment to remember had long become part of the mainstream ethos embracing religious and national holidays.[34] In this cultural context with state-rituals of remembrance expressing respect for those murdered in the Shoah as well as those who died in combat trying to establish the state, the obligation to remember became the most sacred commandment – especially in the secular world, where commemorations developed into complex liturgies featuring certain songs, silences, and other rituals. Within this Jewish Israeli environment with its broad consensus understanding of commemoration as a communal and intergenerational commitment, questioning the obligation to remember can be understood as a form of constructive cultural criticism. This is exactly what Avishai Margalit does in his small but impactful book *The Ethics of Memory*.[35] Among the rich and varied wave of theoretical literature on memory published at the beginning of the twenty-first century, *The Ethics of Memory* stands out. At first glance, Margalit's elementary questions, such as whether there is a moral obligation to remember, seem simplistic. But it is precisely its critical reflection on basic aspects of memory culture, rather than a preliminary equation of remembering with critiquing, that is needed in twenty-first-century religious thought.

Margalit makes a distinction between a morals of memory and an ethics of memory and links the former to "thin" relations between people belonging to different groups and cultures. Remembering, in his view, cannot reasonably be expected to meaningfully occur within the framework of such thin relations, except in the case of crimes against humanity, where the obligation is overwhelming. Other than in regard to such atrocities of global scale, Margalit exposes the primary place of remembering as existing within one's own national or religious group, what he describes as "natural" communities of memory.[36] Can Christianity be regarded as such a "natural" community of memory? As we have seen, a Christian community of memory cannot be simply aligned with a Jewish

---

[34] Idit Zertal, *Israel's Holocaust and the Politics of Nationhood* (Cambridge: Cambridge University Press, 2010).
[35] Avishai Margalit, *The Ethics of Memory* (Cambridge, MA, and London: Harvard University Press, 2002).
[36] Ibid., 69.

community of memory because the two groups' historical experience and power relations problematize any possibility of a simple shared memory. Rather, developing a concept of Christian memory requires a highly differentiated account of narratives shared as well as interpretational traditions developed in complementary or competing fashion. At the same time, any understanding of Christian relations to Judaism as merely "thin" would also be mistaken here, given their sharing of scriptures. In light of the experience of Christian violence toward Jews, harsh anti-Jewish polemics, aggression, and actual violent acts can hardly be described as reflecting a "thin" set of relations. Since for most of their common history, Jews were the target of violence caused or promoted by Christians, the ethics of memory must mean very different things for them. Remembering the history of Jewish–Christian relations with ethical criteria necessarily leads to a critique of Christianity. For Judaism, remembering Christian violence may also facilitate a kind of resilience of identity. The Egyptologist and theorist of memory cultures Jan Assmann has described this feature of Jewish memory culture admiringly.[37] In contrast, Margalit, living in a context where the frequently repeated imperative to remember does not reflect cultural resistance but the most comprehensive consensus, pursues an ethical questioning of the practice of remembering. But for both the Jewish and the Christian community, adding "ethics" to "memory" implies the insight that "memory" in itself does not yet contain a critical theory.

It is no coincidence that Margalit's questioning approach to the ethical value of memory was written in a cultural Jewish-majority context.[38] While both Judaism and Christianity are communities built on narrated memories and the practice of remembrance, the imperative to remember is explicitly constitutive of identity only in the Jewish tradition. Here, remembering constitutes a commandment, or rather, a component of many commandments, e.g., "remember the Sabbath day and keep it holy." Accordingly, critical memory discourse looks very different in contemporary Judaism and Christianity. While in Judaism the commitment to memory reflects a wide consensus among religiously observant and secular Jews, Christians usually see their engagement in the practice

---

[37] Jan Assmann, *Das kulturelle Gedächtnis. Schrift, Erinnerung und politische Identität in frühen Hochkulturen*, second edition (Munich: Beck, 1999), 31.

[38] Barbara U. Meyer, "Die andere Ethik der Erinnerung und die eigenen Erinnerungen. Kritische Überlegungen zu Avishai Margalit," in Inge Hansen-Schaberg and Ulrike Müller, eds., *Ethik der Erinnerung in der Praxis. Zur Vermittlung von Verfolgungs- und Exilerfahrungen* (Wuppertal: Arco Wissenschaft, 2005), 35–49.

of remembrance as expressing a critical approach rather than perpetuating traditional thought and action. In Israeli society, the value of memory has become almost a truism, supported and repeated by political and religious leaders. In this situation, counter-memories flourish and the ethical question of how to remember becomes key. Margalit's critical take on theories of memory thus proves helpful for a Christian reflection on history and historiography. Here, too, what is needed is not a mere invocation of memory as "the secret to redemption" but rather the crucial question of how memory can function as a critical theological category for examining Christian thought. Margalit's suggestion that each community primarily take responsibility for its own memories is certainly not sufficient for the needs of a self-critical Christian theology.[39] At the same time, his overall call to remember evils against humanity demands further interpretation. A Christian obligation to remember would need to be formulated alongside Margalit's division into "ethical" and "moral" realms and thus focus neither on the immediate nor on the world community but on the specific other communities that suffered most under the Christian church.

In the late twentieth century, the sites of Christian memory of the Shoah have multiplied and include among them many local and community efforts. Remembering has evolved as a critical activity of Christian clergy as well as of lay initiatives to express an affirmation of Judaism and to counteract supersessionism. Moreover, as I illustrate later, some traditional Christian outlooks on history that over the centuries had promoted resentment and hatred have been corrected in late twentieth-century interreligious discourse. Can one call this a "mending of memory"?[40] How can distorted, harmful, or even hateful approaches to history be changed through "memory"? After all, we tend to think of memory, even when distorted, as something received rather than created, inherited rather than adapted. Yet, in recent mainstream Church history, Catholic as well as Protestant, we find interesting examples of correcting past views, facilitated by encountering the other's history as narrated by the other. In this regard, Levinas' powerful statement about interpreting pain can be meaningful to interreligious memory: "the justification of the

---

[39] Margalit, *Ethics of Memory*, 82.
[40] See my article "Memory and Moral: The Challenge to Christianity," (Hebr.) in Yotam Benziman, ed., *Memory Games: Concepts of Time and Memory in Jewish Culture* (Jerusalem: Van Leer Institute and Hakibbutz Hameuchad Publishing House, 2008), 153–162.

neighbour's pain is certainly the source of all immorality."[41] Applied to
the Christian remembering of painful events in Jewish history, one could
say that Christian theological rationalizations of Jewish suffering enhance
immorality. Conversely, interreligious ethics can build on listening with
empathy to the other community's historical traumata and painful
memories. Considering an ethics of memory rather than simply equating
memory with ethics is important for any contemporary religious
self-criticism within interreligious discourse. The second half of the twentieth century offers noticeable examples of the mending of memory in an
interreligious setting. As a change in memory is difficult to attest to or
measure within a religious community, I will adduce two examples
here that impacted Christian self-understanding as officially presented
toward Jews.

THE PRESENCE OF MEMORY IN LITURGY

The Jewish fast day *Tisha b'Av* (the Ninth of Av) marks the loss of the
two Temples and was employed to subsume subsequent Jewish tragedies
and atrocities in its litanies, such as the destruction of the Jewish communities in Rhineland by the crusaders. Thus, *Tisha b'Av* served to represent
as well as to structure the most painful Jewish memories of loss. But while
the Second Temple is mourned on *Tisha b'Av*, this very same destruction
has traditionally been justified in the Christian memory tradition, and has
even been celebrated as a divine affirmation of Christian truth, an
example of the most fundamental kind of replacement mentality. The
Lutheran Church calendar formerly included a Sunday dedicated to the
memory of the Temple, with its destruction being commemorated as a
sign of Judaism's spiritual defeat. Interestingly, this "holiday," the "10th
after Trinity" (eleven weeks after Pentecost), would fall in August, and
thus in timely proximity to the Ninth of Av. In the nineteenth century, the
German Lutheran Church regularly donated the offerings of this Sunday
service to the missionary societies targeting Jews for proselytizing. Today
this Sunday is called "Israel-Sunday" and marks a date of repentance for
previous Christian wrongdoings against Jews, with the offerings being
donated to Church-rooted organizations that send volunteers to countries

---

[41] Levinas, "Useless Suffering," in Robert Bernasconi and David Wood, eds., *The
Provocation of Levinas: Rethinking the Other* (London; New York: Routledge, 1988),
156–167, 163. (French: "La Souffrance inutile," in *Giornale di Metafisica*, 4 (1982):
13–26.

that suffered under Germany in World War II.⁴² This example of "mending memory" is remarkable in its liturgical as well as its practical dimensions, a metamorphosis of the most disrespectful of proselytizing rituals into an initiative of practical reconciliation, one which also involves a substantial charitable component.

A far more famous instance of the correction of distorted memories, and one that operates on a global scale, is the Catholic Church's retraction of its longstanding accusation blaming the Jews for Jesus' death. This accusation had never been part of the Christian creed, but its various narratives had nevertheless exerted a strong impact on Christian antisemitism and violence historically directed at Jews. This distorted memory, one of the key ideas behind Christian antisemitism, was explicitly corrected in the famous declaration of the Second Vatican Council, *Nostra Aetate* of 1965. It should be noted that the accusation that "the" Jews killed Jesus, however wrong historically in the first place, always only made sense when Jesus was not remembered as a Jew (analogous to saying the "Americans" killed John F. Kennedy, since of course, Kennedy was no less American than his assassin). The Catholic Church's active and direct correction of a complex tradition and transmission process presents a powerful intervention of critical memory practice on behalf of the victims of violence caused by false witness. With the Vatican II text of *Nostra Aetate*, a distorted memory was corrected in general by displaying the Church's formal authority. For a widespread popular memory to be changed, multiple processes of examining and retelling the story are necessary. Here, Mary Boys' meticulous account of traditions narrating Jesus' death offers a substantial critique of memory that complements and supports the Vatican's statement with historical detail.⁴³ Writing as an academic and at the same time as a member of the Christian community of memory seeking reconciliation between Jews and Christians, Boys presents not just a textual study but also a testimony of applied inter-religious ethics of memory. Interpreted in terms of Avishai Margalit, one might say that Boys exercises both the moral and the ethical imperative to remember – the moral, as the false accusation regarding Jesus' death has led to atrocities, and the ethical as a member of the more recent community of Jewish and Christian scholars engaged in correcting memories.

---

⁴² The organization "Action Reconciliation Service for Peace" sends young adults as volunteers to all the countries that suffered under Germany in World War II.

⁴³ Mary Boys, *Redeeming Our Sacred Story: The Death of Jesus and Relations between Jews and Christians* (Mahwah, NJ: Paulist Press, 2013).

In both Catholic and Protestant Church documents engaged in reformulating the Christian approach to Jews and Judaism, the biblical command to remember is one of the most quoted verses. In the Epistle to the
Romans, we see a remarkable, specifically Christian imperative to remember: "Remember that thou bearest not the roots but the roots thee."
(Romans 11,18). Paul here warns the non-Jewish followers of Jesus
against cultivating feelings of superiority toward Jews. Instead, the Gentiles are reminded to remember the (Jewish) roots of the olive tree at all
times.[44] In recent Church documents committed to revising the Christian
approach to Jews and Judaism, this verse has often served as the heading
or summary statement of a new theology emphasizing and appreciating
Christian indebtedness to Israel. All three of these examples from the
second half of the twentieth century illustrate the corrective potential of
memory, as developed also in contemporary philosophy, for instance, the
concept of "just" remembering developed by Paul Riceour.[45]

While it is important to notice that memory is not in itself an ethical
category, the imperative to remember appears already in the Bible as an
obligation committing the individual or group to an ethical approach.
The Exodus, for instance, is recalled to provide a rationale for the commandment to love the stranger (Leviticus 19,34). Remembering "that
thou bearest not the roots but the roots thee" is apparently intended to
combat an early developing Gentile hubris. In both examples, the Bible
displays a basic ethical grammar of memory: One's own previous lower
status is to be remembered in order to prevent looking down on others as
one's status has improved.[46] The memory of Jesus the Jew is not an
ethical statement or argument in itself. But the effort of remembering
and reminding others of his Jewishness makes sense as a means to
counteract antisemitism that is in line with the biblical grammar of explicit calls to remember so as to avoid arrogance and condescension.

---

[44] The exegetical dispute over who exactly is meant by the "root" – the fathers, the people
Israel, the Jesus-believing Jews – continues until today. For an informative introduction to
traditional versus contemporary readings of Paul, see John G. Gager, *Reinventing Paul*
(Oxford and New York: Oxford University Press, 2000).

[45] See Paul Riceour, "Memory and Forgetting," in Richard Kearney and Mark Dooley, eds.,
Questioning Ethics: Contemporary Debates in Philosophy (London and New York,
1999), 5–11, esp. 11.

[46] Similarly, the phrase "A wandering Aramean was my father" (Dt 26:5) likely refers to
Abraham's modest beginnings, his common ancestry with the peoples of his
Mesopotamian birthplace, and the contingency of his descendants' fates on fulfilling
their covenant with God.

Although the practice of commemoration has been depicted culturally as mainly an ethical enterprise, memory has also been presented as a component of faith traditions. Christian theologians would have chosen this representation due to the general priority of faith over deeds in all mainstream Christianity. Thus, it is telling that the Christian theologian most seriously invested in a theology of memory, Johann-Baptist Metz, builds his theory on the notion of remembrance in the sacrament of the Eucharist. The Catholic Metz is one of the few contemporary German theologians well known to the English-speaking world. Over the course of several decades, he has developed "memory" as a fundamental theological category. In late twentieth-century German intellectual literature, memory became a much-discussed category, with an impressively growing vocabulary of terms like remembrance and commemoration. Metz has added to German memory discourse various supplementary terms and even created new idioms combining the Latin term "memoria" and the Greek "anamnesis." Terms are used inconsistently – sometimes even by those who invented them – and themselves do not necessarily add any content to the discussion. But the phenomenon of the compounding of language is worth interpreting. At the very least, it reflects the growing relevance of the field. In the context of religion, the proliferation of language may indicate an attempt to express an experience of previously unrealized dimensions.[47] In addition to a broad conception of memory with regard to Christianity and Judaism as communities of memory, Metz has also developed a narrow concept of memory as a critical category. To underscore this critical, subversive understanding that is intended to challenge Christian bourgeois complacency, he speaks of "dangerous memory." The choice of the attribute "dangerous" (*gefährlich*) is awkward even in the original German. Metz developed this political language of memory as early as 1969, when concepts like "liberation" and "critical theory" were frequently referred to by theologians, whereas "memory" was still not widely used.[48]

While the category of critical memory has accompanied his theological work since the 1960s, it was not until 2006 that Metz published a full

---

[47] Dietrich Ritschl has described the phenomenon as a heightening of language ("Sprachgewinn"). See Ritschl, *The Logic of Theology* (Philadelphia: Fortress Press, 1987), 174.

[48] Johann Baptist Metz, "Politische Theologie in der Diskussion" (1969), in *Zum Begriff der Neuen Politischen Theologie: 1967–1997* (Mainz: Grünewald Verlag, 1997), 33–61.

monograph on the theme, *Memoria Passionis*.[49] Here Metz's main argument is that the memory of Jesus' suffering holds a key place in Christian tradition. (I will further discuss his vision for a revised approach to suffering in Chapter 5). The claim of critical memory as something Christianity needs possesses a certain circularity when it is presented in relation to the *memoria passionis*, the recalling of Jesus' words "do this in remembrance of me" in the Eucharist. Unfortunately, Metz does not explain whether and why this memory is originally critical, or whether and how it needs to be transformed into critical memory. This lack of in-depth argumentation might be connected to the cultural climate of post-war Christianity, where until the 1990s pleas to remember were identified with critical voices in society and churches alike.

Metz laments that the task to remember is only marginal in Christian tradition.[50] Nevertheless, he finds the basis of Christian memory to reside in the liturgy of the Eucharist, in the verse "do this in remembrance of me" (1. Corinthians 11, 24.25) after the blessing of both the bread and the wine. It is not clear how Metz comes to call this text marginal. The Eucharist is the most repeated sacrament in a Christian's life, and thus the liturgy of the Eucharist is a text most present to Christians. The Corinthian text, transmitted as Jesus' words at the Last Supper, lies at the heart of Catholic, Orthodox and Protestant liturgies alike. The 1. Corinthians text also presents a very special case for a theory of religious memory, as it is poetically composed. It is one of the very few texts Paul quotes, which means that its poetry is earlier than Paul's writings. New Testament scholars broadly agree that the *Sitz im Leben* of this text is in the very early sharing of bread and wine in remembrance of Jesus. Most interestingly, in the letter to the Corinthians, the text is quoted to support communal solidarity. Paul invokes it to bring the Corinthian community that is beset by social gaps back to an original atmosphere of sharing and equality. Thus, in the New Testament setting, the Jesus-imperative to remember already functions as social critique.

---

[49] Johann Baptist Metz, *Memoria Passionis: Ein provozierendes Gedächtnis in pluralistischer Gesellschaft*, second edition (Freiburg i.Br.: Herder, 2006).

[50] Metz, "In der Krise des europäischen Geistes"(1992), in *Zum Begriff der Neuen Politischen Theologie: 1967–1997* (Mainz: Grünewald Verlag, 1997), 142–148, 146.

THEOLOGY BETWEEN COMMUNITIES OF MEMORY

Since, as we have seen, Jewish memory is constitutive for any concept of Christian memory, the Christian community of memory will always relate to the Jewish community of memory.[51] The first memory of Jesus the Jew (when read as *genitivus subjectivus*) refers to the God of Jesus, who is the God of Israel. A clear grasp of the Jewishness of Jesus ensures a clear understanding of this God. The reverse is also true: When Jesus is not remembered as Jewish, God is often conceptualized as an abstract power. Christianity is affected by the contemporary Jewish historiography of the Second Temple period, and the Christian community of memory is challenged as well by individual Jewish voices sharing new insights about the historical Jesus. When the Christian community of memory loses sight of Jewish communities, it easily loses sight of the Jewish Jesus – and thus of Jesus' God.

Avishai Margalit's understanding of "natural" communities of memory explicated as "families, clans, tribes, religious communities and nations" suggests a certain isolation of memory cultures.[52] This model does not fit the Christian interconnectedness in narrative due to Christianity's composition of scripture. Moreover, the biblical practice of memory does not feature a "natural" phenomenon. Instead, we find a didactics of the intergenerational transmission of memories, as in Deuteronomy (Dt. 6:20). Yosef Yerushalmi has elaborated on the fact that the effort to interpret history is not at all a general human feature common to all civilizations. On the contrary, cultures greatly differ in their interest in historiography, and Jews have been outstandingly invested in questioning and understanding the meaning of historical occurrences – which is not in itself the same as writing conventional narrative history.[53]

Can Christianity be described with the concept of a natural community of memory? The Christian community of memory consists of people sharing memories rooted in scripture and dogma, sacrament and liturgy. A unique feature of the Christian community of memory is its continued reference to the Jewish community of memory. From the Christian perspective, the connection between these two distinct communities of memory is theological – in the first sense of the word – since Christians believe that the God of the Bible is Jesus' God and consequently the God

---

[51] With different sets of multiple memories one should perhaps rather choose the plural and speak of "Jewish communities." My use of the singular term suggests an alternative to the even more contested term "religion."

[52] Margalit, *Ethics of Memory*, 69.   [53] Yerushalmi, *Zakhor*, 6.

Christians worship is the God of Israel. Continued reference means that a Jewish memory community is not only historically connected but also of ongoing relevance to Christian recollection and revision; one might call it "anamnetic reasoning." Remembering and considering Jesus the Jew shakes up the suggested notion of "natural" communities of memory. Thus, the Jewishness of Jesus may be best described as a trans-communal memory.

Theologically, the guiding memory of Jesus being Jewish points to the identity of the one God whom Christians clearly see as the creator, but do not always view so clearly as the God of Israel. The Jewishness of Jesus, then, fosters a clear memory of the God of Jesus as the God of the Jews. That Jews and Christians worship the same God has been emphatically affirmed in the *Dabru Emet* declaration of Jewish scholars in 2000.[54] Yet even in the year 2000, this theological statement was controversial among Rabbis of various denominations. To Christians it should have been clear, referring back to their fundamental decision against Marcion about creating an inclusive Christian canon.

Losing sight of the Jewish community of memory can even create theological problems. An interesting example is the case of Christian theologians who try to reformulate Christian thought after the Shoah. It would seem likely that these Christians, who share with Jews not only the basic belief in the God of creation but also the understanding of the Shoah as a paradigm shift, would confront a similar problem when thinking about God after the Shoah. Questions such as how could God let this monumental catastrophe occur, where was God, or how was God affected by it are central to Jewish as well as Christian wrestling with God. But while an engaged and emphatic refusal to defend God has become a central feature in Jewish post-Shoah thinking, Christians do not seem to consider themselves as sharing the same problem. For Jewish post-Shoah thinkers – whether they claim God to be alive, as with Emil Fackenheim, or dead, as with Richard Rubenstein – the problem of theodicy has become a central one. There are good reasons, moreover, to assume that Jews and Christians would at present engage in similar dilemmas in asking about God after the Shoah. Jewish and Christian thinkers have by now shared their convictions in decades-long dialogue, and Christians have phrased most of their critiques of Christianity after listening to Jewish experiences.

---

[54] Andrew S Jacobs, "A Jewish Statement on Christians and Christianity," in Tikva Frymer-Kensky, David Novak, Peter Ochs, David Fox Sandmel, and Michael A. Signer, eds., *Christianity in Jewish Terms* (Boulder, CO: Westview Press, 2000).

Given all this interreligious encounter, academic as well as social, it is astonishing to find a basic lack of communication between Jewish and Christian post-Shoah thinkers in the most theological of all questions, that of theodicy. Jewish post-Shoah thinkers question God's reliability, while otherwise highly critical Christian post-Shoah theologians strongly affirm God's ongoing covenant with the people Israel. Jewish and Christian post-Shoah thinkers do, however, share the impression that traditional answers are not sufficient where God is concerned.[55] In Jewish post-Shoah thought, we can even see a certain switch from questioning God to questioning the notion of theodicy itself. Zachary Braiterman has called this phenomenon "antitheodicy."[56] The term is helpful in pointing out the determination of these thinkers not just to reject the notion of theodicy but to build their thought on this very rejection. The founder of Jewish post-Shoah philosophy, Emil Fackenheim, formulated a "614th commandment" that entails the task of denying posthumous victories for Hitler. In his view, a denial of God would count as such a posthumous victory, as the reality of God is an inherent part of Jewish identity and continuity. Interestingly, Fackenheim's post-Shoah thought refers to religious and secular Jews. Believing is not at all important but giving up the idea of God would damage Jewish existence. Irving Greenberg's post-Shoah thinking is likewise built on a refutation of theodicy. The modern orthodox Rabbi and religious intellectual built his post-Shoah theology on the notion of covenant.[57] Dividing Jewish history into three phases, he describes the first, the biblical, as being led by God; the second, the rabbinical, as a dialogue between God and the rabbis; and the third, after the Shoah, as being led by the people of Israel who no longer rely on God. Remarkably, Greenberg does not make any concluding statement about God. Instead, he expresses his sense of disappointment by ignoring God in the present. In this covenantal concept, God is neither declared alive and in charge nor dead or helpless. Ignoring God to the extent of not offering any comment on God's state of being

---

[55] Hardly any theologian calls him or herself a post-Shoah theologian, which is true also for the Jewish American philosophers Emil Fackenheim and Richard Rubenstein, who were originally labeled "Holocaust theologians," even without the "post."

[56] Zachary Braiterman, *(God)After Auschwitz: Tradition and Change in Post-Holocaust Jewish Thought* (Princeton, NJ: Princeton University Press, 1998), 31.

[57] Steven T. Katz, Gershon Greenberg, and Shlomo Biderman, eds., *Wrestling with God: Jewish Theological Responses during and after the Holocaust* (Oxford: Oxford University Press, 2007), 497–555.

effectively shifts the focus of responsibility to the human side of the covenantal contract.

Although the Christian post-Shoah theologians developed their thinking while in conversation with Jews, they could not avoid theodicy in a similar manner. My impression is that this is due to the centrality of covenant thought in Christian post-Shoah theology. The concept of a Jewish covenant being superseded by Christianity had once been central to supersessionism. In radical critique of this thought pattern, Christian post-Shoah theologians have strongly affirmed Israel's ongoing covenant. The notion of the unrevoked covenant lies at the heart of post-supersessionist Christian theology. Paradoxically, though, a strong affirmation of the presence and future of Israel inherently includes the affirmation of the presence and future of the divine covenant partner. Christian theologians affirming Israel therefore have a hard time questioning God. Apparently, Christians need God alive to affirm the living vitality of Judaism and Jews. But not speaking out against God leads to another unexpected and still little noticed theological problem. A Christian theology that does not protest God after the Shoah will eventually raise a question about the true identity of the God Christians worship. If Christians share the memory of the God of Abraham and Sarah as the God who sent Jesus Christ – against all neo-Marcionite denials – then the Jewish disappointment in this God must affect them too. Sharing the problem, in this case, is required as part of remembering the most fundamental Christian claim of belonging to the same God.[58]

Thus, the first constitutive Christian memory of the one God of Israel and of Jesus, made manifest in the Christian canon, serves as a directive even in contemporary theological interreligious discourse. Marcion had raised the basic question about whether Jews and Christians worship the same God. A post-Shoah theology is committed to affirming the anti-Marcionite position because it offers a fundamental assertion that Christians worship the same God as Jews – though not in the same way. But post-Shoah theologians themselves problematize this assertion, because they cannot follow Jews in overtly questioning God or putting God aside without ceasing to be Christians. And yet Christians have to insist on Jews' right to an anti-theodicy that they themselves do not partake of. Again, the rejection of Marcion lies at the bottom of this responsibility of post-Shoah

---

[58] Barbara U. Meyer, "Theodicy and Its Critique in Christian Post-Shoah Thought," in Beate Ego, Ute Gause, Ron Margolin, and Dalit Rom-Shiloni, eds., *Theodicy and Protest* (Tübingen: Evangelische Verlagsanstalt, 2018), 177–194.

Christian theologians to affirm the legitimacy of Jewish approaches to the shared God without necessarily engaging in those same approaches.

A theory of Christian memory cannot be formulated in contrast to Jewish memory, as Christianity shares large parts of the biblical narratives. On account of this textual basis, it is appropriate to describe Christian memory as inherently interreligious. The Christian equivalent to Yerushalmi's description of Judaism as a "unique fusion of religion and peoplehood" would then be a unique combination of religion and relatedness to Jewish peoplehood.[59] The Jewishness of Jesus can serve as "*anamnesis*," a reminder, but does not in itself provide a sufficient critique. Nevertheless, distorted memories can actually be repaired, both in the case of wrong facts – as to the responsibility for Jesus' death – and with regard to malevolent interpretations, such as the Christian triumph over the destruction of the Temple. I would call this the "anamnetic potential" of the memory of the Jewish Jesus. Taking the mending potential of memory and counter-memories seriously does not mean prioritizing memory over history. In this book, memory functions as a frame of reference helping us to formulate historical questions anew. The dimension of memory-discourse thus adds to the reflection on the Quest for the Historical Jesus and helps to formulate ideology-critiques of this research. Twentieth-century Historical Jesus research alternated between extreme pessimism and unmerited optimism. Scholars often exaggerated in oddly contradictory ways, either claiming to know nothing or expressing certainty over the exact details surrounding Jesus' words and deeds. In this polarized academic debate, the memory of the Jewish Jesus functions as a critical but moderating voice, asking about and assessing historical probabilities. Thus, in the spectrum of scholarly approaches, memory here is closer to historical research than to presenting alternative "narratives."[60] While this study is about the memory of Jesus the Jew, I treat his Jewishness as a historical fact rather than a variable memory.

---

[59] Yerushalmi, *Zakhor*, xxxvi.
[60] Memory, as well as counter-memories discussed in this study certainly have nothing to do with the recently invented idiom of "alternative facts."

2

The Past: History of Halakhah and Dogma

Understanding Jesus as part of the Jewish world rather than in contrast to Judaism has profoundly changed New Testament scholarship in recent decades. While at the beginning of the twentieth century only a few scholars perceived Jesus as an integral part of his environment, fully situating him in his Judean milieu has become the dominant approach of the last thirty years.[1] The so-called Third Quest for the historical Jesus is typically connected to this approach.[2] One cardinal question of this historical research is where exactly to place Jesus within the Judaism of his time – was he a charismatic Galilean, a Pharisee, or perhaps an apocalyptic prophet?[3] Yet interestingly, for the theological understanding of Jesus' Jewishness the question of Jesus' precise placement within Judaism seems to be of relatively minor importance. Systematic theologians reflecting on the meaning of Jesus' Jewishness tend not to dwell on discussions of Jesus' membership in a specific sect within Second Temple Judaism. None of the leading theologians who wrote Christologies that

---

[1] For a highly informative, comprehensive overview of the history of the search for the Historical Jesus, compare Gerd Theissen and Annette Merz, *The Historical Jesus: A Comprehensive Guide* (Minneapolis, MN: Fortress Press, 1998). For a recent overview of Jewish approaches to Jesus, see Walter Homolka, *Jesus Reclaimed: Jewish Perspectives on the Nazarene* (New York and Oxford: Berghahn, 2015).

[2] Ben Witherington has compiled a detailed overview of the main works representative for this approach. Ben Witherington, *The Jesus Quest: The Third Search for the Jew of Nazareth*, second edition (Downers Grove, IL: InterVarity Press, 1997).

[3] I agree with E. P. Sanders that Jews' participation in different literary and legal movements, e.g. "apocalypticism and the Pharisaic interpretation of Sabbath law," need not be mutually exclusive. See E. P. Sanders, *Judaism: Practice and Belief, 63 BCE–66 CE* (Minneapolis, MN: Fortress Press, 2016), 11.

focused on Jesus the Jew – Paul van Buren, Friedrich-Wilhelm Marquardt, Roy Eckardt, and Hans Hermann Henrix – made decisive statements about Jesus' membership in a specific grouping or indicated whether he belonged to any group at all. This should not be seen as reflecting a disregard for history but rather as a clear expression of Christological reasoning: The theological discussion of Jesus' Jewishness is a matter of memory, but it is not about the past. Terrence Tilley, for instance, prefers to speak about the "historic Jesus" as not "a person in the past" but "the person remembered by his followers."[4] The emphasis lies on the role and content of memory in the present.

Still, there are questions raised by the historical research on Jesus' affiliations within Second Temple Judaism that are highly relevant for contemporary Christological and interreligious discourse. The manifold opinions about certain Jewish sects as Jesus' primary groups of reference contain important sub-questions about his words and deeds that might sometimes prove even more significant than his group membership itself. The contrasts and correspondences between Christian and Jewish scholarship on Jesus have offered interesting insights for assessing his Jewishness, from the eighteenth century, as we will see, up through the present. Some twentieth-century Jewish scholars have sought to reclaim Jesus. Their reclaiming of Jesus as a Jew typically went together with high praise for his ethical, legal, and rhetorical creativity. Joseph Klausner (1874–1958), the first Jewish scholar to publish an academic historical account of Jesus in Hebrew, employed his appreciation to critique what he viewed as a widespread Jewish resentment toward Jesus.[5] Zev Harvey has called attention to an astonishingly different perspective presented by the Harvard Jewish intellectual historian Harry Austryn Wolfson (1887–1974) in a generally overlooked introduction, published in 1925, to Joseph Jacob's novel *Jesus as Others Saw Him*.[6] Harvey deserves credit for having rescued this short but insightful text from oblivion, and contrasted Wolfson's account of the Jewish Jesus with Klausner's,

---

[4] Terrence W. Tilley, "Remembering the Historic Jesus – A New Research Program?," *Theological Studies* 68 (2007): 3–35, 3. I agree with the importance of the remembering communities but would not reduce theological references to the memory of his followers.
[5] Joseph Klausner, *Jesus of Nazareth*, trans. Herbert Danby (New York: Macmillan, 1925).
[6] Harry Austryn Wolfson, "Introduction" to Joseph Jacobs, *Jesus as Others Saw Him* (New York: Arno Press, 1973 (1925)). Wolfson was already professor of Jewish medieval philosophy at Harvard. For my study, his later research on Christology as part of his work on the philosophy of the Kalam, his magnum opus in interreligious philosophy, will have special importance (see Chapter 6).

both from 1925.[7] But in contrast to Klausner's characterization of Jesus' moral teachings as outstanding, Harvey notices a completely different reasoning underlying Wolfson's call for a Jewish reclamation of Jesus. It is not because Jesus said anything particularly exceptional, but simply insofar as his teachings qualify him to be considered as one of the early Sages. Wolfson foresees a future Hebrew reclamation of the Galilean Jew in the Land of Israel. I find this moderate evaluation remarkable, as it has the strength of integrating the historical Jesus into the heart of Judaism – something forecast at the beginning of the twentieth century and thus well before the debates of the Third Quest. Among contemporary Jewish Jesus scholars, Amy Jill Levine comes closest to this approach. Written in the context of the advanced Third Quest, where Jesus' Jewishness needs neither proof nor praise, Levine's works display a refreshing freedom from the necessity to evaluate Jesus as a "marginal" or "central" Jew, crediting his teachings as both original and at the same time belonging to a specific context.[8]

REMEMBERING SECOND TEMPLE JUDAISM

There is a growing consensus among systematic theologians and exegetes that the dimension of "memory" is constitutive for Christological reasoning as well as crucial to historical analysis.[9] As an intellectual discipline, memory is not necessarily less scientific than "pure" historical research (in the manner seen by practitioners of the historical-critical method) but can help scholars to better frame historical facts, especially when various communities of memory differ in their fact-finding. At the same time, "memory" does not present an argument in itself nor does it simply fulfill a complementary function for historical research.[10]

---

[7] Warren Zev Harvey, "Harry Austryn Wolfson on the Jews' Reclamation of Jesus," in Neta Stahl, ed., *Jesus among the Jews: Representation and Thought* (New York: Routledge, 2012), 152–158. Harvey notes that the two scholars appreciated each other and suggests that Wolfson had read Klausner's book on Jesus.

[8] Amy-Jill Levine, *Short Stories by Jesus: The Enigmatic Parables of a Controversial Rabbi* (New York: Harper Collins, 2014).

[9] See the title and structure of New Testament scholar James Dunn's Jesus book; James D. G. Dunn, *Jesus Remembered* (Grand Rapids, MI: Wm. B. Eerdmans Publishing Co., 2003.)

[10] Wolfgang Stegemann offers an excellent critique of the languages used to present Jesus as "real," "historical," or "remembered" in his *Jesus und seine Zeit* (Stuttgart: Kohlhammer, 2009), 89ff.

The historical positioning of Jesus within Second Temple Judaism is certainly a matter of both historical research and memory. Jewish and Christian scholars of the Second Temple period have themselves been led by different memories; one might even go so far as to say that for centuries Christian scholars lacked a sense of memory as a force shaping their questions. With the growing awareness of the Jewish Jesus as a kind of suppressed or at least under-utilized memory, this began to change in the mid-twentieth century. Nevertheless, it took Christian scholars considerable time before the growing consciousness of the memory of the Jewish Jesus was matched by the knowledge and skills required to do justice to it. In the 1970s and even the 1980s, the division between Christian and Jewish scholars was for the most part predetermined by the former's inadequate knowledge of early rabbinic literature. Today, serious scholars from both backgrounds read each other's work, and some non-Jewish scholars have achieved mastery in midrashic literature, Mishnah and Talmud. This has transformed the discourse profoundly, and a scholar's view on the Historical Jesus is now not necessarily discernable or even in line with his or her religious affiliation, as we will see.

Two aspects of the historical positioning of Jesus within Second Temple Judaism are important for a theological reflection on Jesus the Jew. The first concerns Jesus' relation to contemporaneous Jewish law, and the second takes into consideration Jesus' uniqueness. Both questions deal with the way Jesus lived and with his deeds rather than with his words.[11] How are we to imagine his social position? Was he just outstanding or actually alone? Was he integrated or disconnected? What did he stand for? Was he a person committed to a certain viewpoint or a contrarian basically arguing with everyone else? Whether there was such a thing as a "Common Judaism" during the Second Temple period remains a highly debated question among historians as well as scholars of Rabbinic Judaism and of the New Testament.[12] Translated to the memory of Jesus, this historical research corresponds to the question of

---

[11] This is the reason why N. T. Wright's view of Jesus as an apocalyptic prophet is not discussed here, although he represents an important voice within the Third Quest. N. T. Wright, *Jesus and the Victory of God* (Minneapolis, MN: Fortress Press, 1997).

[12] Adele Reinhartz and Wayne O. McCready, eds., *Common Judaism: Explorations in Second-Temple Judaism*, second revised edition (Minneapolis, MN: Fortress Press, 2011). E. P. Sanders has coined the term "Common Judaism" and further developed it, especially in *Comparing Judaism and Christianity: Common Judaism, Paul, and the Inner and the Outer in Ancient Religion* (Minneapolis, MN: Fortress Press, 2016).

whether Jesus was near the center or closer to the margins of Judaism.[13] The traditional answer to Jesus' integration into Second Temple Judaism is negative, just as the common view regarding his singularity is generally positive – and both of these prejudgments are connected. Yet in recent years, historical research has been more inclined to see Jesus in the midst of and deeply rooted in Second Temple Judaism and to view him as part of a likeminded community, like the Pharisees if not the Pharisees themselves, a point I will discuss further on.

But one might ask, what theological difference would it make? It has long been suggested, and probably more feared and imagined than proven, that Jesus' full integration into the Judaism of his time would make him something "less" than what he had traditionally been seen as: less special, less revolutionary, and even somehow "less Christian." In fact, an in-depth study of Jesus' Judaism proves just the opposite. Looking closely at Jesus in his religious context leads to new insights about what the Christian memory of Jesus might actually mean to Christians today. Perceiving Jesus not just as a person who could have lived anywhere at any time, but learning about him as a Jew with a specific practice, narrative, and tradition, actually helps to revitalize his humanity. And his humanity is generally of unquestioned importance to any Christian past and present. It is not a secondary or negligible aspect of the Christ story. Rather, that Jesus has indeed lived is essential to the Christian faith. In fact, the historicity of Jesus is ingrained and fixed in the creeds of the early Church, as explicating his humanity. In the Chalcedonian creed, for instance, his birth is narrated as a twofold matter: according to his divinity he is begotten before all ages, but according to his humanity he is "in these latter days, for us and our salvation, born by the virgin Mary."[14] According to the ecumenical creeds of the early Church, the humanity of Jesus Christ is no less dogma and truth than is his divinity. And the Church Fathers considered the denial of his true humanity a heresy to be clarified and clearly rejected. By the fifth century, the divinity of Jesus Christ was well established and constitutive for the Christian faith, although attempts to reduce the humanity of Jesus were still being

---

[13] John P. Meier, *A Marginal Jew: Rethinking the Historical Jesus, Volume 3: Companions and Competitors* (New York: Yale University Press, 2001). Somewhat predictably, the thesis of Jesus' marginality has been succeeded by one that emphasizes his centrality. See Andre LaCocque, *Jesus the Central Jew: His Times and His People* (Atlanta: SBL Press, 2015).

[14] For the original text and accurate translation, see Norman Tanner, ed., *Decrees of the Ecumenical Councils* (Washington, DC: Georgetown University Press, 2017).

articulated and continued to demand explicit repudiation. For this reason, the historical imaging and illumination of Jesus is unthinkable without reference to his Jewishness. Being Jewish stands for a specific way of life and a particular narrative and tradition, a certain unique daily practice, a distinctive time structure, and probably even a unique approach to God that was in no way disconnected from the Jewish practice of the era.

How Jewishness was practiced and experienced is a question of intensive and ongoing research.[15] One particularly striking example of the implications of Second Temple history for Jewish–Christian relations is research on the Pharisees. The texts of the Gospels portray legal conflicts between Jesus and the Pharisees, and Christian tradition subsequently produced a hostile view of this group, which because of its resemblance to the later rabbis substantively compounded future Christian anti-Judaism. Yet individual scholars, as early as Abraham Geiger (1810–1874) and as recent as Harvey Falk (*Jesus the Pharisee*, 2003), linked Jesus closely to the Pharisaic movement.[16] In the second half of the twentieth century, Christian scholars reversed the negative image of the Pharisees and emphasized the group's positive social values and legal creativity. Christian theologians engaged in a revised approach to Judaism, emphasizing Jesus' closeness to the Pharisees together with his observance of Torah.[17] Consequently, the "reputation" of the Pharisees changed from the most contested to the most appreciated sect in Ancient Judaism, thus interestingly reflecting the shifting Christian approach to Jewish Law from one of contempt to one of respect.

More research on the Pharisees' legal reasoning promises to further strengthen this new Christian affirmation of Jesus as Torah-observant. But the increasing consensus over Jesus' observance is not necessarily proportionate to his identification with Pharisaic halakhic judgment. The historian Yair Furstenberg, for instance, has recently emphasized Jesus' disagreements with the Pharisees on matters of ritual purity.[18]

---

[15] See Sanders, *Judaism*.

[16] See Susannah Heschel, *Abraham Geiger and the Jewish Jesus* (Chicago: The University of Chicago Press, 1998); Harvey Falk, *Jesus the Pharisee: A New Look at the Jewishness of Jesus* (Eugene, OR: Wipf & Stock Publishers, 2003).

[17] The use of the term "Torah" is manifold: In the narrow scriptural sense, Torah means the five books of Moses only, but it is also used for the whole Hebrew Bible. In its still broader sense, Torah comprises the "oral tradition" of Jewish legal discourse, meaning the Mishnah and its great commentaries, the Jerusalem and Babylonian Talmud.

[18] Yair Furstenberg, "Defilement Penetrating the Body: A New Understanding of Contamination in Mark 7,15." *NTS* 54 (2008): 176–200.

Subsequently, Daniel Boyarin interpreted this legal difference as reflecting the contrast between the traditionalism of Jesus versus Pharisaic innovation.[19] In this manner, scholars of Jesus and Jewish Law have come full circle: from initially depicting Jesus as someone opposed to the Law and the Pharisees embodiment of it, to the effort to reduce the gap between Jesus and the Pharisees, and finally to this most recent view of Jesus as protecting biblical law against Pharisaic innovation. For the memory of Jesus the Jew, his historical relationship to the Pharisaic movement is particularly important, as the Pharisees represent the only sect of Second Temple Judaism that continued long after the destruction of the Temple and helped constitute rabbinical Judaism. Thus, the projection of the Pharisees as *the* Jews par excellence – a clearly distorted New Testament interpretation that presupposes Jesus' lack of Jewishness – somehow does make sense as a rabbinical memory. Jewish as well as Christian scholars engaged in the project of overcoming New Testamental anti-Jewish prejudice that clearly indulged in claiming Jesus as a Pharisee. Of course, Jesus need not belong to this sect in order to prove their treatment in New Testament texts unjust. However close or distant the historical Jesus was to the Pharisees, the redactors of the gospels, especially Matthew, clearly had no intention of presenting them fairly. David Flusser pointed out that "the wording of the Gospels exaggerates the clashes between Jesus and the Pharisees."[20] He suggested that while Jesus might not have identified as a Pharisee, his views were close to the Pharisaic school of Hillel. Giving an account of the memory of Jesus the Jew, his identification with the historical Pharisees' respective legal positions is less relevant than Jesus' being clearly invested, interested, and actively engaged in legal discourse and questions of observance. Pointing out Jesus' divergences and agreements with the Pharisees may promote a clearly anachronistic tendency to project the Pharisaic sect as halakhically uniform rather than discursive. But there are very good historical reasons to view them as a group discussing questions of law that were not yet decided on.

[19] Daniel Boyarin, *The Jewish Gospels: The Story of the Jewish Christ* (New York: The New Press, 2012), especially chapter 3.
[20] David Flusser, "Jesus," *Encyclopedia Judaica*, vol. 10 (Jerusalem: Keter Publishing House, 1972).

JESUS AND THE LAW: BOUND AND BINDING

David Flusser (1917–2000), Rabbinics and New Testament scholar at the Hebrew University, showed in his path-breaking 1969 work that Jesus lived according to the Torah and did not break its laws.[21] This account of Jesus was not entirely new; contemporaries like Geza Vermes had come to similar views somewhat earlier.[22] Indeed, as early as 1783 the Jewish Enlightenment philosopher Moses Mendelssohn had presented an impressive exegesis relating to both categories of history and memory:

Jesus of Nazareth was never heard to say that he had come to release the House of Jacob from the law. Indeed, he said, in express words, rather the opposite; and, what is still more, he himself did the opposite. Jesus of Nazareth himself observed not only the law of Moses but also the ordinances of the rabbis; and whatever seems to contradict this in the speeches and acts ascribed to him appears to do so only at first glance. Closely examined, everything is in complete agreement not only with Scripture, but also with the tradition. If he came to remedy entrenched hypocrisy and sanctimoniousness, he surely would not have given the first example of sanctimoniousness and authorized, by example, a law which should be abrogated and abolished. Rather, the rabbinic principle evidently shines forth from his entire conduct as well as the conduct of his disciples in the early period. *He who is not born into the law need not bind himself to the law; but he who is born into the law must live according to the law, and die according to the law.* If his followers, in later times, thought differently and believed they could release from the law also those Jews who accepted their teaching, this surely happened without his authority.[23]

Writing in the late eighteenth century, Mendelssohn's Christian contemporaries, including some who had previously expressed admiration for his work, either declined to take seriously his account of Jesus as Torah-observant (like Kant, assuming Mendelssohn was engaged in a clever ruse) or else regarded it as a hostile attack on Christianity.[24] Of course, Mendelssohn was not speaking with the academic authority of a university professor, which was not an option for Jews in Europe until the end of the nineteenth century – and not in the field of New Testament studies until the late twentieth. His scholarship was highly regarded in

---

[21] David Flusser, *Jesus*, third edition (Jerusalem: Hebrew University Magnes Press, 2001), especially 56–80.

[22] Geza Vermes, *Jesus the Jew: A Historian's Reading of the Gospels* (Minneapolis, MN: Fortress Press, 1973).

[23] Moses Mendelssohn, *Jerusalem, or On Religious Power and Judaism,* translated by Allan Arkush (Hanover, NH: Brandeis University Press, 1983), 134.

[24] Alexander Altmann, *Moses Mendelssohn: A Biographical Study* (London: Litman Library, 1998), 532–552.

almost all fields – except, one might say, for his views on Jesus, despite his knowledge of rabbinics and in a way because of it.

Approximately two hundred years later, David Flusser in a sense ratified Mendelssohn's intentions when he taught New Testament texts and studies of the Historical Jesus at Jerusalem's Hebrew University. Coming from a recognized scholar belonging to Jerusalem's Orthodox community, Flusser's writings proved a shock to his Jewish colleagues in Israel as well as to Christian scholars abroad.[25] John Gager has interpreted Flusser's view of Jesus as based on good interfaith intentions.[26] I understand his scholarship as profiting from knowledge of rabbinic literature that New Testament scholars of his generation seldom had. Since Flusser, recognizing Jesus as observing Halakhah,[27] the Jewish religious law of his time, has led to major shifts in New Testament exegesis and Historical Jesus research. In many cases, the study of rabbinic literature exerted a profound impact on the readings of New Testament texts by young Christian scholars visiting the Hebrew University in the sixties, among them E. P. Sanders, Peter Schäfer, and Michael Krupp. These scholars became major influences in New Testament research and Jewish studies, and their books about Jesus exhibit their first-hand understanding of the pharisaic and rabbinic contexts.[28]

Flusser emphasized that Jesus himself did not break any contemporaneous Jewish laws, which is not disconnected but still distinct from the question of the observance of the disciples as well as the question of whether Jesus held specific opinions as a legal scholar.[29] Sanders, today representing mainstream New Testament scholarship, summarizes the point as follows: "The synoptic Jesus lived as a law-abiding Jew."[30]

---

[25] It is hard to decide for whom this was more difficult to digest. The Christian New Testament scholars were asked nothing less than to turn their research upside down. The Israeli reaction might be understood by the fact that the Hebrew translation of his groundbreaking book *Jesus* (German: 1968; English: 1997) appeared in 2009.

[26] John G. Gager, "Scholarship as Moral Vision: David Flusser on Jesus, Paul, and the Birth of Christianity," *Jewish Quarterly Review* 95 (2005): 60–73.

[27] Halakhah is the term for the discussion and practice of religious law in Judaism. Accordingly, Judaism can be described as a "halakhic religion."

[28] E. P. Sanders, *Jesus and Judaism* (London: SCM Press, 1985); Peter Schäfer, *The Jewish Jesus: How Judaism and Christianity Shaped Each Other* (Princeton, NJ and Oxford: Princeton University Press, 2012); Peter Schäfer, *Jesus in the Talmud* (Princeton, NJ: Princeton University Press, 2007); Michael Krupp, *Jesus und die galiläischen Chassidim* (Tübingen: TVT Medienverlag, 2014).

[29] E. P. Sanders does not regard Jesus as a legal scholar or "Rabbi." See Sanders, *Jewish Law from Jesus to the Mishnah* (Minneapolis, MN: Fortress Press, 2016), 4.

[30] Sanders, *Jewish Law from Jesus to the Mishnah*, 125.

I regard the view of Jesus himself as fundamentally observant as constitutive for any discourse on Jesus the Jew. Nevertheless, while the notion
of a halakhically observant Jesus has altered the historical scholarship of
Christians, it has thus far been absorbed into the thought of only a very
few systematic theologians committed to a revised Christian understanding of Judaism. Strikingly, if not surprisingly, the few theologians who did
focus on a law-bound Jesus were those who had themselves struggled
with a particular antinomian background, such as the Lutherans Dietrich
Bonhoeffer, Friedrich-Wilhelm Marquardt, and Katharina von
Kellenbach.[31] Marquardt opens his Christology with an extraordinary
account of non-Christian perceptions of Jesus worldwide.[32] They converge in but one aspect of his life: Jesus' conflict with and opposition to
the law.[33] Of course, what is referred to generally as "the law" will
always be the Jewish law, Halakhah. This fact is significant: The non-
Christian world knows little about Jesus, and non-Christians hardly
know him as a Jew. But they all have heard about him being opposed
to Jewish law! Marquardt shows that presenting Jesus in opposition to
Jewish law is connected to an anti-Jewish profile of Jesus. Thus, he
concludes that there is a specifically Christian responsibility for these
widespread anti-Jewish conceptions of Jesus that have long transcended
Christian borders.[34] I would add here my own evaluation that Christian
anti-Judaism today is expressed mainly in depreciating law theologically.
This kind of Christian anti-Judaism does not need to refer to Jews or
Judaism explicitly and thus is especially problematic since it is typically
more subtle and less overt than what preceded it.[35]

While Marquardt tries to integrate law back into Christianity, I would
formulate the Christian task in a slightly different way: How can Christianity as a non-halakhic religion express true appreciation for the Other's
religious law? A first step would be the very recognition of Jesus as a

---

[31] Friedrich-Wilhelm Marquardt identified with the earlier Reformations. See Marquardt,
Prolegomena, 1988, 9. Another example of a Lutheran-based theologian reflecting
critically on Christian approaches to law is Katharina von Kellenbach. She was the first
feminist theologian to sharply analyze the pattern and pitfalls of anti-Judaism promoted
by feminism: The eagerness to claim Jesus as treating women equally is established by
exaggerating the Law's discrimination against women in Second Temple Judaism. See
Katharina von Kellenbach, *Anti-Judaism in Religious Feminist Writing* (Atlanta: Scholars
Press, 1994).

[32] Friedrich-Wilhelm Marquardt, *Das christliche Bekenntnis zu Jesus, dem Juden. Eine
Christologie*, Vol I, (Munich: Kaiser, 1990).

[33] Marquardt, *Christologie I*, 92–93.   [34] Ibid., 94.

[35] And exceeds the context of Jewish–Christian relations.

practicing, Torah-observant and halakhically committed Jew. In a second move, Jesus' sayings about Jewish law should be understood as demonstrating his participation in discussions over laws, not his deprecation of Jewish law per se. Whatever Christians traditionally marked as Jesus' "criticism of Jewish law" as such should now be understood as his embrace of a given position within the halakhic discourse, of which there was a wide spectrum at the time.[36] In traditional as well as popular exegesis of the Gospels it has long been agreed that Jesus was on the moderate side of the juridical spectrum, meaning that he would generally opt against a strict interpretation of the law. Placing Jesus in proximity to the school of Hillel, famous for legal teachings that were depicted as moderate, has been a Jewish historical tendency going back to Abraham Geiger (1810–1874).[37] Yet, a close reading of the Sermon on the Mount clearly shows that Jesus is not actually lifting the burden of commandments but rather presenting a stricter interpretation than that of his putative opponents, as for example regarding divorce. In later Christian traditions and especially those promoted by Luther, these Jesus-sayings were interpreted as intentionally taking the law *ad absurdum*. But historically and in context of early rabbinical reasoning, it seems improbable that Jesus meant to lighten the weight of commitment by showing that full observance is impossible. Jesus' interpretation of law in the Sermon on the Mount shows him closer to the stricter school of Shammai than to Hillel, with whom he is usually affiliated for emphasizing the centrality of the commandment to love one's neighbor.[38] Chana Safrai (1946–2008), a scholar of Rabbinic Literature and the New Testament, found support for Jesus' closeness to Shammai in their shared legal favoritism toward women.[39] This affinity to the stricter school of legal reasoning increases

---

[36] Lawrence Schiffman has emphasized that despite Josephus's descriptions of the various Second Temple sects as differing primarily over beliefs, in truth their major conflicts surrounded matters of halakhic practice. See Lawrence Schiffman, ed., *Texts and Traditions: A Source Reader for the Study of the Second Temple and Rabbinic Judaism* (Hoboken, NJ: Ktav, 1998), 233.

[37] Susannah Heschel, *Abraham Geiger and the Jewish Jesus*. Geiger's claim of similarity between Jesus and Hillel was greeted smugly by nineteenth-century Christian scholars.

[38] There is a long research history connecting the two, reaching from Abraham Geiger to David Flusser. James H. Charlesworth and Loren L. Johns, ed., *Hillel and Jesus: Comparisons of Two Major Religious Leaders* (Minneapolis, MN: Fortress Press, 1997).

[39] Chana Safrai, "Bet Hillel and Bet Shammai," in *Jewish Women's Archive. Encyclopedia* (jwa.org). The article does not refer to Jesus, but Safrai often mentioned the Shammai–Jesus alliance in her teaching.

the gap between Jesus and any antinomianism traditionally projected onto him. Based on more recent research of Jesus in the Jewish context, the historical authenticity of a saying attributed to Jesus increases in likelihood when he positioned himself as "*maḥmir*," which is the technical Hebrew term for choosing the respectively stricter alternative in halakhic discourse. Harry Austryn Wolfson humorously picks up this question of Jesus' affiliation in the aforementioned text of 1925, envisioning an obituary of Jesus in a Galilean synagogue citing his rulings about divorce: "O Rabbi Jesus, verily thou art a Shammaite; but we have long decided to follow the more lenient views of Hillel."[40]

The Christian relationship to law has always been complex and multifaceted. In the Protestant and especially the Lutheran tradition, the doctrine of justification has served as a theological means to subordinate law to belief. But while the doctrine of justification was formulated only in the sixteenth century and is held to be central only by Protestant Christians, the priority of faith is a Pauline idea and thus relevant for all Christians. Since Christian identity was first formulated in 325 (the Nicaean Creed), it has not been praxis or law but rather the content of belief that has defined Christian belonging. What Christians worldwide have in common is expressed in the language of faith. There is a certain tension between this assumption of the overall superiority of faith and the Jew Jesus who probably did not regard faith as higher than law or, rather, separable from it. But in theological terms, the observant Jesus of history and the priority accorded to faith by Christianity need not be seen as contradictory. A deeper reflection reveals that the observant Jesus is included in fourth-century ecumenical dogma: "truly human," as confessed in Nicaea, means truly a specific flesh-and-blood human from a particular time and place – a Galilean, a man, a teacher, a healer, a Jewish person who observed Shabbat. Thus law – observance – is a characteristic that helps us to perceive Jesus' humanity in accordance with the earliest dogma, even illuminating it by making humanness more concrete. The commandment to both remember and keep the Shabbat strongly expresses the biblical connection between memory and law. As one of the halakhic practices doubtlessly important to Jesus, he appears as a Jew remembering and observing.

Another ecumenical Christian question is whether Jesus' observing the law and "fulfilling the law" (Mt 5,17) need to be seen as conflicting, in

---

[40] Harry Austryn Wolfson, "Introduction," in Jacobs, *Jesus as Others Saw Him.*

terms of the historical versus the theological, or whether they can be interpreted as synonymous statements. Observing the law is a repetitive, ongoing, never-ending process, whereas fulfilling the law implies its one-time-only perfect realization in Jesus. I would suggest the following distinction: Jesus the Jew observed the commandments of the Torah, and Jesus Christ fulfilled the Torah without abrogating it. The first is a historical and the second a Christological statement. Both are part of the Christian belief that comprises the humanity and the divinity of Jesus Christ. Jews will approve only of the first part and not of the second, due to their own commitment to Torah. For Christians, perceiving the Torah as holy is not only a matter of recently learned respect toward Judaism. In Paul's Epistle to the Romans, Torah is declared holy (Rom 7,7).[41] Paul's theological reason for maintaining the Torah's holiness still commits today's Christians to hold Torah holy, even though they are not obser-vant of Jewish Halakhah: It is one and the same God who gave the Torah and who sent Jesus Christ, the same God who created the world and made a covenant with Israel. This God is characterized by Paul as not taking his gifts back (Romans 11, 29), neither the covenant nor the Torah. Christians as believers in this God of the Bible – and not an abstract Godhead – witness Israel's ongoing covenant and hold the Torah holy, while they themselves do not follow contemporary Jewish law.

This revised Christian approach to Halakhah is not simply an act of modern religious tolerance. Rather, Christian memory bears witness to Torah-observance as the way Jesus lived the covenant even though Chris-tians live and observe the covenant differently. Contemporary Christians without Jewish family background – in Paul's words, Gentile Christians – find themselves here experiencing the covenant differently from their savior. In the history of Christian thought, the positive significance of Jewish law for Christian faith has been neglected – with the important exception of Marquardt, who expressed the highest esteem for Halakhah and aspired to develop Christian dogmatic thought as "Evangelical Hala-khah."[42] He did not intend to turn Christianity into a halakhic religion, but he did want to reconsider the status of commandments and religious practice versus theory within the frame of Christian dogmatics.

---

[41] The letter to the Romans as Paul's theological testament is here given priority over his polemics in his earlier letter to the Galatians, but compare Boyarin, who takes the opposite path. See Daniel Boyarin, *A Radical Jew: Paul and the Politics of Identity* (Berkeley and Los Angeles: University of California Press, 1994).

[42] Marquardt, *Prolegomena*, 166ff.

My proposal is to maintain the dissimilarity of observance between Jesus and his followers today and to explore the spiritual value of this difference. That is to say, there is a limit to the imaging of Jesus. "Thou shalt not make any graven image" concerns first of all God, but Jesus too is more alive when not reified by Christian thought. Thus precisely as the law-bound Jew, Jesus gains freedom for Christians. A Jewish man of the Second Temple period, he lived according to the Jewish law of his time. Torah-observance was his way of living the covenant. Christians today hold the Torah holy, both as their own text and as the tradition and law of another community, the Jews. Yet there is no need to appropriate Halakhah in order to express Christian respect for Jewish law. I would go as far as to say that the opposite is the case: Christian respect for Jewish Halakhah is not well expressed by an attempt at assimilation. Torah observance is a specifically Jewish way of living the covenant. Christians trying to make this way their own actually risk compromising the dignity ascribed to the particularly Jewish commitment. But while Torah observance is the specific Jewish way of living the covenant, Christians are bound to the scriptural basis of Jewish Torah, the Five Books of Moses. Textually, the Christian relation to law is highly complex, as the Christian canon entails many legal texts, both in the New and the Old Testament. Both text groups are connected to Jesus. The laws in the books of Exodus, Leviticus, Numbers, and Deuteronomy, but also Torah hymns in the Psalms, are part of the historical Jesus' holy text. The Gospels witness Jesus discussing Jewish law, and central texts like the Sermon on the Mount are actually halakhic discussions; they are interpretations of Torah commandments.[43]

This paradox of Christianity's being a non-halakhic religion and its textual rootedness in law has been widely overlooked in systematic theology. The memory of Jesus as an observant Jew can actually help to reconcile this disparity without falling into the old pitfall of supersessionism. Perceiving Jesus as a participant in the halakhic practice and discourse of his time can encourage Christians not only to be witnesses to the ongoing covenant of the people Israel, as already professed in numerous Church declarations, but also to affirm the concrete commitment to

---

[43] Christianity in general and the Lutheran Reformation in particular went according to Paul, or more precisely, according to an antinomian reading of Paul. But today a majority of New Testament scholars agrees that Paul perceived the Torah as God-given. Even Lutherans who preferred the polemics in Galatians over Paul's in-depth theological analysis in Romans still had to deal with the fact of a large corpus of law texts being part of Holy Scripture. See my discussion on contemporary readings of Paul in Chapter 6.

Jewish covenantal existence today. Thus, to give but one example, Christians would not be neutral regarding Jewish opportunities for the observance of kashrut, the dietary laws, but would act as witnesses for this concrete Jewish way of living the covenant, thus helping to enable a practice that is not their own, but that they know of as holy according to their own sources. (This witness does not imply a Christian preference of Orthodox over Reform post-halakhic interpretation of kashrut). A similar argumentation can be applied to questions and current controversies over circumcision, as we will see in Chapter 4.

The Christian memory of Jesus as law-observant is not limited to remembering a practice that is not Christian. But there is also a tradition, at least a long-established Christian counter-tradition, of taking Jesus' practice seriously: for instance, monistic traditions that refrain from owning property in remembrance of Jesus' poverty. The understanding of Jesus as committed to Halakhah helps us to see his practice as a part and even a realization of his God relationship. This memory is helpful for a Christian revision of the hierarchy between belief and ethics in Christian theologies.[44]

ONLY JESUS: UNIQUENESS AND BELONGING

The second historical aspect that bears theological relevance concerns the uniqueness of Jesus as a Jew of the Second Temple Period. Since the eighteenth century, Christian scholarship has shown increasing interest in research on the historical Jesus. New Testament scholars have been continuously revising the methods and criteria for the so-called Quest for the Historical Jesus.[45] The overall objective of this research was to differentiate between the authentic and the secondarily transmitted sayings of Jesus. Methodologically, his Jewish context was important in a rather ironic manner. In the 1950s, the German Protestant theologian Ernst Käsemann suggested the criterion of dissimilarity as a methodology to identify the actual words of Jesus. With regard to Jesus' Jewishness, this

---

[44] Emmanuel Levinas has called for ethics as first discipline of philosophy and it would certainly be a great challenge to extend this call to Christian systematic theology, as I have suggested in my book on post-Shoah Christology. See Barbara U. Meyer, *Im Schatten der Shoah – im Lichte Israels. Studien zu Paul van Buren und Wilhelm-Friedrich Marquardt* (Zürich: Theologischer Verlag Zürich, 2004).

[45] It is common to differentiate three phases of this research. The First Quest for the Historical Jesus was concluded by Albert Schweitzer in 1906. The Second Quest started in 1953 with Ernst Käsemann, and the third began in the 1980s.

meant that any sign of his rootedness in Judaism was viewed as less authentic than any attested opposition to it! This method, although presented as a historical-critical tool, exhibited a strong bias against the integration of Jesus into the Jewish world of his times.

In the second half of the twentieth century, while still at times utilizing the criterion of dissimilarity, the attitude toward a pointedly Jewish Jesus began to change. But it was only in the 1980s, strongly promoted by New Testament scholar E. P. Sanders, that the Jewish context of Jesus' biography became central. This initially academic outsider position eventually became mainstream. Toward the end of the second decade of the twenty-first century, the importance of Second Temple Judaism as the primary context of the historical Jesus has been acknowledged by the overwhelming majority of New Testament researchers. Of course, this change was not just facilitated by a newly positive Christian attitude toward Jews, but by an expansion of information about Second Temple Judaism. For example, both in traditional and previous academic exegesis, Jesus had been portrayed as breaking the law by healing on Shabbat. Now, the study of rabbinic literature has demonstrated that the principle of *pikuaḥ nefesh*, the priority of saving lives, was already widely known in the Second Temple period; hence Jesus' choice was not opposed to but rather in line with much contemporaraneous Halakhah. Obviously, Jewish law then was not the same as Halakhah today. But major concepts, such as *pikuaḥ nefesh*, appear already to have been well established at the time.[46] Other exegetes have noted that Jesus' healing does not involve any transgression since he heals by words. With the knowledge of parallel rabbinic texts, two flaws of traditional exegesis could thereby be corrected: the negative imaging of Jewish law as not promoting healing, and a cheap elevation of Jesus at the cost of demeaning Judaism.

Understanding Jesus within rather than against his Jewish context did not necessarily weaken the estimation of his historical impact. On the contrary, deepening the understanding of his involvement and rootedness in Judaism helped to anchor him anew in history. This is best shown with the example of New Testament scholar Rudolf Bultmann (1884–1976), in contrast to early twentieth-century Jewish scholars like Joseph Klausner.[47] Bultmann's studies on the historical Jesus were characterized by an overall skepticism regarding the historicity of Jesus as such.

---

[46] See 1 Maccabees 2; M Yoma 8; (BT Yoma 80a–84b).
[47] Joseph Klausner, *Jesus of Nazareth: His Life, Times, and Teaching* (London: Allen and Unwin, 1925.)

Bultmann had even proposed that we simply cannot be sure whether there had ever really been a historical Jesus.[48] But his most famous statement on the matter was a Christological one: Bultmann claimed that it was not important whether Jesus had a historical existence, important for the Christian belief was the "thatness" of Christ having been sent (*das "Daß" des Gekommenseins*). In sharp contrast to this withdrawal from history, early twentieth-century Jewish scholarship exhibited little doubt as to Jesus' historical existence.

Noting this disparity, the Christian theologian Marquardt contrasted the "historical-critical minimum" with the "Jewish maximum" and explained the Jewish trust in Jesus' historical being with reference to the specific character of the Jewish memory chain.[49] Jewish existence is remembered from generation to generation, Marquardt notes, and the memory is credible in the sense that the Jewish person doing the remembering sees himself or herself as a link in the chain of generations. Thus Marquardt presents Jews' assumption of Jesus' historicity as a reflection of Jewish memory. Marquardt's hypothesis is fascinating. No matter whether secular, Reform, or Orthodox, Jewish scholars did not tend to share Bultmann's skepticism. They were aware (also here, secular, Orthodox, and Reform alike) of Jesus having been a Jew and sometimes reach out to defend Jesus against a Christian view of him. It is a commonplace that Jews do not accept Jesus' messiahship, let alone his divinity. Interesting is the fact, however, that even young Israeli students who grew up in a Jewish majority context and without any encounter with New Testament texts still display a certain knowledge of Jesus. It may be explained as a collective memory of the unconscious kind, since in Israeli education there is very little information transmitted regarding Jesus, either positive or negative.[50] Different from Jewish students in Christian majority cultures, who inevitably pick up tidbits of information through common cultural references, Israeli youth scarcely know any of the stories, or attributed sayings, of Jesus. Rather, their

---

[48] Interestingly, Bultmann was not questioning Jesus as a historical person in his early Jesus book from the twenties. In this short, well-written book, Bultmann displays an unusual familiarity with rabbinical Judaism and describes Jesus as rabbi! This early publication of Bultmann thus supports my thesis of the Jewishness ensuring Jesus' historicity. See his *Jesus* (Berlin: Deutsche Bibliothek, 1926).

[49] Marquardt, *Christologie I*, 135–138. In traditional Judaism this "memory chain" is known as *shalshelet hakabbalah*, chain of tradition.

[50] The Jewish religious and secular school systems do not differ much in this.

fragmentary knowledge is composed of images: the image of Jesus walking on water, transmitted humorously, and the image of Jesus on the cross.[51]

It is remarkable, indeed, that an Israeli student almost entirely lacking in textual knowledge would more often than not seek to defend Jesus against Church "misunderstandings." Nothing comparable can be seen with Buddha, whom secular Israelis tend to admire, or Muhammad, whom they usually do not admire. Israeli students might like or criticize Buddha and Muhammad in light of their representations in the respective traditions referring to them. But they will often refer directly and with astonishingly sure judgment to Jesus. Were we to pursue these admittedly anecdotal perceptions more systematically and scientifically, we would need to ask in return how these students' criticism of Jesus might be different from typical Western perceptions of Jesus as a barefooted pacifist or hippie or as an outsider misconceived by a power-hungry church? Jewish Israeli students seem to perceive Jesus as a rebel or reformer, as a prophet or a Reform Rabbi. Marquardt probably had Jewish scholars like David Flusser in mind when he developed his theory of Jewish memorial attestation to Jesus' historicity: Israeli professors who had themselves received a broad European education. The fact that the Jewish recognition of the Jew Jesus transcends time and place – the generations as well as the Diaspora–Israel gap – supports Marquardt's impressive intuition for the transmission of Jewish knowledge. The Jewish act of recognizing Jesus does not at all imply recognition of the Church's understandings of Jesus, but, on the contrary, is usually connected to a criticism of the traditional Christian view.

In most of the Historical Jesus literature, the uniqueness of Jesus has been presupposed rather than presented as a result of actual research. Impressions are different when Jesus' actions are evaluated through the prism of rabbinical literature. Shmuel Safrai (1919–2003), like Flusser an Orthodox Jewish professor at the Hebrew University of Jerusalem, drew attention to remarkable similarities between Jesus and Second Temple Hasidim, charismatic Galileans,[52] as did Geza Vermes.[53] Talmudic texts tell of such charismatics

---

[51] The 2004 Israeli film "Walk on Water" is a good example of the resonance of New Testament images in contemporary Israeli culture.

[52] Shmuel Safrai, "Jesus and the Hasidim," *Jerusalem Perspectives* 42–44 (1994): 3–22.

[53] Geza Vermes, *Christian Beginnings: From Nazareth to Nicaea* (New Haven, CT: Yale University Press, 2014), esp. the first two chapters. For a detailed history of the Hasid Theory within Jesus research, see Hilde Brekke Moller, *The Vermes Quest: The Significance of Geza Vermes for Jesus Research* (London and New York: Bloomsbury T&T Clark, 2017), esp. chapters 9–11.

as Hanina ben Dosa, who likewise performed miracles, engaged in healing, and were recognized as especially dear to God. A version of the story of the famous Honi "the Circle-drawer" (Honi ha-Meagel) appears as early as the Mishna (Taanith 3.8), the first rabbinic text body and far closer to Jesus' time. The historical Honi lived before Jesus, during the first century B.C.E. One of the striking features of this text is the description of Honi as son of God. The narratives about these charismatic personalities coincide with what is told about Jesus in several aspects. They were itinerant preachers and healers in the Galilee and led a simple, ascetic lifestyle. They healed people and occasionally faced halakhic problems in their contact with the sick. Unusual for mishnaic literature that typically centers on men's study of the law, there are many stories about Hasidim healing and helping women. Safrai explained this by noting that these miracle-men acted outside the house of study, and so, most naturally, came across women in need of help. Outstanding are their prayers, individually formulated and demonstrated in front of audiences who confirm the effectiveness of the charismatics' petitioning of God. The parallels between these charismatics and Jesus are not limited to minor similarities like geographical and social settings.[54] They include also characteristics once assumed to belong exclusively to Jesus, like the use of the father and son metaphor special connection to God of the pious. Safrai argues that "in Hasidic circles the relationship of a Hasid to God was not just one of 'child of God', but of a son who can brazenly make requests of his father that someone else cannot make. The Hasid addressed God as '*abba*', 'my father', or 'my father in heaven', and the LORD responded the way he responded to 'Hanina, my son'."[55] Safrai also notes that the Hasidim were the sole addressees for the cure of illnesses: "It should be stressed that all the stories indicate that people turned to the Hasidim and to no other group to effect cures or exorcise evil spirits. People may occasionally have turned to more mainstream sages to pray for rain within the framework of the ceremonies connected with drought, but they went only to the Hasidim to cure illness or chase away spirits."[56]

---

[54] The displays of magical and healing properties are not the only examples of significant Second Temple Judaic parallels with Jesus. Josephus himself catalogued a number of messianic pretenders who proliferated in the first century. On this topic more broadly, see Richard A. Horsely, *Bandits, Prophets, and Messiahs: Popular Movements at the Time of Jesus* (Salem, OR: Trinity Press, 1999). The difference in the case of figures like Honi is that some of them were later legitimized by the Rabbis. The only contemporary messianic figure who partly fit this model was Simon bar Kokhba, and then only possibly and momentarily by some leading Rabbis, most notably Rabbi Akiba.

[55] Safrai, "Jesus and the Hasidim," 7.   [56] Ibid.

How is the notion of Jesus' uniqueness affected if he did not only have disciples but also colleagues: charismatics, recognized as God's beloved and likewise performing miracles? Here it is helpful to differentiate between uniqueness and singularity. The discovery of historical personalities similar to Jesus, the Jewish Galilean itinerant charismatics, does not compromise his uniqueness. Generally, the existence of colleagues does not call into question one's uniqueness but rather changes one's social situation from solitude to interconnectedness. Not his uniqueness, but Jesus' singularity is called into question by the research on Second Temple Hasidism. Like other types of contextualization, situating Jesus in his "professional" religious environment only intensifies his rootedness in Jewish history. But as noted, the historical fact that there were Jews who lived like him, who were close to God, capable of performing miracles and dedicated to healing the sick, does not serve as an argument against Jesus' uniqueness. E. P. Sanders has pointed out that Jesus' uniqueness is not and should not be based on sayings uniquely related to him.[57] It is fascinating that a scholar of exegesis and not of dogmatics made this important Christological statement.

I would like to extend this observation even further. Jesus' uniqueness is not and should not be based on words or deeds solely related to him. Let me illustrate this point by approaching it from a dogmatic theological perspective.

The uniqueness of Jesus is only a traditional Christian notion. It is not in itself dogma. Christ's sonship, of course, is unique, but it is not uniqueness that is professed by the Christian believer but sonship! In strictly dogmatic thinking, the claim of uniqueness for the historical Jesus could even be seen as promoting dynamism, an approach that the Church Fathers marked as heresy. In dynamism the divinity of Jesus Christ was seen as a secondary acquisition of a figure who had been born "less" or even non-divine and was only later divinely empowered. The official Christian belief, first formulated in Nicaea at the beginning and then approved in Constantinople at the end of the fourth century, knows of Jesus Christ as *always* having been the Son of God. There is no need to claim uniqueness for Jesus' human existence, but in strictly dogmatic argumentation such a claim could be even misleading. Jesus

---

[57] E. P. Sanders, *The Question of Uniqueness in the Teaching of Jesus* (London: The University of London Press, 1990).

Christ is unique in Christian belief insofar as only he is the Son who is both human and divine. The claim of a historical uniqueness of Jesus preceding his uniquely being Jesus Christ does not serve Christian dogma.

Jesus Christ was fully human and he was not alone. There were others who shared his views, his practices, his questions and discussions. He was not remote but deeply involved in his surroundings, listening to others, talking to them, learning and teaching. This is exactly what fully human means: engaging with people, committing to others, withdrawing, reaching out, finding friends, building trust, earning recognition, experiencing disappointment. Full humanity is lived in communion with others. Together, involved, connected – and also alone: Jesus surely had original views and ideas of his own and possibly did proclaim messages not heard before. In today's language, he might be assumed to be an individualist, listening to his own inner voice, not assimilating to mainstream opinion, not adapting other people's judgments. He was his own person, and being fully human also means precisely that: to be yourself. He was irreplaceable, there was no one like him; he was the only one of his kind. And, as is typical for an individualist, he probably felt lonely at times, misunderstood, not fully recognized, and not always appreciated for what he himself wished to be acknowledged for. At times he no doubt felt like a stranger, sometimes even isolated. Living in communion with other people and feeling at times isolated are not contradictions but markers of the full spectrum of the social experience. All these characteristics conform to another phrase from the Chalcedonean Creed of 451: "in all things like unto us." Jesus' full humanity comprises his being integrated and his being estranged. He is different and he fully belongs at the same time. In traditional readings of the Gospel, Christian exegetes would have typically emphasized Jesus' estrangement over his belonging and presented it in terms of distance from Judaism. Historically, though, it makes more sense to prioritize his cultural bond. However, all of these modern characterizations, individualism and integration alike, need to be employed cautiously to avoid anachronism.

The category of Jewishness, though heterogeneous in itself for this period (as for our own), is still the most helpful in order to limit if not prevent such anachronism. Jesus can be described as an individualist within Jewish culture. His personal independence and originality did not change the fact of his religious belonging. So, instead of playing out Jesus' singularity against his Jewishness, it is historically appropriate to describe his special personality within the parameters of Jewish identity.

Although it is difficult to reconstruct precisely what being Jewish meant for the Second Temple period, historical and archeological research can help to frame an outline of "daily" Jewishness, for example, around the halakhic and spiritual reality of Shabbat.[58]

THE HISTORICAL JESUS AND CHRISTIAN DOGMA

Paradoxically, in the academic world trust in the reality of a historical Jesus is sometimes expressed more confidently among Jews than among Christians. The fact that Jesus is remembered and recognized as a Jew also by scholars (and students) of today's Jewish community bears theological significance in itself. The rootedness of Jesus in the covenant of Abraham and Sarah and his belonging to the Law of Moses and Miriam as perceived and approved by the followers of Mosaic Law – this truly binds today's followers of Jesus to the people of the covenant.

Hence the historical research on Jesus has far-reaching and highly complex theological implications. Historical insights into the Jewishness of Jesus are fully compatible with – indeed, integral to – Christian belief in Jesus Christ. Even more so, the study of Jesus' historical context even strengthens Christian dogma. The historical research on Jesus has dogmatic significance, and the focus on his Jewishness increases this by rooting him more deeply in Second Temple Judaism. The more characteristics and features we learn about his time, the more details are available for describing his true humanity. To estrange Jesus from a concrete historical context and to doubt Jesus' historicity means to doubt his full humanity. The Church Fathers were strongly concerned about ensuring the full humanity of Jesus in the creed, against popular views that presented him as being only seemingly human, a heresy known as "Docetism." According to the patristic authors, to diminish Jesus' humanity is a heresy. It can be said that describing Jesus' humanity in Jewish terms is a further prophylactic against Docetism. And illustrating how Jesus lived as a Jew deepens this anti-Docetic impetus.

---

[58] In her book about Jesus' mother Mary, Elizabeth Johnson has beautifully portrayed what it meant to be a Jewish woman at that time. Elizabeth Johnson, *Truly Our Sister: A Theology of Mary in the Communion of Saints* (New York: Bloomsbury Publishing, 2006).

The discourse about Jesus' specific placement within Second Temple Judaism is not irrelevant for theology, especially when discussing Jesus' approach to Torah. But more persuasive than Jesus' particular legal opinion or whether or not he held specific legal opinions is the fact that Jesus lived a life of Torah. This recognition opens up dogmatic discourse to fresh understandings of Jesus Christ and Torah as deeply connected in history.

The dynamic interaction between Jewish and Christian scholars in this field has been extraordinary. Since Marquardt's assessment of the Jewish historians who doubted Jesus' historicity less than some Christian New Testament scholars, the dynamics between Jews and Christians in Historical Jesus research have only become more complex. A Christian (Michael Krupp) as well as a Jewish (Geza Vermes) scholar favor the view of Jesus as Galilean charismatic. At the same time, Rabbi Harvey Falk strongly supports, while the scholar of early rabbinics Jacob Neusner (1932–2016) strongly rejects, the notion of Jesus having been a Pharisee.[59] One might say that a difference remains in the vehemence of the argument and the confidence of its presentation – Christian scholars are typically more hesitant in their historical assessments. Another recent development in the academic Jewish–Christian debate about Jesus is that Jewish scholars do not always wait for their Christian colleagues to formulate Christological challenges following from new research, but at times do so themselves – as e.g. Walter Homolka, who has laid out some of the ways in which Jewish Jesus Research challenges contemporary Christology.[60] Thus, in the historical search for Jesus, Jews and Christians have built an interreligious academic community of research and memory, conducting an ongoing discussion about texts and contexts, methods and interpretation. In this fascinating research community, Jewish and Christian scholars hold opinions not always predictable through reference to their own religious backgrounds. Until the mid-twentieth century, Christian theologians typically declared Jesus unique and Jewish historians saw him as part of the world around him. Today, after half a century of interreligious study, scholarly positions have become highly differentiated and often employ an impressive level of inside knowledge of texts that are not

---

[59] Jacob Neusner, *A Rabbi Talks with Jesus* (McGill Queens University Press, 2000). The fact that Jacob Neusner, a rabbinical scholar who authored hundreds of books, turned toward the end of his life to writing about Jesus, is remarkable in itself.

[60] See Walter Homolka, *Jewish Jesus Research and Its Challenge to Christology Today* (Leiden, Boston: Brill, 2016.)

part of their own traditions' canon. In twentieth-century historical research, we have seen multiple cases of an obvious and intended impact of "Jewish" on "Christian" scholarship.[61] Even more fascinating are the manifold unintended byproducts of interreligious comments on historical evaluations. As in the case of Harry Austryn Wolfson, they can present interesting material for theological thought. Wolfson's avoidance of superlatives and his unusual acknowledgment of Jesus' sayings devoid of over-estimation are echoed in contemporary Jewish Jesus scholarship by Amy-Jill Levine, who approaches Jesus' teachings as worthwhile, interesting, and meaningful – without the need to categorize them as either paralleled or non-paralleled,

> Jesus of Nazareth dressed like a Jew, prayed like a Jew ..., instructed other Jews on how best to live according to the commandments given by God to Moses, taught like a Jew, argued like a Jew with other Jews, and died like thousands of other Jews on a Roman cross. To see him in a first-century Jewish context and to listen to his words with first-century Jewish ears do not in any way undermine Christian theological claims. Jesus does not have to be fully unique in order to say something or do something meaningful.[62]

Beyond the catagorizations of Jesus as a 'marginal' or a 'central' Jew, I find him best described as a 'halakhic Jew.' Knowledgeable about the written and oral Torah, observant of contemporaneous Jewish law, and an active, even passionate, participant in halakhic discussion.

---

[61] At the beginning of the twenty-first century, these categories are also blurred. Jewish scholars might be unaffiliated, not every non-Jewish scholar of Jewish Studies is Christian, and some "Christian" scholars might describe themselves as "post-Christian," etc. For this study, it is not the contrast or clear divide between Jewish and Christian scholars that is important but their often complementary work and discussions.

[62] Amy-Jill Levine, *The Misunderstood Jew*, 51.

3

The Present: Jesus and Jewish Continuity

The Christian reference to Jesus Christ in the present tense opens an array of challenging questions when confronted with a Jewish Jesus. In this chapter, I follow two major lines of thought that are generated by speaking about the Jewishness of Jesus in a manner not restricted to just the past. One line traces an obvious competition of identities, exemplified in African American Christian traditions that sometimes identify Jesus as black, while at least one black theologian, James Cone, draws an explicit link between a historical Jewish Jesus and a black Jesus of the here and now. Similarly, the post-Shoah recovery of the Jewish Jesus challenges Palestinian theologies today – though not always in ways that 'Westerners' expect. The presence of Jesus the Jew not only complicates but also intensifies the efforts of Christians today to make Jesus "one of us."

My second line of inquiry is perhaps untypical but is also clearly indebted to the interreligious dimension of our topic. If the Jesus whom Christians believe to be alive has not left all his Jewishness behind but is Jewish also in the present, the elementary question of what constitutes "Jewishness" remains to be filled with content. What connects the Second Temple, the era of the historical Jesus, and today's Judaism? Speaking about Jesus in the present tense seems to belong to an exclusively Christian confessional language. But here we see that Christology is not just concerned with historical Judaism but also has a stake in contemporary Jewish self-understanding as well as in everything that happened in between – from post-Second Temple Jewish history to the present. Thus, the question of Jewish continuity becomes important to Christian thought, even if this importance has not been widely recognized. An ironic inversion is the fact that today it is often Jewish academics rather than Christians who eschew the notion of Jewish continuity over the millennia. In what follows, I will examine the connecting lines between Second Temple and contemporary Judaism by looking at the continuities inherent in textual memories.

WHAT DOES IT MEAN TO SAY THAT JESUS *IS* JEWISH?

Does it make sense to say that Jesus *is* Jewish? The formulation of this question indicates a move from a Jesus of history to a Jesus as remembered by Christians in the present time. In the Christian language of faith, Jesus is referred to as the risen Christ – and, accordingly, is believed to be alive right now. But even that conclusion cannot be taken for granted. Dietrich Ritschl – a Swiss systematic theologian, whose works connect the European and American theological worlds – has shown how theologians of the Western church tended to relegate even the risen Jesus to the past.[1] In contrast, Ritschl's work on both classical and contemporary Christ-ology gives an outspoken priority to the present tense.[2] According to him, Christology needs to take as a starting point the "Christus praesens" of the Church, who enables Christians to "hope backward" and "remember forward."[3] Yet it is precisely this *Christus praesens* who connects Christians to God's history with Israel.[4] This temporal preference regarding Christology was shared by Ritschl's American colleague and close friend Paul van Buren.[5] Two decades after the publication of Ritschl's 1967 *Memory and Hope*, van Buren added a theological move by connecting the presence of Christ to the presence of the Jewish people's ongoing covenant. He proposed that Israel's covenant in past and present be understood as the appropriate context to think through Christology

---

[1] Dietrich Ritschl (1929–2018), who was trained in Basel, taught dogmatics and ethics in Canada, Australia, North-America, and Germany. His theological work is committed to an ecumenical approach as well as philosophy of language and thus significantly transcends the inner circle of theologies of Jewish–Christian relations. Dietrich Ritschl, *Memory and Hope: An Inquiry Concerning the Presence of Christ* (New York: Macmillan, 1967), xii.

[2] This does not mean that God's spirit is less present in Israel. Ritschl, *The Logic of Theology* (Philadelphia: Fortress Press, 1987), 186.

[3] Ritschl, *Memory and Hope*, 13.

[4] And, remarkably, it is the law of Israel that keeps the *Christus praesens* from becoming timeless, and thus serves as a criterion for ethics. Ritschl, *Memory and Hope*, 199.

[5] Both were students of Karl Barth whom they left behind when they got involved with philosophy of language but to whom they still maintained a certain proximity with regard to their redeveloping of Christocentric systematic theologies.

today.[6] This contemporary contextualization serves as a basic presupposition in his 1988 Christology *Christ in Context*: "Every proper Christological statement will make clear that it is an affirmation of the covenant between God and Israel."[7] In this sense, to return to this chapter's opening question, Christ not only was Jewish but remains so today.[8]

The Christian proclamation of Israel's covenant as alive has become a central topic in Church declarations since the second half of the twentieth century; one could call it the theological marker of post-supersessionist Christian thought that has now become mainstream Church theology. Here, the present tense serves as an expression of interreligious recognition.[9] Van Buren's Christology is special in implying an interconnectedness between the living covenant of the Jewish people and Christ being alive. This suggested present synchrony of the Other's covenant and Jesus Christ is a remarkable concept that has not yet received the acknowledgment it deserves. Not only is the Jewish people here theologically recognized, but Christian faith is made dependent on precisely this recognition.

Emphasizing the presence as the first mode of Christology signals a priority of dialogue over definition. The answer to Bonhoeffer's famous question – "who is Jesus Christ for us today?" – cannot sufficiently be given by Christians alone. Taking seriously the interconnectedness of the living Christ – as held in dogma – and the living covenant of the people Israel – as preserved in the Pauline Epistle to the Romans – points to a contemporary Jewish witness of the Jewish Jesus. The extraordinary component of this faith-relevant witness is its interreligious character: Today's Jews recognize the Jewishness of Jesus. Christians believe in the presence of Christ as well as the presence of the Jews' covenant. Christologically formulated, there is a contemporary Jewish witness of Jesus the Jew – though without Jews witnessing Christ. The proclamation that

---

[6] Paul van Buren, *Christ in Context*, 29.   [7] Ibid., xix.

[8] Barbara U. Meyer, "The Dogmatic Significance of Christ Being Jewish," in Philip A. Cunningham, Joseph Sievers, Mary C. Boys, Hans Hermann Henrix, and Jesper Svartvik, eds., *Christ Jesus and the Jewish People Today: New Explorations of Theological Interrelationships* (Grand Rapids, MI: William B. Eerdmans Publishing Company, 2011), 144–156.

[9] I adopt the term "recognition" from contemporary philosophy and social theory. The translator's note to one of Axel Honneth's books on the topic, lays out the double meaning of the English term, namely "re-identification" as well as "the granting of a certain status." For my take on interreligious recognition both understandings work together when Christians not only affirm Judaism but also acknowledge Jewish traditions based on their own sources. See Joel Anderson, "Translator's Note" in Axel Honneth, *The Struggle for Recognition: The Moral Grammar of Social Conflicts* (Cambridge, MA: MIT, 1996).

Jesus *is* Jewish is not a Jewish but a Christian statement of faith. It relies on Jewish memory that Jesus was Jewish and on Christian belief that Jesus Christ is alive today.

BLACKNESS AND JEWISHNESS

Apparently, there is a world of difference between saying that Jesus was and that he is Jewish. The temporal hierarchy is bluntly illustrated in James Cone's Christological statement: "He *is* black, because he *was* Jewish."[10] The African American theologian James Cone (1936–2018) – he too was a student of Karl Barth – applies the different time modes in order to mark a soteriological hierarchy: In this systematic theology the present tense signifies divine presence. Cone's Christology clearly emphasizes and favors a "black" Jesus. But instead of presenting Jesus being black as an alternative to his being Jewish, Cone links the two attributes in a piece of affirmative logic. In this case, blackness does not simply supersede Jewishness. Rather, blackness builds on Jewishness. Both connect as markers of the oppressed, or maybe as markers of a memory of oppression. Cone connects both Jesus' blackness and Jewishness to the biblical narrative:

The affirmation of the Black Christ can be understood when the significance of his past Jewishness is related dialectically to the significance of his present blackness. On the one hand, the Jewishness of Jesus located him in the context of the Exodus, thereby connecting his appearance in Judea with God's liberation of oppressed Israelites from Egypt. Unless Jesus were truly from Jewish ancestry, it would make little theological sense to say that he is the fulfillment of God's covenant with Israel.[11]

The black and the Jewish memory of Jesus have often been contrasted, but I see Cone's formulation as open to a variety of interpretations: The exodus memory is constitutive for both black and Jewish culture and the experience of oppression has shaped both poetic and political self-expression. As Cone writes: "By electing Israelite slaves as the people of God and by becoming the Oppressed One in Jesus Christ, the human race is made to understand that God is known where human beings experience humiliation and suffering."[12] Yet I wish to question the equation of black

[10] James Cone, *God of the Oppressed*, revised edition (Maryknoll, NY: Orbis Books, 1997), 123.
[11] Ibid., 123f.
[12] James Cone, *A Black Theology of Liberation* (Philadelphia: Lippincott, 1970), 67.

and Jewish identity with oppression and to argue for a more complex understanding that allows for greater agency and collective responsibility.[13] Both blackness and Jewishness describe complex cultures that are not exclusively defined by oppression or even the memory of oppression. Do Jewishness and blackness belong to the same category of collective identities? Jewishness and blackness are certainly very different constituents of identity, but a comparison is helpful and may highlight their difference when ascribed to Jesus.[14] The first difference comes to mind on paper: Jewishness is written with capital J, while blackness is usually not capitalized. Apparently, Jewishness is, among other things, a religious categorization in English, while blackness evidently lacks any religious or national specificity. And yet Cone identifies Jesus as both Jewish *and* black, albeit not necessarily at the same time. What does he mean?

Cone expresses his understanding of Jesus' Jewishness in covenant language: "Unless Jesus were truly from Jewish ancestry, it would make little theological sense to say that he is the fulfillment of God's covenant with Israel."[15] Blackness, he repeatedly asserts, is not a matter of skin color. In fact, according to Cone, "the *literal* color of Jesus is irrelevant."[16] Underscoring this point, Cone does not claim for communities that are neither "black" nor "white' – as e.g. Native Americans (sometimes) referring to themselves as "red" – a need to adopt the black Jesus. At the same time, however, the blackness of Jesus *is* relevant for African American Christians as a marker of positive identification and self-affirmation, and, in a different, far more critical way, for "white" Americans as well, as a constant reminder of their own privileged and comfortable position vis-à-vis "non-whites" and especially African Americans. Nevertheless, other questions arise here: For instance, is the blackness of Jesus important in the same way for African Christians? Or, has the meaning of blackness changed in South Africa since the defeat of Apartheid? The notion of Jesus' blackness echoes a specifically African

---

[13] Barbara U. Meyer, "The Dogmatic Significance of Christ Being Jewish," 144–156, 149.

[14] In musicology and especially twentieth-century history of American music, blackness and Jewishness are often discussed together, as sometimes exchangeable, sometimes connected or competing identities with a set of more and less variable cultural components. See, for instance, Jeffrey Melnick, *A Right to Sing the Blues: African Americans, Jews and American Popular Song* (Cambridge, MA: Harvard University Press, 2001).

[15] Cone, *God of the Oppressed*, 124.

[16] James H. Cone, *A Black Theology of Liberation*, Twentieth Anniversary Edition (Maryknoll, NY: Orbis Books, 1990), 123.

American experience, a cultural reference connected to the memory of loss, exile, slavery, racism, discrimination, the civil rights movement, poverty, music, and prayer. Cone does not limit his thoughts to a fixed definition of blackness. But clearly, in his connecting of Jesus and blackness, oppression is central and outweighs the more creative aspects of black culture, as found in musical, poetic, as well as political traditions.[17] Instead, Cone underlines Jesus' clear-cut opposition to discrimination and oppression. The statement that Jesus himself is black – added to the claim that Jesus is opposed to discrimination – pays tribute to the historical African American struggle against a "white" Jesus that rose together with an expansion of slavery in the early nineteenth century.[18]

Another typically overlooked aspect of Cone's argumentation creates an interesting solidarity between advocates of the black and the Jewish Jesus. He refers to criticisms of his black Christology as failing the universal message of Jesus. "I contend that there is no universalism that is not particular." Cone defends a black Jesus in opposition to a universal (ethnically indistinct) Jesus whom he correctly depicts as not biblical. "As long as they can be sure that the gospel is *for everybody*, ignoring that God liberated a *particular* people from Egypt, came in a particular man called Jesus, and for the particular purpose of liberating the oppressed, then they can continue to talk in theological abstractions."[19] The Biblical Jesus is rooted in stories told as particular. With the particularity both of the Exodus event and the incarnation itself, Cone presents blackness in line with the story of the people Israel. Particularity though is not a value in itself but refers to oppression and the need to be liberated. The womanist theologian Jacquelin Grant distributes color differently: As she states in the programmatic title of her book, the black women's Jesus is black, while the white women's Christ is white.[20] Grant's argument belongs to an inner feminist discourse between advantaged and disadvantaged women that was prefigured in nineteenth-century Christological discussion when "Christ" was associated with the mainstream church,

---

[17] The discussion about the centrality of oppression in "christologies of color" continues. Xompare, for instance, Brian Bantum, *Redeeming Mulatto/a: Theology of Race and Christian Hybridity* (Waco, TX: Baylor University Press, 2010).

[18] Edward Blum and Paul Harvey have discovered this interconnectedness: Compare Edward Blum and Paul Harvey, *The Color of Christ: The Son of God and the Sage of Race in America* (Chapel Hill: The University of North Carolina Press, 2014).

[19] Cone, *A Black Theology of Liberation*, 126.

[20] Jacquelyn Grant, *White Women's Christ and Black Women's Jesus: Feminist Christology and Womanist Response* (Atlanta, GA: Scholars Press, 1989).

power, and privilege, while "Jesus" stood for the "true" Gospel, one of marginalization and social protest. Unlike Jacqueline Grant, James Cone does not draw a clear line between "Jesus" and "Christ."[21] But if he did, blackness would be ascribed first of all to Christ, as Christ stands for the present tense and only secondarily to Jesus! Cone's Christological thinking consistently privileges the present tense. His speaking of Jesus' blackness in the present tense suggests that he does not think primarily of a merely historical figure. Cone is deliberately developing Christology and thus complying with the inner grammar of Christological language that values the present over the past.

An obvious difference between the category of blackness and Jewishness identified with Jesus is their explicitness in Scripture. Jesus is clearly, explicitly, and unquestionably portrayed there as Jewish. While there is no mentioning of "whiteness" in the New Testament, the black Jesus is a matter of interpretation, an ascribed additional identity of Jesus not presented as exegesis but as a certain Church-critical reading. In most of the Church declarations of the late twentieth century, the Jewishness of Jesus is presented with a similar self-critical intention and as a datum implying an ethical content in itself. But suggesting the Jewishness of Jesus as a moral statement in its own right makes sense only with reference to the European history of anti-Judaism. While blackness is introduced to the Christological discussion in order to engage Christology against racism, Jewishness is emphasized to fight anti-Semitism.

Apart from their famous teacher Karl Barth, the systematic theologians Dietrich Ritschl, Paul van Buren, and James Cone have another theological predecessor in common: Dietrich Bonhoeffer. They all quote his key question "Who is Jesus Christ for us today?" as a criterion for Christology and see their own Christological critique as a critical response to his. Bonhoeffer himself mentioned Jesus' Jewishness in 1942 in a deeply prophetic statement: "The expulsion of the Jews from Europe will lead to an expulsion of Jesus. For Jesus was a Jew."[22] Bonhoeffer here uses the past tense to ascribe Jewishness to Jesus, but the warning about an

---

[21] Cone shares the "assumption that there is no radical distinction between the Jesus of history and the Christ of faith." Cone, *God of the Oppressed*, 237.

[22] Bonhoeffer, *Ethics* (New York: Touchstone, 1995), 51. Bonhoeffer probably wrote this in 1940.

upcoming expulsion of Jesus as a consequence of the expulsion of the Jews shows that his formulation is meant to be as acute and present as can be.

Within the theology that I have been discussing in this chapter, Jewishness and blackness both comprise dimensions of a critical Christology – critical of power-relations, discrimination, oppression, and intergroup violence. One could say that engagement against racism and anti-Semitism mark the core contexts of proclaiming a black or a Jewish Jesus. Despite this parallel, however, it is important to remember that the Jewish and the black Jesus belong to fundamentally different Christological categories. First, there is a difference regarding historical research. The historical Jesus is undeniably Jewish. In contrast, there is no scriptural or early interpretational tradition referring to Jesus as black – which by no means delegitimizes such a reading.[23] But the most important difference lies in the *Christus praesens*. The contrast here is palpable. The blackness of the risen Jesus is affirmed in the black church, while the Jewishness of the risen Jesus is affirmed in the non-Jewish Christian Church. Nor is this a difference of mere identity politics. With the black Jesus, the black church challenges white supremacy, western discrimination, and global racism. It affirms and empowers itself in this struggle. Meanwhile, the Jewish Jesus is intended to confront anti-Semitism, and, possibly, racism in general. Yet at the same time, the Jewish Jesus can never be in the Christian's domestic domain.[24] Black women and womanist theologians express great familiarity and closeness in their knowledge of the black Jesus. Their Jesus-talk, i.e., talking of Jesus as a friend, can be understood from a Christological inner perspective. The Jewish Jesus does not have comparably close "friends" among the non-Jewish Christians. This difference is not just relevant on an intellectually reflected Christological level but also in spiritual and liturgical reference to Jesus Christ. Black Christian spirituality has deep ties to the black Jesus, expressed in music and art and poetry. The black Jesus is close to his black sisters and brothers, in a relation of intimacy with them through prayer and worship. This intimacy is apparent to all – whether it can or cannot be shared by non-black Christians. The Jewish Jesus, however, does not enact closeness

---

[23] Though this by no means delegitimizes such readings. For further exploration of this topic, see the articles collected in Cain Hope Felder, ed., *Stony the Road We Trod: African American Biblical Interpretation* (Minneapolis, MN: Fortress Press, 1991).

[24] Except for people of Jewish family background and Christian belief, whether they understand themselves as Christian Jews or Jewish Christians.

for non-Jewish Christians and is not expected to provide immediate spiritual or social empowerment. On the contrary, the Jewishness of Jesus entails challenges and even unforeseeable difficulties for the believing non-Jewish Christian. And while the meaning of the black Jesus is different for black and non-black followers of Jesus Christ, one may extend the notion so that the black Jesus can stand for any other disadvantaged particularity, and this might be in line with James Cone's theology: "The 'blackness of Christ,' therefore, is not simply a statement about skin color, but rather, the transcendent affirmation that God has not ever, no not ever, left the oppressed alone in struggle. He was with them in Pharaoh's Egypt, is with them in America, Africa and Latin America, and will come in the end of time to consummate fully their human freedom."[25]

To understand the difference between the Christological discourse about the black and the Jewish Jesus, the language of otherness may prove helpful. The Jewish Jesus presents a certain otherness to his non-Jewish followers. The black Jesus takes sides with the black Other ("othered" in the American context), and empowers black and criticizes white Christians, which bears a considerable significance for predominantly white churches. The blackness of Jesus is meaningful to those who are "othered" on account of their color, and, differently, to those participating in the othering of people according to color. The latter applies to a majority of non-black Christians in Christian majority societies worldwide, who may, also as non-racists and even as engaged anti-racists, consider themselves as inadvertently profiting from such othering or simply acknowledge privilege in a society with overlapping categories of class and color. Thus, blackness presents a framework to critique Christology. Still, there are contexts where "otherness" and oppression are not primarily bound to color. Blackness is empirically connected to discrimination and poverty, but it is not necessarily so. Is Jesus' blackness affected by affluent and empowered black societies? Would the attribute "black" change its meaning with the achievement of full equality – or would it even lose it? There is no definite answer to these questions since there is no political entity yet that privileges blacks over non-blacks, and there is no geographical unit characterized by the full economic equality of black communities.

Jewishness has likewise been seen as an epitome of being "othered" and medieval Jewish history especially has been told in the framework of

---

[25] Cone, *A Black Theology of Liberation*, 126.

this recurring parameter of oppression.[26] But in sharp contrast to blackness, the meanings of Jewishness have here undergone major social changes. There is a Jewish majority context for comparative reference: The modern state of Israel privileges Jewish identity in an official as well as unofficial manner. Jewishness is sharply disconnected from any "otherness" in the Jewish state. Being Jewish is connected to the right to immigrate and constitutes a privilege also as regards pre-immigration work permits. For many of Israel's non-Jewish residents (and those halakhically not recognized as Jews), "Jewishness" marks an advantaging identity. Thus, the connecting line between Jewishness and blackness consisting of a common marginalization, discrimination, and economic disadvantage is severely disrupted by the example of the modern Jewish state.

JEWISHNESS BETWEEN THE FIRST AND THE TWENTY-FIRST CENTURIES

If Jesus is alive and Jesus is Jewish, does he relate only to Second Temple Judaism or is he recognizably connected to contemporary Jewish life? Political actualizations of the Jewish Jesus by Christians today have been diverse, ranging from "Christ at the Checkpoint"[27] to "Jesus would be a settler."[28] Given this wide array of appropriations of Jesus, is it possible to formulate any criteria for a specifically Jewish actualization of Jesus? We will return to this important question shortly. But for the present discussion, it is first of all remarkable that contemporary Jewish scholars and writers of very different geographical backgrounds, levels of observance, and knowledge of text traditions agree on Jesus' Jewishness – whether they portray him as close to or far from their own Jewish experience.[29] This begs the question, what is "Jewishness" over the time span of two millennia? After all, if we propose to say that Jesus is Jewish also in

---

[26] David Nirenberg tells the story of medieval Jewish–Christian relations as an ongoing othering of Jews. Nirenberg, *Anti-Judaism: The Western Tradition* (New York: W.W. Norton & Company, 2014).

[27] This was the title of an evangelical conference hosted by the Bethlehem Bible College, Bethlehem, in March 2012.

[28] Michael Oren, *Jerusalem Post*, July 22, 2015.

[29] Neta Stahl, *Other and Brother: Jesus in the 20th Century Literary Landscape* (New York: Oxford University Press, 2012).

the present, we have to assume and make explicit a notion of Jewish continuity over time. It is ironic that Judaism had been depicted as stagnant and unchanging in supersessionism, a view that could not acknowledge any degree of Jewish development, transformation, evolution, and change after Jesus' death. But now the situation is quite the opposite of that of the pre-modern Church. Today non-supersessionist Christians clearly must acknowledge a history of Jewish dynamism and development over time, of Jewish creativity and continuous renewal. It is precisely this acknowledgment that raises the question of what it is exactly that connects the Judaism of the century of Jesus with the Judaism of our time.

Traditionally, Jewishness has been conceptualized in religious and ethnic terms, and there has always been a tension over which of these is paramount (Sylvia Barak-Fishman). Theologically, the notion of chosenness has often been seen as providing the continuous content of Judaism (David Novak). Yet at the same time the assumption of uniqueness has prompted criticisms among contemporary Jewish scholars, and in some recent writings critical Jewish historians have tended to mark Jewishness as a "construct" (e.g. Shaye Cohen, Aaron Hughes). I will first examine the arguments against conceiving of "Jewishness" as an identifiably continuous phenomenon. Taking this recent skepticism of the term "Jewishness" into consideration, I will then begin anew from a minimalist basis and sketch out what first-century and twenty-first-century Jews may possibly share.

The historian Shaye Cohen follows the development of the terms "Jew" and "Jewishness" throughout antiquity.[30] He shows that initially the ethnic designation had priority over the religious. A Jew was a member of the Judean polity, as initially constituted by Persian imperial rule. Especially through the agency of Hellenization, this ethno-political designation evolved into a more conceptual and religious one. The Greeks influenced Jews to formulate their beliefs and practices in terms of being a religion among others. According to Cohen, this marked an extraordinary turn. "The development of Iudaios from 'Judean' to 'Jew' testifies to a momentous development in the history of Judaism, the growth of a non-ethnic conception of Jewishness."[31] The move from "Judean" to "Jew"

---

[30] Shaye J. D. Cohen, *The Beginnings of Jewishness: Boundaries, Varieties, Uncertainties* (Berkeley: University of California Press, 2001).
[31] Cohen, *The Beginnings of Jewishness*, 342.

was significant: once Jewishness ceased to be an exclusively ethnic identity, a Gentile could aspire to and actually become Jewish.

But this apparent open-endedness was closed off in the period after the destruction of the Temple in 70 CE, especially through the rise of Christianity and Islam during the course of the first millennium. With the gradual displacement of Jews from Palestine, a process that occurred over many centuries but was largely complete by the seventh or eighth centuries, and their essential transformation into an entirely diasporic people, Cohen sees the conceptualization of Jewishness as now determined by more reified social boundaries. "[W]hen Christians and Muslims define themselves over against Judaism," Cohen argues, Jews no longer need to engage in the same process of self-definition.[32] In other words, Jews' minority status within majority non-Jewish civilizations now functioned both to define and forcibly impose the contours of Jewish identity. The situation for modern Jews again altered the basis of Jewish definition and self-definition. The "quid pro quo" for Jewish emancipation entailed a relinquishing of all "national" components of Jewish identity, e.g. the self-governing Jewish community, or the continued use of specifically Jewish languages like Yiddish or Ladino, in return for the acquisition of modern citizenship in the new polities emerging in the wake of the French Revolution. Now Judaism, at least in theory, was to be considered a religion only and Jews would be considered French or Poles "of the Mosaic persuasion." But this shift proved difficult at best. It was challenging for even the most determined Jew to acculturate or assimilate entirely, but especially so in the face of new forms of anti-Semitism that questioned the sincerity and – with the emergence of scientific racism – even the capacity of Jews to integrate into the new nation-based cultures and polities. In part as a reaction to this ethno-nationalism, the last third of the nineteenth century in Europe saw increasing numbers of Jews embracing a range of nationalist and collectivist orientations of their own, such as Zionism. Finally, in the post-Shoah Jewish world, according to Cohen, the prevailing "uncertainty of Jewishness" bears resemblance to the identity questions that were characteristic for antiquity.[33] The not-very-satisfying conclusion to this history of Jewishness is that Judaism describes – in Benedict Anderson's now well-worn words – an imagined

---

[32] Ibid., 344.

[33] Cohen compares this to the Middle Ages, where boundaries were built by Muslims and Christians. For Jews, there was no necessity then to define their boundaries. Ibid., 8.

community:[34] "Jewishness," Cohen concludes, "has no empirical objective verifiable reality to which we can point and over which we can claim:
This is it! ... [It] will remain a social construction – a variable, not a
constant."[35]

Cohen's was neither the last nor the first effort by Jewish historians to
grapple with the problem of continuity. Amid the nineteenth-century
battles over emancipation, a number of theories were advanced to demonstrate not so much Jewishness's continuity as its adaptability. The
Church's image of a stultified or ossified and tradition-bound Judaism
was seen as a threat to Jews' own claim that nothing in their religion
precluded their acculturation and loyal membership in modern nation
states. In the face of both emancipatory and missionary pressures, a
number of Jews felt it necessary to identify a set of constants that they
believed characterized Judaism from its Sinaitic inception to the present.
In this endeavor, Jewish thinkers were aided by some of the contemporary
philosophical approaches being developed in mid-nineteenth-century
Europe, particularly Germany. A small group of Judaic scholars centered
in Berlin and identifying themselves as the *Verein für Cultur und Wissenschaft der Juden* adopted a historicist approach to understanding the
dynamic relationship between a posited fixed and permanent "essence" of
Judaism and those elements that arose in the face of momentary, temporal
challenges.[36] The theories of Judaism identified such concepts as monotheism and the Jews' ethical mission to humanity as its possible fixed
elements. Interestingly, both classical Reform Judaism and Modern
Orthodoxy drew on many of the same philosophical premises despite
their often radically different conclusions. For instance, both reinterpreted
traditional Jewish messianism in terms of an ethical mission of Jews to
serve as a "Light unto the Nations." But they differed profoundly on the
status of Halakhah, ritual, and the nature of community.[37]

These expedient nineteenth-century theories defining an "essence of
Judaism" were radically redefined in the twentieth, but some of their ideas
still prevailed. Thus, even beyond the Jewish nationalist orientations of
the so-called Jerusalem School of Jewish historiography, we still find

---

[34] Benedict Anderson, *Imagined Communities: Reflections on the Origin and Spread of
Nationalism* (London: Verso, 1983).

[35] Cohen, *The Beginnings of Jewishness*, 5, 10.

[36] Ismar Schorsch, *From Text to Context: The Turn to History in Modern Judaism*
(Hanover, NH: University Press of New England, 1994).

[37] Michael A. Meyer, *Response to Modernity: A History of the Reform Movement in
Judaism* (New York: Oxford University Press, 1988).

today persistent variations of the "essence" paradigm.[38] The intellectual historian Michael Meyer, for instance, comes to the conclusion that at the present time the "sense of Jewish peoplehood" provides the strongest ingredient to Jewish identity.[39] Similarly, the philosopher David Novak's latest book presents Zionism as a central component of today's Judaism. Novak, a scholar of theology and law, centers his account of Judaism on the traditional notion of chosenness. Referring to its biblical reasoning, Novak emphasizes that chosenness is not pointed to the past, but to the future.[40] Despite their ingenuity, such efforts to identify meta-features of Jewishness appear to be swimming against the tide. The post-modernist sensibility bristles at the assertion of continuity over the course of millennia. They not only tack against the historicist commitment to contextualization and contingency but might also imply an underlying genetic driver of Jewish survival and destiny.[41]

I wish now to challenge the conclusion that any attempt to identify continuity over the longue duree is necessarily essentialist. First, it is not necessary to narrowly define Jewishness in order to make sense of the word. A tradition need not be stagnant in order to detect lines and motifs of continuity over centuries. In the twenty-first century, it has become a commonplace to present identity as something constructed and imagined. Indeed, any view challenging this insistence has to defend itself against the essentialist reproach. Moreover, the anti-essentialist approach to Jewish identity seems particularly convincing since essentialism has often gone together with stereotypes and prejudgments, infamous anti-Semitic characterizations of behaviors, characteristics, or physical traits labeled as typically Jewish. Certainly, anti-essentialism is a necessary reaction or antidote to anti-Semitism, although the attribution of Jewishness has undergone remarkable changes, even in popular language. For instance,

---

[38] On the Jerusalem School, which retrospectively projected Zionist conceptions back onto all ages and epochs of Jewish history, see David N. Myers, *Re-inventing the Jewish Past: European Jewish Intellectuals and the Zionist Return to History* (New York: Oxford University Press, 1995).

[39] Michael A. Meyer, *Jewish Identity in the Modern World* (Seattle and London: University of Washington Press, 1990). Meyer speaks of "Zion," presumably to underline the built reality of Zionism rather than just the movement that led to it.

[40] David Novak, *Zionism and Judaism: A New Theory* (Cambridge: Cambridge University Press, 2015).

[41] For a more nuanced expression of this overall approach, see David B. Goldstein, *Jacob's Legacy: A Genetic View of Jewish History* (New Haven, CT: Yale University Press, 2008).

in the Israeli context, as well as in today's American Jewish community, the judgment that "this is not Jewish" is now mostly applied as a criticism, with the behavior labeled "Jewish" representing what is deemed to be appropriate and desirable!

Cohen's attempt to present Jewishness as like any other ethnic identity, emphasizing its boundaries while neglecting any specific, meaningful content, proves not particularly helpful to describing Jewish religious creativity – nor does it accord much cultural agency to generations of Jews. Even Jews who historically did not have the choice to either reinforce boundaries or otherwise assimilate did have the opportunity to be culturally active or passive. The composition of a monumental work like the Babylonian Talmud cannot be explained mainly as a matter of reinforcing a religious or ethnic boundary, as Cohen suggests. It is the cumulative creation of generations of Jews actively involved in continuing, discussing, and transforming their narratives and legislation. These learned people did not devise a "construct" but a magnum opus, an epic of world literature; they were not part of an identity-construct, but of an intellectually dynamic community. And this suggests that one possible significant element of continuity is the discursive tradition in Judaism (so evident in the Babylonian Talmud), a point to which I will return.

The "construct" theory is itself a construct, but with little explanatory power in accounting for Jewish productivity and far too little credit given to the cultural reflectivity of the rabbinical discussants and authors. These interlocutors were consciously referring to a collective textual and ritual past and building a new corpus of literature, composed both in a traditional and innovative manner. The emergence of rabbinic literature can be described as Jewish reinvention or revolution, but either way the rabbis appear to have been actively aware of what they were doing and saw themselves within the chain of the people Israel's generations.[42]

It is a comparatively easy task to describe Jewish continuity since the beginnings of rabbinic literature. Daniel Boyarin famously speaks of "Judaism" as meaningfully existing only since the period of rabbinic transformation. This allows him to refer to Christianity as older than

---

[42] Indeed, the term *shalshelet ha-kabbalah* (chain of tradition) would come to constitute a particularly crucial genre of rabbinic literature. See Gerson D. Cohen's introduction to the *Sefer Ha-Kabbalah of Abraham ibn Daud* (Philadelphia: JPS, 1967). For an overview encompassing the creation of the Babylonian Talmud, its gradual dissemination in different regions of the diaspora, and its ongoing relevance today, see Barry Scott Wimpfheimer, *The Talmud: A Biography* (Princeton, NJ: Princeton University Press, 2018).

Judaism[43] – a provocation that has very different connotations for Jewish and Christian scholars. But it also curiously parallels the traditional supersessionist views of the Church, the denial of Jewish continuity from the Hebrew Bible through rabbinic literature and until the present. I give preference to Jewish continuity as perceived by a majority of Jews who see themselves in a generational chain since biblical times. These chains are difficult to prove – but also the disconnection is not historically evident. Admittedly, my position is not completely independent of Christianity's changing approaches in this field. Among the strongest components of Christian supersessionism was the claim of Jewish discontinuity. Of course, the Christian error of supersessionism does not inadvertently prove the notion of Jewish continuity. The here presented notion of continuity is text and interpretation based. To understand Judaism as an emerging community of text interpretation does not mean suggesting clear limits of these interpretational efforts and methods. It does mean remembering that the texts interpreted in this community were broadly defined. The canon was not closed but its main parts were outlined. Thus, when I regard rabbinic Judaism as part of a developing community of text interpretation since biblical times, I credit the interpretational self-understanding of the Sages more than the Christian supersessionist view. It is to be noted here that Boyarin does take the Rabbis' self-understanding as continuing Second Temple Judaism into consideration: "The Rabbis see the first-century Pharisees as their spiritual ancestors."[44]

My outline of the textual continuities does not at all mean to propose an early dating for canonization. But long before finalizing the border lines of the textual corpus, there already existed texts that delineated the borders of the canon, such as the Pentateuch and the Prophets.[45] Since the theological meaning of Jesus' Jewishness is tied to the discussion of Jewish continuity between the first and the twenty-first century, it is necessary not to start with the Mishnah, but to show continuity as well with earlier Jewish literature and thought. In fact, this is not difficult to demonstrate, for what would become the six orders of the Mishnah – juridical discourse

---

[43] See Daniel Boyarin, *Dying for God: Martyrdom and the Making of Christianity* (Stanford, CA: Stanford University Press, 1999), 5. Most recently, Boyarin has claimed that the concept of "Judaism" itself originates in Christianity; see Boyarin, *Judaism: The Genealogy of a Modern Notion* (New Brunswick, NJ: Rutgers University Press, 2018).

[44] Daniel Boyarin, *A Radical Jew: Paul and the Politics of Identity* (Berkeley: University of California Press, 1994), 2.

[45] Daniel Boyarin, *Border Lines: The Partition of Judaeo-Christianity* (Philadelphia: University of Pennsylvania Press, 2004).

about liturgy, purity, family, property, worship, and agriculture – was in the first century already being discussed and transmitted as oral tradition.[46]

Jewishness can obviously not be an unchanging "constant." One of the most striking features of Jewish identity is, indeed, its transformability. But the lack of constant content and form does not exclude continuity. On the contrary, dynamics and variety need to be included in any theory of a developing Jewishness.[47] My point is that the denial of a fixed, limited, clearly defined view of Judaism does not mean that all notions of Jewish continuity are equally "constructed" (artificial) and thus have no basis in history. On the contrary, it is a characteristic of Jewish belonging that its components and expressions vary widely in their composition and yet still retain consistent features.

Sylvia Barak Fishman has come closest to capturing this complexity by pointing to multiple Jewish identities rather than trying to formulate a single definition of Judaism.[48] Her broad array of lived ways to be Jewish shows that the claim of Jewishness as being merely a construct actually presupposes a narrow definition of Jewishness and is thus not an alternative to traditional views of Judaism but a variation on them.

The topic of "Jewishness" ought not be abstracted from actual Jews who live, perceive, discuss, practice, and interact within what they themselves recognize as "Jewishness."[49] Hannah Arendt leveled the criticism that the term "Jewishness" had often replaced the traditional word "Judaism." She understood the term "Jewishness" as lacking religious and political content, and thus leading to an understanding of "Jewish" as a quality. But in this case, Arendt misspoke and the truth is exactly the opposite: Jewishness is a term that can but need not necessarily encompass the Jewish religion. It is a broad term, a big tent. Arendt privileged the religion Judaism not because she herself was a believer but because she regarded religion as the most authentic and original content of Judaism. That is understandable, but it is not necessarily true. Here I am not using the word "Jewishness" as a replacement for "Judaism," nor in any pre-

[46] E.P. Sanders, *Jewish Law from Jesus to the Mishnah* (Minneapolis, MN: Fortress Press, 2016)

[47] Moshe Rosman, *How Jewish is Jewish History?* (Liverpool: Liverpool University Press, 2008).

[48] Sylvia Barack Fishman, *The Way into the Varieties of Jewishness* (Woodstock, VT: Jewish Lights Publishing, 2008).

[49] Non-Jews contribute to this discussion today – especially when they are aware of the history of non-Jewish discourse on Judaism that has been mainly anti-Jewish and at times philosemitic.

defined way. My use of the term is as open as "Jewish belonging." Referring to Arendt's critique, I do, however, find it helpful that "Jewishness" is less defined by Jewish religion than is Judaism, as I try to make room for the various understandings of Jewish belonging based on faith as well as tradition, culture, and ethnicity.[50]

Michael Meyer draws attention to the fact that Jewish intellectuals as non-traditional and diverse as Martin Buber and Sigmund Freud found Jewish identity "manifestly present in individual consciousness, but darkly beyond definition."[51] While it is difficult to describe the phenomenon called "Jewishness," its mere existence was beyond doubt for these thinkers, a point that needs to be taken seriously. It suggests that even profound minds conditioned to pursue essences and origins did not hesitate to accept, in this case, a feeling, or perhaps a commitment, as sufficient. Meyer bases his account of contemporary Jewish identity on Jewish majority opinion. Here, the "concern for the future of the *Jews* seems to run deeper than concern for the future of the *Jewish religion.*"[52]

One thing has profoundly changed during the last third of the twentieth century: Jewish identity is highly appreciated and also desired by many non-Jews.[53] In North America, Jewishness is regarded by many as an attractive identity, and outreach programs that invite children of interfaith marriages to participate in Jewish educational institutions have become increasingly successful. In New York and many other major American cities, Jewish identity is manifold and generally positively embraced by new generations of Jews, even those lacking any institutional affiliation. The major Jewish holidays are prominently presented in various media, so that not only secular Jews but also many non-Jews are aware of the Jewish calendar.[54] This account may be too optimistic, and

---

[50] Sociologically, the complexities and dynamics of Jewish belongings have been well researched. See, for example, Harvey E. Goldberg, Steven M. Cohen, and Ezra Kopelowitz, eds., *Dynamic Belonging: Contemporary Jewish Collective Identities* (New York: Berghahn Books, 2011).

[51] Michael Meyer, *Identity*, 4.   [52] Ibid. 57.

[53] In the state of Israel, suggesting that someone may not be Jewish is considered an insult – and this understanding is often applied institutionally. Ironically, one of the few questions that airport security in Israel usually does not ask travelers is: "Are you Jewish?" They instead ask whether one has relatives in Israel, when one started to learn Hebrew, or whether anybody in the family knows Yiddish. But even airport security is not a reason to question someone's Jewish identity.

[54] There are no classes, for instance, on the Jewish New Year and Yom Kippur at many of the schools in the State University of New York (SUNY) system.

I do not at all wish to downplay the anxiety that demographic concerns about declining affiliation or identification raise among American Jews. The point I am making here, however, is that the connotation of "Jewish" in the twenty-first century is no longer that of "oppressed" or "marginal" but in many ways of an accepted or even admired identity option – not along the lines of traditional philosemitism, defined as a "prejudice in favor of the Jews," but as a positive approach based on positive experience.[55]

Jewish belonging thus describes a highly complex identity, including an ethnic component, a religious center, a manifold culture, and, I would add, a shared memory. For the individual members of the global Jewish community the various aspects – ethnicity, religion, culture, and memory – are prioritized differently, while each of these components is complex in itself. Jewish ethnicity is manifold, religion is not necessarily centered on belief but often perceived of as observance, and the importance of memory varies even between families. Given all this, it is indeed a remarkable phenomenon – and not a predictable necessity – that Jews who define themselves along such different lines would still commonly identify with such a vague, complex, and dynamic collective description as Jewishness.

Drawing a line of Jewish belonging from the Second Temple period until today is indeed fraught. We do not know how people in the first century felt about their Jewish belonging. One eminent scholar of this period insisted on referring to its plural "Judaisms." But even if we accept Jacob Neusner's notion of a very divided Jewish world at the time of Jesus, it is telling that he still labels all of these varieties Judaism![56] At the same time, scholars no longer widely assume that the sectarianism that beset that era characterized the majority. Most contemporary Judeans and Jews were not strong adherents of any particular sect but held certain basic things in common: a sense of common ancestry, a shared commitment to Mosaic laws, especially Shabbat, kashrut, and circumcision, a sense of Jerusalem, and even the sometimes controversial Temple as the axis mundi – at least of their world – even when hailing from the diaspora. Literacy was not yet a high priority for non-priests or those

---

[55] Jonathan Karp and Adam Sutcliffe, "Introduction" to Karp and Sutcliffe, eds., *Philosemitism in History* (New York: Cambridge University Press, 2011).

[56] E.g. Jacob Neusner, William Scott Green, and Ernest S. Frerichs, *Judaisms and their Messiahs at the Turn of the Christian Era* (New York: Cambridge University Press, 1987).

not included among the Pharisaic sect, but learning as commanded by Deuteronomy 11:17 ("and you shall teach them to your children"), in the sense of the imbibing of teachings from the Torah, was undoubtedly an assumed component of Jewish identity.[57]

This loose, broad, disorganized situation of a kind of voluntarist Jewishness, comprising ethnic elements, observances, a hope for the future restoration of past glories, and some basic convictions, probably likewise characterized the majority of Jews in the period between the destruction of the Temple and the promulgation of the Babylonian Talmud, a period comprising almost a millennium. Most scholars no longer believe that rabbinic Judaism conquered the majority of Jews either in or outside of Palestine in the century or two after the redaction of the Mishnah; rather, the rabbis' consolidation of authority was likely far more gradual, regional, wavering, and uncertain than long assumed.[58] In this sense, the situation of Jewish modernity, in which we find a similar fragmentation of Jewish authority and singularity, appears somewhat as a restoration of the prolonged pre-rabbinic status quo ante. And that too suggests a kind of continuity.

There have also been recent attempts to formulate theological accounts of Judaism without being essentialist. One especially interesting example was written with the explicit intention of speaking to liberal as well as traditional Jews. For this project, called *The Future of Jewish Theology*, Steven Kepnes chose "holiness" as the leading motif and prism.[59] From the biblical imperative "you shall be holy" through the holiness of Shabbat, Torah, and kashrut, Kepnes interprets Judaism as a "cultural linguistic system."[60] In striking contrast to traditional approaches in Comparative Religion, Kepnes understands holiness as comprising both a spiritual and an ethical dimension.[61] Holiness, according to Kepnes, is "equally a matter of thought and action," "a way of life that needs to be learned and practiced."[62] The Bible-based concept of holiness serves here

---

[57] On a recent effort to identify the rabbinic demand for literacy as a turning point in Jewish history, see Maristella Botticini and Zvi Eckstein, *The Chosen Few: How Education Shaped Jewish History, 70–1492* (Princeton, NJ: Princeton University Press, 2012). But see also the strong reservations expressed by Shaul Stampfer in his review, "The Chosen Few," *Jewish History*, 29 (2015): 373–379.

[58] Seth Schwartz, *Imperialism and Jewish Society: 200 B.C.E. – 640 C.E.* (Princeton, NJ: Princeton University Press, 2001).

[59] Steven Kepnes, *The Future of Jewish Theology* (Malden, MA: Wiley-Blackwell, 2013).

[60] Ibid.,19.   [61] Ibid., 9.   [62] Ibid., 4.

as an outline to understanding liberal and traditional Jewish communities as complementary. Holiness is lived by both caring about ritual purity, as taken seriously in traditional Judaism, and engaging in *Tikkun Olam*, as pursued in the various liberal Jewish approaches.[63] In a highly original though non-polemical move, Kepnes brings together these two major ways of practicing Judaism. Understanding both caring about kashrut and helping refugees as acts of holiness, Kepnes expresses the highest possible respect for both halakhic and ethical concerns. My interpretation of Kepnes' Jewish theology is that Judaism always needs the practice of the other Jewish community!

My own account of Jewish belonging between the first and the twenty-first century offers no single definition of Judaism – partly because defining-as-limiting-interpretations are very much contrary to what Jewish hermeneutics have traditionally stood for. In this sense, defining Jewishness is literally a contradiction in terms. Rather, if anything constitutes a truly Jewish approach, manner, or method, then it is the ever-unfolding commentary, the yet additional opinion added to the discussion, the continuously open discourse. In seeking to deconstruct the charge of essentialism we can show hints of continuity built by a constant textual frame of reference dating back as early as the biblical period. The body of biblical texts is in itself manifold in style and diverse regarding content. Many of these texts – most strikingly the Prophets but also texts from the Pentateuch – display a remarkable level of self-reflection and even collective self-criticism. It cannot be proven that this self-reflectivity directly leads to the dialogical style of rabbinic literature, but the two are also not disconnected: Rabbinic literature presents itself as interpreting biblical law. The connecting characteristic between collective self-reflectivity in biblical texts and halakhic discourse in rabbinic literature could be described as a kind of polyphony. Menachem Fisch has used this term to describe the dialogical character of Talmudic culture.[64] I would like to expand this characterization by applying it to the biblical texts as well. Clearly, the biblical text entails a more clear-cut

---

[63] Ibid., 12.

[64] Menachem Fisch, "Judaism, and the Religious Crisis of Modern Science." In J. M van der Meer and S. Mandelbrote, eds., *Nature and Scripture in the Abrahamic Religions: 1700–Present* (Leiden: Brill, 2008), 525–567, 545.

message: the true prophet is right to criticize the majority of the people, and kings are judged in terms not of their political, military, or economic policies but solely by reference to their dedication to the one God. The plurality of rabbinic discourse, where minority opinions are mentioned and often not even rejected, marks another stage in this Jewish dialoguing, but the roots of this polyphony can already be found in the two major segments of the Hebrew Bible, the Torah and the Prophets, both of which were part of Jesus' cultural socialization.[65]

One example is the weaving of narrative, the instruction of memory and law in the Book of Exodus. The motif of the Exodus is not simply told as a one-dimensional myth of ethnic origin. Rather, a story that entails a narrative and a collection of narrative-referring laws are woven into each other. The instruction to remember previous slavery is directly connected to a social ethics of concern for the stranger. The Exodus narrative itself is not the story of heroes, but a memory of rescue. The main content of the biblically instructed memory is not a heroic but an enslaved past. Memory is thus deployed to enforce the rights of the socially disadvantaged. The biblical prophetic literature is centered on the individual critical voice. The critique of mainstream practices like the exploitation of the poor and injustice is reported as God-supported. Thus, the very phenomenon of prophetic criticism echoes theological ethical discourse where minority opinion and marginality matters.[66] Both Pentateuchal and Prophetic texts do not explicitly display a plurality of opinions, as will be found in rabbinic literature. Clearly, this polyphony increases over the course of Jewish history. But I would use the term "implicit polyphony" to describe the different dimensions present in biblical texts. Polyphony becomes explicit in rabbinic discourse but is already present in the divergent literary genres comprising the biblical text. In the New Testament, polyphony is most apparent in the composition of four gospels telling Jesus' story in differing style, language, and narrative. I would go as far as to call

---

[65] The scholarship of David Weiss Halivni should also be mentioned in this context. This path-breaking scholar of the Talmudic editing process shows that argument for argument's sake is a consistent – though not invariable – feature of Jewish religious culture. See especially his *Midrash, Mishnah and Gemara: The Jewish Predilection for Justified Law* (Cambridge, MA: Harvard University Press, 1986).

[66] The Bible scholar and theologian Walter Brueggemann is perhaps the leading exponent of the notion of a polyphonic biblical text. Among his many works exploring the "plurality of voices" in the Hebrew Bible, see *Theology of the Old Testament: Testimony, Dispute, Advocacy* (Minneapolis, MN: Fortress, 1997).

this literary form the "most" Jewish aspect of the New Testament, echo-
ing biblical style and prefiguring the rabbinic notion of different opinions
that are likewise God's word.[67]

So far, my description of Jewishness as based on a continuous tradition of textual reference is mainly hermeneutical. Is Jewishness only a
plural way of understanding or is it merely a more multi-dimensional
interpretation of reality? Is it better described as method and form rather
than as content? While the latter seems a logical possibility, on the other
hand, listening to minority opinions is more than just a method. It
demonstrates and also perpetuates an ethics. One might say that this
would be mainly an ethics of discourse. But the prophetic text that is
listening to the experience of the disadvantaged clearly supports social
justice. Moreover, the Exodus motif, transmitted as a memory of slavery
that endorses a solicitous approach to strangers, offers a clear agenda of
moral engagement. Both collective self-reflections promote a critique of
power as well as self-criticism of peoplehood. Jewish peoplehood is here
not constituted by heroism or an idealized Golden Age – although the
stories of exodus and early statehood could be told that way. The
biblical self-critical tradition does not exclude or prevent later diverging
representations of the same stories.[68] The Passover Haggadah, composed in the Middle Ages, also includes aggressive aspects of the memory
of survival (e.g. exhorting the Lord to "pour out thy wrath on the
gentiles").[69] And among today's messianic and chauvinistic groups the
memory of David's reign can be louder than Nathan's critique of David's
reign. My theory of the continuous frame of textual reference does not
exclude the existence of power-adoring phenomena in contemporary
Jewish political culture. But it relativizes them as marginal – at times
gaining considerable attention, but in no way reflecting the core of
Jewish tradition.

---

[67] "Elu ve-elu divre elohim hayyim" ("these and these are [both equally] the words of the
living God," a statement found in tractate Eruvin 13b). The composition of four gospels
was anything but self-evident. Marcion suggested one gospel, based on Luke, proving
that not just regarding content but also regarding form he aimed at an un-Jewish
scripture!

[68] Related ideas are explored in Michael Walzer's *Exodus and Revolution* (New York: Basic
Books, 1986).

[69] On both Christian influences on and anti-Christian polemics within the Haggadah, see
Israel Jacob Yuval, *Two Nations in Your Womb: Perceptions of Jews and Christians in
Late Antiquity and the Middle Ages* (Berkeley: University of California Press, 2006).

JESUS THE JEW BETWEEN THE FIRST AND TWENTY-FIRST CENTURIES

What can be said then about Jesus' understanding of Judaism on the basis of this textual frame of reference, without essentializing Judaism and without psychologizing the historical Jesus? It is true that we do not know how Jesus perceived his Judaism intellectually, and how he reflected about law and faith. But we know that the historical Jesus read the texts of Torah and Prophets, lived according to the Jewish law of his time, and participated in its discussions. This law is not identical with today's Halakhah, but it nevertheless constitutes its foundation. Connecting halakhic lines between the first and the twenty-first centuries includes laws of purity, dietary laws, agricultural regulations, and laws about time, such as Shabbat and holidays. Observance characterized Jesus' daily life, certainly his week and his year. Shabbat was different from other days, and the year was structured by the three festivals of Passover, Shavuot, and Sukkot. The three holidays were marked with pilgrimages to Jerusalem, and they connected his life to the biblical narrative of exodus, the wilderness, and the receiving of the law. Already in Jesus' time, these holidays mark the most important memories of the people Israel's history with the God of Israel. There is a text telling a story, entailing instructions for the memory of that story as well as reflections on the significance of that memory. That means that there is collective identity being built, an identity held dynamic by collective self-reflection. This is phenomenologically different from the typical tale of origin common to many peoples and cultures.[70]

We cannot, of course, know what precise influence these texts had on Jesus, but we can describe the particular qualities of these texts and then see him as a person exposed to these narratives and memories – a person who understood himself as connected to them by reading the texts aloud in a synagogue, by actually undertaking a pilgrimage to Jerusalem, by marking holidays and Shabbat in his own life. There is no way to know what Jesus thought about these traditions, but we have good reason to believe he was part of them. His interpretations – sayings and speeches – transmitted in the Mark, Luke, and Matthew narratives – are entangled with traditions of the communities collecting and editing the materials of which the Gospels were composed. But although we do not have historical

---

[70] Anthony Smith, *The Ethnic Origins of Nations* (Oxford: Blackwell Publishers, 1986).

evidence of Jesus' explicitly relating to these textual traditions, contemporary historical research would support Jesus' participating in traditions and discussions of law. Historical Jesus research has tried to place Jesus within the halakhic discourse – but most certainly, the halakhic method as such, weighing different arguments in order to come to a conclusion that is in line with previous basic law, had an impact on Jesus' discussions of law. Whether Jesus was radical, liberal, strict, or engaged in transgressing the law, he was nevertheless part of a culture that was at the same time observant and discursive. Jesus' Jewishness can thus be best described as a set of hermeneutics – not hermeneutical principles yet, but rather an open platform inviting interpretation and discussion. It is the method rather than a certain content that may be described as Jewish. But juxtaposing "method" and "content" is insufficient here. The method is not just the form, not just something exterior to an interior set of materials. What I here describe as "polyphony" is not just a method, and even the more comprehensive term "hermeneutics" is not quite sufficient to express the open meaning of multilayered, self-reflective narrative and law – and both intertwined, as in the book of Exodus.

To describe Jesus' Jewishness with the help of a horizon of textual reference means that his way of life – and thought – was to determine the right measurement in accordance with the textual tradition of the Pentateuch and the Prophets. More than functioning as an adjective or attribute, Jewishness here describes activities of self-reflection, memory, and discussion. Within this horizon of Jewishness as discursive practice, certain social Bible-based commitments seem to be dominant in most of the Jesus texts, namely, those that indicate consideration for the underprivileged, with roots in Torah law, especially regarding the widow, the orphan, and the "ger" (stranger), as well as in the social criticism characteristic for most of the biblical books of prophecy.

The Jewishness of Jesus is not easily described in terminologies of twenty-first-century Judaism, but it is also not simply disconnected. It is impossible to trace such multi-faceted expressions of Jewish identity down to a singular concept – but its "multifacetedness" will certainly be part of the key. The question whether a continuity or discontinuity of Jewishness across the ages should be given preference ought at least to be shared with today's diverse Jewish communities. A majority of religious, observant, secular, Israeli and Diaspora Jews perceive and present themselves as Jewish and see themselves connected to a chain of generations going back to rabbinic as well as biblical times.

The question of Jewish continuity opens up an interesting realm of interreligious reasoning. Christological thought committed to the Jewishness of Jesus is informed by contemporary Jewish discussion about Jewishness. A most specific "Other" is taken seriously as a primary source of revelation (understood as insight into divine matters) for theological questioning within a particular faith community and a particular interfaith relationship.

Palestinian theologians find themselves on the other side of the map of Jewish continuity. But the christological clash is not taking place between Jews and Palestinians hoping to win a future for themselves, arguing who was first in the land. The argument provoked by Jesus the Jew is a competition between post-Shoah and Palestinian theologians about who remembers him best. Just as with regard to Black theologians, Palestinian Christians are typically suspected of "having a problem" with the Jewishness of Jesus. Rather than stating a "problem" for theologies that are not considered mainstream, I want to explore the intensification of discourse when Jesus is re-remembered as Jewish.

The theological tension between post-Shoah and Palestinian theologians needs to be examined in the context of emerging Christian post-supersessionism. After the Shoah, many European and American theologians could no longer identify with a Christian theory of Jewish displacement. Looking for alternatives, post-supersessionist thought developed in a manner closely interwoven and supported by the Pauline epistles, especially Romans. The biblical language of the covenant proved helpful to express affirmation of the Jewish people instead of their replacement. Thus, Christian theologians critical of displacement theologies formulated their revised view of Judaism as "the unrevoked, living covenant."[71] When reflecting critically on themselves they applied Paul's metaphor of the olive tree (Rom 11). They identified themselves with those addressed in Paul's admonition to remember that it is not you who supports the root, but the root that supports you (Rom 11:18).[72] Christians affirming Judaism began to perceive themselves as "engrafted

---

[71] Among the many publications, see for example Simon Schoon, *Onopgeefbar verbonden* (Kampen: Kok, 1998) or Norbert Lohfink, *The Covenant Never Revoked: Biblical Reflections on Christian–Jewish Dialogue* (New York: Paulist Press, 1991).

[72] The exegetical dispute over who exactly is meant by the "root" – the fathers, the people Israel, the Jesus-believing Jews – continues until today. For an informative introduction to traditional versus contemporary readings of Paul, see John G. Gager, *Reinventing Paul* (Oxford and New York: Oxford University Press, 2000).

branches." The avoidance of replacement thought and a grateful affirmation of Judaism were elementary to this theology and spirituality, and
they were certainly appropriate sentiments to counteract a long tradition
of Christians claiming spiritual superiority. But while European and
American theologians established a theological commitment to dialogue
with Jews and Judaism, Palestinian theologians have found themselves
overlooked and disadvantaged. With growing interdenominational consensus, mainstream Western Churches have reformulated their self-
understanding and especially their understanding of Christ. Christians
no more see themselves as substituting for Judaism and negating Jesus'
Jewishness. They no longer define themselves negatively, by repudiating
and distorting Judaism. In fact, the distortion of Judaism began to appear
to them as a distortion of Jesus himself. Even the notion of a unique Jesus
was seen by some as supporting Christian claims of superiority and thus
degrading Judaism.

Together with a new Christian self-understanding as post-supersessionist,
the accentuated Jewish Jesus was now proclaimed for all Christians to
remember. But Western Christians forgot to ask whether Palestinian Christians too had themselves actually forgotten and needed to be reminded of
this. Amid a struggle over national self-determination waged against a
professedly Jewish state, they may have not been in the mood for such
reminders perceived as "Western." Moreover, the Pauline metaphor of the
engrafted branch, most appropriate for Christians' embrace of self-criticism,
did not much resonate with Palestinian Christians. Many Palestinian families live with intense memories of expulsion or fear of expulsion from their
homes. Actual olive trees of Palestinians have been and even continue to be
literally uprooted. In contemporary Palestinian culture, the olive tree stands
for rootedness in the land, in history and tradition. The theological question
is whether Palestinian Christianity may represent a special branch of the
olive tree, not an engrafted one. The Christological question is whether Jesus
the Jew is an Other in Palestine.

Perhaps this tension can best be illustrated through a personal anec-
dote. A few years ago, I was asked to give a talk about the Jewish Jesus to
a group of Palestinian theologians connected to the Kairos document.[73]

[73] For the text of the Kairos document, written by an interdenominational group of
Palestinian theologians, see "Kairos Palestine: A Word of Faith, Hope, and Love from
the Heart of Palestinian Suffering." In Rifat Odeh Kassis, ed., *Kairos for Palestine*
(Ramallah: Baday/Alternatives, 2011), 177–197. The document aims to empower
Palestinian Christian identity and the pursuit of justice. Strikingly, but generally

The setting was prepared by Jews and Christians engaged in Jewish–Christian dialogue. To lecture Palestinian theologians about the Jewishness of Jesus is, of course, an act of chutzpah. This is not because "all the Jews they know are soldiers and settlers," as is often stereotypically stated by self-acclaimed advocates of Palestinians, but because it is patently arrogant to suggest that a Christian does not know his or her Bible. My talk did not at all seek to claim that anybody was denying Jesus' Jewishness, but the awkwardness of the topic for this particular setting created its own dynamic. During the feedback, every participant opened with a declaration of insistence at not having a problem with Jesus the Jew. But what followed was more interesting. I had talked about Jesus' otherness, his distance and difference from his followers today. Nobody picked up on the otherness of Jesus as a Jew. None of the Palestinian participants in the meeting problematized Jesus as Other. Everybody referred instead to the theme of proximity, even immediacy: "Yes, he was Jewish, he was here, he walked on the land, he was shaped by the landscape"; "Of course, a Jew. No problem. He breathed the air I breathe he smelled the flowers that I smell, he ate the olives I eat." "Sure, Jewish. Jesus was Mediterranean. A warm person. Tradition was important to him, family. Like for me." These Palestinian theologians expressed a strong sense of identification with Jesus the Jew, a sense of his proximity and his likeness to them as an indigenous person.

The Christian memory of Jesus the Jew as different from them is likely to be most appropriate for Western Christians and their revision of inclusivism conveying superiority. Western Christians required a long time to recognize the value of difference.[74] But then, difference became a central term in interreligious relations, at times even referred to as an ideal.[75] In contrast, emphasizing "difference" as an interreligious value does not necessarily promote justice between Palestinians and Jews. Over decades, Palestinian theologians have developed a broad variety of contextual theologies, drawing on methods of liberation theology as well as other models of theological and political reflection. As with other

overlooked, is the fact that the authors mainly quote the biblical prophets to support their call for justice.

[74] Distance as a strong form of relatedness still presents a challenge to the Christian side of Jewish–Christian relations. See Friedrich-Wilhelm Marquardt, *Was dürfen wir hoffen, wenn wir hoffen dürften? Eine Eschatologie*, Vol. I (Gütersloh: Kaiser, 1993), 183.

[75] Jonathan Sacks, *The Dignity of Difference. How to Avoid the Clash of Civilizations*, second edition (London: Bloomsbury Academic, 2003).

liberation theologies, justice has been at the center of their interpreting the Bible and the political situation.[76] The focus of justice is most impactfully expressed in Naim Ateek's book *Justice and Only Justice*, arguably the classic theology in the Palestinian context.[77] While in my reading and listening to contemporary Palestinian voices the Jewish Jesus is not just remembered as caring about justice; interestingly, it is Jesus the Jew – not simply Jesus the Palestinian – who is remembered as siding with those who encounter injustice.

Just as there are many mansions in God's house (John 14:2), there are many branches on the olive tree. Palestinian Christians can look back to a very specific form of Christian continuity. They may identify as the roots or the trunk of the olive tree, the special branches, or the olive-wooden crèche that hosts the incarnation of the hope for justice. Their closeness to Jesus, its immediacy, the direct, non-transmitted knowing of Jesus ironically reminds me most of all of Jewish scholars who sometimes demonstrate a similarly immediate understanding and clear judgment of Jesus, though through the texts more than through the land.

The textual dimension is given a forceful interpretation in Mitri Raheb's account of memory, where the author closely interconnects biblical and church history.[78] Raheb describes the people of the Bible as "people of the Land" and views himself as one of them. "Throughout Palestinian history," writes Raheb,

empires have occupied the land for a certain number of years but were then forced to leave. Most of the time an empire departed only to make space for another empire. The majority of the native people of the land seldom left. Throughout history and starting with the Assyrian Exile, only a small minority was deported, and only a small percentage decided to leave. The vast majority of the native people remained in the land of their forefathers (2Kgs 25:12). They remained the *Am Haaretz*, the native 'People of the Land,' in spite of the diverse empires controlling that land.

---

[76] A detailed introduction is offered by Uwe Graebe, *Kontextuelle palästinensische Theologie. Streitbare und umstrittene Beiträge zum ökumenischen und interreligiösen Gespräch* (Erlangen: Erlanger Verlag für Mission und Ökumene, 1999).

[77] Naim Stifan Ateek, *Justice and Only Justice: A Palestinian Theology of Liberation* (Maryknoll, NY: Orbis Books, 1989).

[78] Mitri Raheb, *Faith in the Face of Empire: The Bible through Palestinian Eyes* (Maryknoll, NY: Orbis Books, 2014).

"This is why in this book," the author continues, "I choose the *people of the land* as the description for the native inhabitants throughout history, for it is they who are the enduring continuum."[79]

Raheb's argumentation is ingenious, and he certainly has a point. In the Hebrew Bible "People of the Land" can refer alternatively to the generality of the Judean and Israelite population or to foreigners and colonists, such as those forcibly resettled in the former northern kingdom following its conquest by Assyria in 721 BCE. In the books of Ezra and Nehemiah, the term is used pejoratively to refer to foreigners who have intermarried with the returned Judean exiles from Babylonia following the Emperor Cyrus's decree in 539 BCE. But some modern Bible scholars have claimed that these "people of the land" are deliberately conflated by Ezra and Nehemiah with a different Deuteronomic concept: the seven Canaanite nations, those peoples whose intercourse with Israel God explicitly proscribes (Hittites, Girgashites, Amorites, Canaanites, Perizzites, Hivites, and Jebusites).[80] For these scholars, and for Raheb apparently, the "people of the land" so mischaracterized by Ezra and Nehemiah were actually Judeans who were never exiled by Babylonia but who remained as peasants in their country, only to be cast as aliens by the repatriated Judean leaders.

Still, the concept of the "people of the land" remains a problematic interpretation from the standpoint of the identity of people who *were* exiled. One might ask, for instance, how Raheb sees Palestinians who were expelled in the second or third generation. What happens to their identity if they are no longer in the land? How is Palestinian diaspora identity to be maintained? Since Raheb's memory of continuity is built on the Bible, one might also ask how he views the biblical authors. To Raheb, the identity codes "Judaic" or "Jewish" are just variables in a long list of shifts; "from Canaanite, to Hittite, to Hivite, to Perizzite, to Girgashite, to Amorite, to Jebusite, to Philistine, Israelite, Judaic/Samaritan, to Hasmonaic, to Jewish, to Byzantine, to Arab, to Ottoman, and to Palestine." I find the biblical authors, who shaped, arranged, and redacted biblical memories and transformed them into narratives, chronicles, and legal texts, unrecognized in this list. These authors explicitly did not identify with the Canaanites, the Amorites, and Philistines alike. Rather,

---

[79] Raheb, *Faith in the Face of Empire*, 12.

[80] Deuteronomy 7:1. On the Am Haaretz in Ezra/Nehemiah, see Aharon Oppenheimer, *The 'Am Ha-Aretz: A Study in the Social History of the Jewish People in the Hellenistic-Roman Period*, trans. I. H. Levine (Leiden: E.J. Brill, 1977), 83–84 and n. 50.

they tell a story of a people and the personalities whom they themselves regard as predecessors. The perspective of that story is not the continuity of the place but of a people whose most profound memories include displacement. Especially as a memory of protest, Raheb might actually underestimate the critical powers of self-reflection that accompany people in times of exile.

Most remarkably, for both Palestinian and black theologians the memory of Jesus the Jew leads to a reinforcement of strong identification. Jesus the Jew is not perceived as further away than a Jesus carrying a universal message. On the contrary, Jesus the Jew shares their specific place in a situation of social or political struggle. One might sum up the Black and Palestinian memory of his Jewishness as signifying that Jesus is "on our side." In both cases, the Palestinian and the African American, increased identification with Jesus the Jew is not primarily expressed with regard to Jewish scholars but toward Christian theologians who had been explaining (maybe "West-splaining") to them what they themselves had just been re-learning, namely that Jesus is Jewish. For Christians seeking an alternative to the aggressive nature of inclusion, traditionally expressed in proselytizing, remembering Jesus' Jewishness goes together with learning distance. African American and Palestinian Christians are more familiar with the aggression of exclusion. With regard to Jesus, one could say that Jesus the Jew does not distance them, nor does he reinforce their exclusion. On the contrary, I would imagine, Jesus the Jew knows of their exclusion. And they have their special knowledge of him. Jesus the Jew is not remembered a stranger to these Christians but as one of them. Thus, in some respects, the African American and the Palestinian Christian witness of Jesus' Jewishness is similar to Jewish post-Shoah presentations.

Reminding Christians of Jesus' Jewish belonging has played a major role in Jewish post-Shoah thought and art – as, for example, in Chagall's famous painting "White Crucifixion" that shows Jesus on the cross wearing a *tallit*, a Jewish prayer shawl.[81] Moshe Gershuni's 1987 work *There/Name* that illustrates the cover of this book is far more subtle. Here, the cross is signed by the Hebrew word שם, that can be read as "shem," meaning "name," or "sham," which means "there." "Ha-Shem," the name, is a rabbinical term for God. "Sham," there, has been used by survivors in Israel to name the worst places of history. There is no

---

[81] Raheb's book shows a shawl resembling a kaffiye!

body of a blatantly Jewish Jesus nailed to the cross here. Rather, one might interpret that a yellow cross is nailed to the question of God's presence.[82]

The Jewish witness of Jesus' Jewishness is not supposed to sponsor Church Christology. But Christological discourse is advanced by critical Jewish voices. Christological thought committed to the Jewishness of Jesus is informed by contemporary Jewish discussion about Jewishness. But how can Jewish self-definition be constitutive of a certain Christology? Nostra Aetate begins with the estimation that "in our age" people get "closer." In many of the "50 years after Nostra Aetate" reviews, this approach has been treated with certain alienation, or at least skepticism. The here-developed interreligious Christology does not build on closeness in the sense of diminishing differences. But interreligious theology pays tribute to an interconnectedness that is not reciprocal.

The contemporary Jewish witness to Jesus the Jew discussed here has Christological relevance for Christian thought. It does not, of course, serve as an affirmation of Church Christology. Jewish collective memory, which helps identify Jesus as Jewish and even welcomes Jesus into the Jewish chain of generations, serves Christians as a critical memory – in the original meaning of "critical" as indicating an act of differentiating. There must be a clear division between Jews recognizing Jesus as Jewish and Christian interpretations of his Jewishness. His Jewishness has been postulated as a critical question by Jews of different epochs. Certainly, the most painstaking questions have been posed with regard to the Shoah. Here, Jesus' Jewishness obviously arises as part of an answer to a question posed by Emil Fackenheim: "Where would Jesus of Nazareth be in 1942 if he had lived in Europe?" For Fackenheim, answering this question marks the beginning of Christian *tikkun* – repair.[83] The expected answer – that he would most likely be found in a concentration camp, as Paul van Buren proposed – implies Jesus' Jewish identity, one that had been neglected or ignored by European Christians.

The logic of post-supersessionist covenant Christology invites and welcomes the Jewish witness to Jesus the Jew. The diverse expressions of this witness, picturing Jesus as Jewish carpenter, Galilean peasant, or

---

[82] See Amitai Mendelsohn, *Behold the Man: Jesus in Israeli Art* (Jerusalem: Magnes, 2017).

[83] Emil Fackenheim, *To Mend the World: Foundations of Post-Holocaust Jewish Thought* (New York: Schocken, 1989). The concept of "tikkun" that is rooted in the Kabbalah, has become central in North American Jewish thought since the last third of the twentieth century. Fackenheim's use of the concept is highly unusual in applying the ethically transformed term also to Christianity: "Christianity is ruptured by the Holocaust and stands in need of a *Tikkun*," 278.

Israeli pioneer, correspond to the manifold Jewish expressions from
Second Temple Judaism to the present. Only some of the types of Jewish
outreach to a Jewish Jesus engage specifically with Christianity, however.
Jews have plenty of reasons for engaging with a Jewish Jesus that have
little or nothing to do with Christianity. Many of the twentieth-century
Jewish scholars and writers who emphasize Jesus the Jew have been
secular. Their reference to Jesus the Jew serves many rather diverse
causes, ranging from Jesus the ethical reformer to the land-bound
Zionist.[84]

Christian theology pays tribute to Jesus by being responsive to these
manifold Jewish voices. They do not define Jesus Christ for the Church,
and do not lead Jesus out of the Church, but Christians nevertheless have
a responsibility to be aware of them. As Dietrich Ritschl described the
connection between Jesus Christ and Christology, "Jesus Christ is not the
answer, however paradoxical, to our Christological questions, but he is
the calling into question of our questions, presuppositions and
answers."[85] The rediscovered Jewishness of Jesus is not an answer to
theological questions about Jewish–Christian relations. Rather, picking
up on Ritschl's formulation, the Jewish Jesus is calling into question
presuppositions and answers about him and about Christian faith in
him. Christian and Jewish historians have tried to define what Jewishness
consisted of during the Second Temple period and have successfully
shifted Historical Jesus research as a whole. The Jewish Jesus Christ, as
the "Christus praesens," is continuously calling into question Christological presuppositions, and incessantly calling into dialogue Jewish questions and answers about Jewishness today.

---

[84] Neta Stahl, ed., *Jesus among the Jews: Representation and Thought* (New York:
Routledge, 2012); Matthew Hoffman, *From Rebel to Rabbi: Reclaiming Jesus and the
Making of Modern Jewish Culture* (Stanford, CA: Stanford University Press, 2007).
[85] Dietrich Ritschl, *Memory and Hope*, 204.

4

The Future: Regarding the Human

As early as 1974, at a premature stage of theologies born out of Jewish–Christian dialogue, Rosemary Radford Ruether formulated a brilliant analysis of the connection between Christology and Christian aggression toward Jews and Judaism.[1] In her path-breaking book *Faith and Fratricide* she described the phenomenon of confusing past and future, in Christian scholarship referred to as "realized eschatology."[2] By shifting what is promised for the end of times to the present, the church becomes more aggressive to those personifying the notion that salvation remains remote. Presenting the promises of salvation, the "not yet" as "already here," sharpens the conflict with a Judaism that stands for the "not yet." Ruether's analysis has convinced numerous theologians,[3] who in response have re-emphasized the future as a time of salvation: Reconciliation has begun, but still needs to be forstered and the reconciliation of all remains in the distant future, though not independent of Christians' reconciling activity.

Among contemporary systematic theologians, Friedrich-Wilhelm Marquardt's dogmatic theology especially reflects this shift.[4] A fair amount of

---

[1] Rosemary Radford Ruether, *Faith and Fratricide: The Theological Roots of Anti-Semitism* (Eugene, OR: Wipf&Stock, 1997).

[2] Ibid., 246.

[3] See especially John T. Pawlikowski, "The Historicizing of the Eschatological," in Alan T. Davies, ed., *Antisemitism and the Foundations of Christianity* (New York: Paulist Press, 1979), 151–166.

[4] Of the seven volumes presenting his dogmatics, three volume titles include the term eschatology. See Marquardt, *Was dürfen wir hoffen, wenn wir hoffen dürften? Eine Eschatologie*, three volumes (Gütersloh: Kaiser, 1993–1996).

99

Christological thought found in Marquardt's volumes is described as eschatology, which displays his commitment to a "theological repentance" (*tshuva*). In Marquardt's formulation, the future of Jesus Christ is about justice. This is his task as a judge, according to the Christian creed. Marquardt's ideas about judgment may be best described as Levinas-inspired post-Shoah ethics. On judgment day, everybody arrives with his or her respective Other. Judgment is individual, but people are not isolated.[5] Relying on the Bible alone, Marquardt emphasizes the significance of works and deeds. This needs to be understood over and against the background of his Lutheran heritage, where practice is treated as secondary, while belief is upheld as the leading Christian obligation. Influenced by Jewish–Christian dialogue and intense Talmudic studies, Marquardt aims at reversing this hierarchy and returns to the biblical preference for praxis. Thus he emphasizes that judgment is according to works (Romans 2,5–6), which is a provocation to Lutherans but one significantly prompted by an unabashed reevaluation of Christianity's relation to Judaism.[6] Marquardt's readers, moreover, German Lutherans and theologians of other denominations interested in Jewish–Christian relations, would have been used to a wide range of modern liberal theologies that all favor a language of love and forgiveness but not of works and deeds.[7]

Combining both of these ideas, that is, underscoring the theological significance of deeds while projecting reconciliation or redemption into the distant future, has been explored by systematic theologians other than Marquardt, particularly Dietrich Ritschl, who speaks of the "unfulfilled talk about reconciliation."[8] Instead of stating and insisting that the most important change – whether it is called reconciliation, the forgiving of sins, or salvation – has already happened, it is now projected into the distant future. The more that is shifted to the future, the more there remains to be done in the present. At the same time, this shift describes

---

[5] Ibid., III, 165.   [6] Ibid., III, 120.

[7] Christologies insisting on the core of salvation as already accomplished could also be dressed in very progressive language. An example is Paul Tillich, who describes the Christ event as "New Being" that changes "alienation," since Christ could live existence without being alienated. The Christ believer likewise can participate in this New Being. With all his existential language, Tillich states that the New Being, in principle, has already begun. See Paul Tillich, *Systematic Theology, vol.2, Existence and the Christ* (Chicago: University of Chicago Press, 1957).

[8] Ritschl, *The Logic of Theology*, 167.

a move from dogma to ethics. The less that has been accomplished by divine agency, the more human agency is still needed.

The traditional Christological insistence that the most significant change has already happened is even less convincing from a critical post-Shoah perspective. In post-Shoah awareness, Emil Fackenheim's challenge to traditional Christianity needs to be taken seriously: "Has the Good Friday, then, overwhelmed the Easter? Is the Good News of the Overcoming itself overcome?"[9] Remarkably, the Jewish Canadian philosopher was here turning to Christians and deploying Christian language. Christianity has been preaching the "victory" of Easter all along, often broadly generalized as a victory of life over death. Jesus' death and his resurrection have been part of the Christian creed since the Council of Nicaea in 325. Both events are listed in the Christian creed and thus belong to the first order set of beliefs in all Christian denominations. In contrast, the interpretation that death is vindicated is not a dogma, although it developed as something central to Christian belief as a faith tradition.[10]

The Christian creed that Jesus died and has risen from the dead is in itself not necessarily offensive toward Judaism.[11] While Jews do not share the belief in Jesus' resurrection, the idea of the resurrection of the dead is originally Jewish and served as a major theological divide between the leading Second Temple groups, the Pharisees and Sadducees. Nevertheless, to Roy Eckardt a triumphalist voice inevitably comes through the Christian proclamation of the resurrection. In an unusual turn, Eckardt suggests the postponement of the notion of Jesus' resurrection:

...That young Jewish prophet from the Galilee sleeps now. He sleeps with the other Jewish dead, with all the disconsolate and scattered ones of the murder camps and with the unnumbered dead of the human and the nonhuman family. But Jesus of Nazareth shall be raised. So, too, shall the small Hungarian children of Auschwitz. Once upon a time, they shall again play, and they shall again laugh.[12]

---

[9] Emil Fackenheim, *To Mend the World: Foundations of Post-Holocaust Jewish Thought* (New York: Schocken Press, 1989), 286. This is his second of three Christological questions.

[10] This differentiation between dogma and its traditional interpretation is particularly important in the case of Jesus' death, as we will see in Chapter 5.

[11] Against the Alice and Roy Eckardt conviction of the early eighties: see A. Roy Eckardt and Alice L. Eckardt, *Long Night's Journey into Day: Life and Faith after the Holocaust* (Detroit: Wayne State University Press, 1982), 150, 132.

[12] Ibid., 150.

This poetic post-Shoah critique of resurrection is not in line with Christian dogma, which is probably why Eckardt eventually withdrew his negation of resurrection.[13] I still see his text as a powerful individual expression of solidarity with Jews and victims of the Shoah. Instead of taking back his relegating of the resurrection to the future, Eckardt could have modified his statement along the following lines. "One might speak about Jesus being resurrected twice – once in the past at Golgotha and once in the future on the Day of Judgment. This, in fact, might be Eckardt's intent: The Christ arose at Golgotha and the 'young Jewish prophet from Galilee' will arise in the future."[14]

It is remarkable that the most outstanding Christian post-Shoah theologians – Roy Eckardt and Friedrich-Wilhelm Marquardt – with their different national and denominational backgrounds, choose the category of future to discuss the memory of the Shoah, and both – the two theologians who have wrestled hardest with the Shoah and the implications of its Christian witness – use a language of hope, with Eckardt hoping for resurrection and Marquardt hoping for God.[15]

A mindful and memory-committed Christology will speak more thoughtfully and hesitantly about the good that happened 2,000 years ago, and more intensely about the evil that occurred in the twentieth century. Emil Fackenheim's question can be understood as suggesting that asserting a victory of life over death in principle has a cynical ring for people deeply conscious of the Shoah. One need not be Jewish to share this sensitivity. It is rather a universal phenomenon that insistence on an overall good will be painful to those experiencing an overall evil. But apart from solidarity in thought, something that Jews have good reason to expect from Christians, Christian truth itself is also in question here. Even if one turns to metaphors like eclipse,[16] or an overshadowing, or a cloud, the questions remains: What lasting value and ultimate significance has Easter if it can be overshadowed? Fackenheim's question is not about

---

[13] Eckardt, "The Shoah and the Affirmation of the Resurrection of Jesus: A Revisionist Marginal Note," in *Bearing Witness to the Holocaust 1939–1989* (Lewiston, NY: Edwin Mellen Press, 1991), 313–331.

[14] I owe this fascinating interpretation of Eckardt's take on resurrection to one of the anonymous readers of my manuscript.

[15] Hoping for God is the critical post-Shoah idea behind Marquardt's last volume that he frames as utopia. See Marquardt, *Eia, wärn wir da – eine theologische Utopie* (Gütersloh: Kaiser, 1997).

[16] See Martin Buber, *Eclipse of God: Studies in the Relation between Religion and Philosophy* (New York: Harper, 1952).

theodicy; it is about the actual impact of the Christ event. I do not wish to say that Auschwitz has simply "ruled out" or overruled Easter – this would be as superficial as the notion that the aftermath of the Shoah must necessarily conclude with the end of God. Yet the Christian problem here is different from a theodicy question that is even partly shared with Judaism.[17]

The problem is that many statements of Christian belief overload the positive aspects of the Christ event. Not only is that not in accordance with Christian dogma, but it can even be seen as in tension with it. That the resurrection covers up all memory of the wounds and pains of death is actually close to the heresy of Docetism – as if death had not really happened to Jesus. Thus, one might conclude, the notion of a principal "victory" over death actually diverts from Christian dogma. To say it differently, the notion of vulnerability is important in combatting Docetism.[18]

What does it mean that Jesus Christ will be Jewish? He, the one person, will be Jewish. His divine and human nature, in their undefined togetherness, remain one person. This person is Jewish – and will be Jewish. We do not know how Jewishness will be expressed at the end of times. Jewishness was differently expressed in the first and twenty-first centuries, as we have seen. What we do know, however, is that this Jewish self-expression will not be disconnected from other Jewish lives – a thought that connects to Eckardt's notion of postponed resurrection. His interpretation of conditioning the Christian content of belief by the life of Jewish children is thus a valid Christian statement, although it seems not to be in line with dogma in a literal sense. We do not know how Jews will perceive and articulate Jewishness in the far future – but Christian belief tells us that Jewishness matters and will not dissolve.[19] This means that Jesus' otherness for Christian non-Jews will not be dissolved either.

---

[17] Theodicy after the Shoah presents a different set of questions to Jews and Christians, but the questioning of God is a shared matter. See my article "Theodicy and Its Critique in Christian post-Shoah Thought," in Beate Ego, Ute Gause, Ron Margolin, and Dalit Rom-Shiloni, eds., *Theodicy and Protest* (Tübingen: Evangelische Verlagsanstalt, 2018), 177–194.

[18] I will continue the discussion of vulnerability in Chapter 6.

[19] Against far-spread evangelical ideas of a "final" dissolving of Jewish difference.

THE FUTURE OF OUR HUMANITY

The question of His humanity is entangled with the future of our human-ity. Marquardt suggested that the Christian theological question after the Shoah is not whether God exists but whether God is "humane."[20] A variation of the theodicy question is how do we regain faith in human-ity after the Shoah? Again, we are thrown back to Emil Fackenheim's questions to Christian theologians. While Fackenheim's first question recalls Jesus belonging to the Jewish people and the second criticizes Easter-triumphalism, his third question can really get under our skin. It entices a different discourse that has in recent years spread to the philo-sophical world, although Fackenheim addressed it specifically to Chris-tian theologians: "Could Jesus of Nazareth have been made into a Muselmann?"[21] The so-called Muselmann poses a painful memory, transmitted through survivors' literature, especially the Italian author Primo Levi.[22] The term "Muselmann" was used in Auschwitz and other camps[23] to describe the state of mind and body of those who had lost all signs of vitality: "non-men who march and labour in silence, the divine spark dead in them, already too empty to really suffer. One hesitates to call them living: one hesitates to call their death death, in the face of which they have no fear as they are too tired to understand."[24]

While it is often overlooked that no interpretation of Jesus' death has effectively become dogma, the notion of his death is itself part of the Christian creed.[25] Following Primo Levi's testimony that "one cannot call their death death," Christology must meet the challenge of disrupted death. Death has lost its dignity – this is a central theme for Emil Fackenheim – and it affects Christian faith, in particular. Until recently, the phenomenon of the so-called Muselmann had not received much attention in historical literature and research about the Shoah. In contrast,

---

[20] Marquardt, *Prolegomena* (1988), 144. I will further explore this statement in the following chapter about Two-Nature Christologies. The word used in the German original is "menschlich," which means both human and humane – the double meaning might be intended here.

[21] Fackenheim, *To Mend the World*, 286.

[22] See especially Primo Levi, *The Drowned and the Saved* (New York: Simon & Schuster Paperbacks, 2017).

[23] Synonyms included "Camels" (Neuengamme), "Crippels" (Stutthof), and "Muselweiber" (Ravensbrück). Agamben, *Remnants of Auschwitz: The Witness and the Archive* (Brooklyn: Zone Books, 2000), 44.

[24] Primo Levi, *If This Is a Man* (London: Abacus, 1987), 96.

[25] The account of his death is of utmost importance to all thought-leading Church fathers as it is the fundamental statement against Docetism.

the phenomenon is central in survivors' accounts, in their written as well as oral testimonies.[26] Despite an abundance of explanations, the etymology of the term is not at all clear. The word "Muselmann" itself is an old German word for Muslim.[27] Clearly, a negative view of Islam was constitutive in its development, although not necessarily in a conscious way.

Giorgio Agamben has called attention to the fact that in Auschwitz "Jews were made into Muslims," and Gil Anidjar has picked up on this weird semantic encounter. In Anidjar's attempt to write a European history of the enemy, "the Jew" and "the Arab" approach each other in their common victimization by "Europe."[28] But in Anidjar's discussion, the notion of the "Muselmann" gets lost in metaphoric and semantic speculations. Anidjar's identification of Europe as the source for Jewish–Arab conflict in the present is a legitimate historical political proposition. But for a history of Nazi-occupied Europe there is no need for complicated metaphors in order to identify the perpetrators. Here, we need to analyze the mechanisms of evil, rather than semantic dynamics. The statements that "Jews died as Muslims" or "Jews knew they wouldn't die as Jews in Auschwitz" are highly problematic. While the etymological history is not settled, "Muselmann" was apparently not a Nazi term. The concept as we know it from the survivors' testimonies comprised the sum of what every camp prisoner was afraid of: the loss of personhood, agency, emotional capacity, and personal will. This is what Primo Levi described as worse than death, and according to testimonies such a state of being was commonly feared by the prisoners more than death itself. But by translating the term "Muselmann" to "Muslim" – a translation that would be semantically correct prior to the twentieth century – personhood is taken away from Jewish prisoners of the concentration camp. To say that Jews did not die as Jews in Auschwitz is a statement that gives in to Nazi logic of the eradication of Jewishness as well as actual Jews.

Developing the word "Muselmann" as the term for a state of apathy previously not known in humanity surely bore the weight of a long-internalized European anti-Muslim attitude. Still, historically, this

---

[26] Giorgio Agamben has pointed out this discrepancy; see Agamben, *Remnants of Auschwitz*, 52.

[27] The word as such would still be used in some traditional children's songs, but German children today would not know the meaning – and would probably not sense a resemblance of the word "Muslim."

[28] Gil Anidjar, *The Jew, the Arab: A History of the Enemy* (Stanford, CA: Stanford University Press, 2003).

wrongdoing remains in the realm of language. It is unlikely that many, if any, real Muslims suffered concrete harm because of this designation, although real Muslims certainly did suffer from Nazism. The main problem with Anidjar's focus on this offensive terminology is that it portrays the development and use of "Muselmann" as the essential crime and thus, inadvertently, diminishes the horrific suffering inflicted on Jews and other victims of Nazism. Jews were not victimized because they were made into Muselmänner; rather, many were made into Muselmänner because they were Jews.

Fackenheim's question about the Muselmann is important, as it focuses on the question of humanity, its limits, challenges, and conditions. The Shoah has been described as an attack on God, but it was also an attack on humanity. The phenomenon of the Muselmann threatens our understanding of the human in an unprecedented way. In Paul van Buren's logic, the prospect of Jesus in the mental, physical, and emotional state of a Muselmann should not be more appalling to God than that of any of his children experiencing such horror. Still, Fackenheim's intriguing question tests the Christian understanding of Jesus' full humanity that has been dogma since the beginning of the fourth century. The most serious defense of Jesus' humanity can be found in the creed formulated by the council of Chalcedon (454): Jesus is truly human, as already proclaimed in Nicaea (325), and his humanity is complete, not partial or in any way different from other human beings – just without sin. That Jesus was without sin was a strong and very early conviction, and not a new emphasis of Chalcedon. Nor had the divinity of Christ been seriously questioned since situating the Son before creation in Nicaea ("there was no time when he was not"). His humanity, though, was still challenged by variations of Docetism, such as the notion that Christ was not fully human and that instead of a human soul Jesus had the Logos (Apollinarianism), or by Eutyches' conviction that in Christ the human was absorbed by the divine. Against these challenges, the Council of Chalcedon insisted on the full humanity of Christ, not one absorbed into or assimilated to his divine nature.

There is no choice but to concede that if Jesus Christ's humanity is completely like our own – just without sin – then he indeed could have been made into a Muselmann. For having been made a Muselmann was not a sin or a failure on the part of the victim. While people in the concentration camps had very different medical constitutions that made them more or less vulnerable to physical disease, there was no instant defense against the condition called "Muselmann." There were no particular personality traits or practices that could guarantee that one would be spared this terrible fate. The apathy of the Muselmann is not a consequence of a previous apathy. Testimonies and literature of survivors clearly show that the state of the so-called Muselmann could strike anyone. Thus the responsibility for this attack on humanity lies solely on the perpetrators' side.

This leads to a second aspect here that bears Christological relevance: The phenomenon of the Muselmann defines a new chapter in the history of evil caused by humans. Turning a human being into a Muselmann is a descent into the deepest level of sin. If Christ had come to take sin on his shoulders, could such a sin also be included? The Western church built theories (and churches!) on the notion of the treasure of Christ's merits. Since Jesus Christ was without sin, there was abundant grace. This notion had been cynically abused on the eve of the Reformation (*indulgentia*) but it was not in itself cynical: It meant that in the universal balance grace outweighs sin.

After the Shoah, however, it would be cynical to claim there is a surplus of grace. The evidence of the twentieth century – not to mention the short twenty-first century – makes the preponderance of evil difficult to deny or downplay. The world is in need of grace, but it might be more appropriate to say that what the world needs is the prevention of ultimate sins. The prevention of genocide should be a specific Christian task for the twenty-first century – not because Christians are better at genocide prevention than non-Christians, but because there are good theological reasons to assume this particular responsibility. Replacement-theology promoted Christian evil against Jews and as a whole represents a theology based on eliminatory thought. Christian post-supersessionist and anti-supersessionist awareness would consequently be a protest against eliminatory thought and action that leads inexorably to the commitment of genocide prevention.

THE FUTURE OF OUR DIVINE SPARK: NATALITY

In order to be true to the future of Jesus Christ, which means to care about the future of both the human and the humane, Christology cannot express itself in solely positive terms. The Shoah was, among other things, also a dehumanizing attack on Christ,[29] one that cannot be papered over by the

---

[29] This sentence is meant to urge a specific Christological revision necessitated by the Shoah and the loss of humanity in the concentration camp. The formulation "attack on Christ" is not meant as metaphorizing or Christologizing the real murder of real Jews in the Shoah.

current embrace of Christological positivism. On the other hand, Christology must not occlude hope.[30] Hope, in this view, is not an illusion that helps to cover up a problematic reality, but on the contrary, a quality that sharpens the perception of what needs to be and can be repaired with human power in the present. The source of hope after the Shoah, according to Emil Fackenheim, is Jewish survival and continuity.[31] Many survivors see every birth of a grandchild as victory over Hitler. Christians can join in the celebration of the continued covenant as grace bestowed on all children of the God of Abraham and Sarah. The covenant of Israel is for most continued by birth.[32] The future of Jesus Christ is bound to the future of this covenant.

Few systematic theologians have thought deeply about the implications of this ongoing interconnectedness.[33] One of the exceptions is Paul van Buren, who has considered the social and familial dimension of the Christological affirmation of the Jewish covenant in terms of the actual lives of individuals. Thus, van Buren invested careful thought in the belonging of children born to families with Christian mothers and Jewish fathers – children who would not be recognized as Jewish by Orthodox Halakhah. Writing in 1983, at the very moment when the American Reform movement in its "Resolution on Patrilineal Descent"[34] recognized patrilineal descent as sufficient for belonging to the Jewish people, van Buren addressed parental choices regarding the religious and educational affiliations of the child of a Christian mother and Jewish father. Here van Buren insists that, as he put it pithily, "if Israel truly gains, the church

---

[30] On Dietrich Ritschl's connection of ethics and hope, see Ritschl, *The Logic of Theology*, 260 f.

[31] Fackenheim, *To Mend the World*, 299 ff.

[32] And for some through conversion to Judaism.

[33] Phil Cunningham has pointed out that the future of covenantal life is interconnected: "Through Christ, through the crucified and raised Jew, the Church continuously encounters God's sustaining invitation to and empowerment of covenantal life. Jesus Christ brings the Church into ongoing covenantal life with Israel's God." Philip A. Cunningham, "A Covenantal Christology." *Studies in Christian-Jewish Relations* 1 (2005–2006): 41–52, 49.

[34] "Reform Judaism: Resolution on Patrilineal Descent," March 15, 1983. Remarkably, in this document, *mitzvoth* play a central role for the manifestation of Jewish identity. This foreshadowed a renewed interest in Halakhah in the traditionally non-halakhic Reform movement. Rachel Adler, who uses the term "Halakhah" for the contemporary liberal and "traditional Halakhah" for the orthodox view, seeks to reclaim halakhic language as vocabulary for praxis in the Reform community. See Rachel Adler, *Engendering Judaism: An Inclusive Theology and Ethics* (Boston: Beacon Press, 1999).

cannot lose."[35] This theological statement constitutes the deepest expression of post-supersessionist Christian thought: Christians are not replacing the people Israel, and there is no theological reason for competition in the social unit most important to Judaism, the family. A truly post-supersessionist Christian approach thus celebrates any birth of a child with a Jewish parent as continuation of the covenant.

Birth is also a universal sign for the future of humanity. The philosopher Julia Kristeva has shown that this is a core idea of Hannah Arendt's philosophical work: "... no matter how far science may progress, women will continue to be the mothers of humanity."[36] According to Hannah Arendt, nothing less than the future of humanity is bound to humans being born by women: "the miracle ... that saves the world ... is ultimately the fact of natality." Arendt continues her praise of natality with the most famous example of the transmitted news of a birth: "... It is this faith in and hope for the world that found perhaps its most glorious and most succinct expression in the few words with which the Gospels announced their 'glad tidings': 'A child has been born unto us.'"[37] It is remarkable that it is not a Christian theologian but the Jewish philosopher Hannah Arendt who quotes the gospel to underline the notion of birth as a miracle. In fact, while "birth" has not generally been a theme in modern theology, for the dogmatic discourse of the early church, Jesus' birth carried definite theological meaning and salvific significance. The origin of Jesus presented the first major dispute of the early Christian church, one that actually led to the formulation of the first Christian creed that characterized the Son as "begotten, not made." To Athanasius, and subsequently orthodoxy, it was key that the Son was not "created," not part of creation, but "begotten" (Nicaea, 325). A century later, at the council of Chalcedon (451), when Jesus' humanity was perceived to be in need of defense and explication, the historical birth "born by the virgin Mary" was added to the concept of "begotten before all ages." It is Jesus' birth – not his death – that bears the main salvific significance in this creed: His birth exemplifies his humanity. And it is precisely here that we are reminded of his Jewishness. It is to the credit of Hans Hermann

---

[35] Van Buren, *A Christian Theology of the People Israel* (San Francisco: Harper & Row, 1983), 340.

[36] Julia Kristeva, *Hannah Arendt* (New York: Columbia University Press, 2001), xiv.

[37] Hannah Arendt, *The Human Condition* (Chicago: University of Chicago Press, 1958), 247.

Henrix to have discovered the name of Jesus' mother Mary as the trace of his Jewishness in the creed of Chalcedon:

Mary's giving birth to Jesus marks him unmistakably as the son of a Jewish mother, from whom he takes on 'flesh'. The presence of Mary's name stands for the birth of a Jewish human being and recalls the concreteness of becoming human as a Jew. The text indirectly echoes this concreteness when, at the end, it places Jesus within the prophetic tradition. By speaking of the Son's second birth from Mary, the text shows that Israel is the latent context of Chalcedon's christology.[38]

The name of his mother qualifies Jesus' birth as his human beginning in a specific historical place and time. Here, in this creed most central for Christology, Jesus' Jewishness and humanity come as close as possible. His birth, according to the Christian creed, indeed saves the world.

But what does Hannah Arendt actually mean by saying that the miracle of birth saves the world? Arendt's is far from a post-feminist philosophy attributing to women the special task of motherhood. It seems necessary to first underline how very unusual this idea is for Arendt, whose thinking is as far from idealism or idealizing mothers as can be. In fact, her understanding of the phenomenon of birth is highly original. For Arendt, natality, the most common ground of human beings, contains the possibility of new beginnings. "The very capacity for beginning is rooted in natality, and by no means in creativity, not in a gift but in the fact that human beings, new men again and again appear in the world by virtue of birth."[39] By rooting the capacity to begin anew, to take the initiative and to act in the fact of birth and natality rather than in creativity and special talent and giftedness, Arendt makes an unusual political-philosophical statement. Julia Kristeva finds that the "theme of life" accompanies and shines through all of Arendt's thought.[40] I suggest that this can also be understood as part of Arendt's post-Shoah and post-totalitarian thought. Her thinking about natality is part of her book *The Human Condition*, a philosophical study of forms of human activity and work.[41] This theory of praxis came at

---

[38] Hans Hermann Henrix, "The Son of God Became Human as a Jew: Implications of the Jewishness of Jesus for Christology," in Philip A. Cunningham, Joseph Sievers, Mary C. Boys, Hans Hermann Henrix, and Jesper Svartvik, eds., *Christ Jesus and the Jewish People Today: New Explorations of Theological Interrelationships* (Grand Rapids, MI and Cambridge: William B. Eerdmans Publishing Company, 2011), 114–129, 126.

[39] Hannah Arendt, *The Life of the Mind* (New York: Harcourt, 1978), 217.

[40] Kristeva, *Hannah Arendt: Life Is a Narrative* (Toronto: University of Toronto Press, 2001), 4.

[41] The Latin title of the German translation summarizes her view of human destination: *Vita activa*.

a moment in Arendt's thinking when she experienced profound disappointment at the political capacities of human intellect. German academia had failed, she concluded, together with German philosophy and the humanities. In her essay from 1964, *Responsibility and Judgment*, for instance, Arendt finds that neither education nor special talent but rather inner dialogue enables resistance to dictatorship. It is the capacity to imagine oneself as continuing to live with one's deeds that makes it possible to refuse cooperation with evil.[42]

When Arendt discusses the origin of the capacity to act and to take initiative, she treats a central political-philosophical question. Her answer, that the capability to begin anew and initiate is rooted in natality, comes over against conditioning initiative by special talent or education. Similar to her article on judgment, Arendt does not credit intellect for the desired human behavior. In *The Human Mind*, she does not even credit creativity but instead opts for the common denominator of having been born as the prerequisite for acting. So rather than finding a special task for women, I interpret her notion of natality as humanity's common ground. To take action, to begin anew, to make an initiative can be expected by everyone by virtue of their birth. Christina Schues has interpreted the fact of natality itself as a call to responsibility.[43] This is not Arendt's language, but nevertheless an interesting and perhaps "Levinasian" reading of her work. Kristeva characterizes Arendt's *The Human Condition* as a "vehement defense of life" and "a hymn to the uniqueness of each and any birth."[44] I would read Arendt's view of natality as part of her political philosophy of the human deed. The status of "acting," of deeds versus mere thoughts, has changed in the post-Shoah situation. After all, many intellectuals and philosophers failed to rise to the occasion. The question of what is needed in order to act humanely in an extreme situation is answered in Arendt's "Responsibility and Judgment" in a minimalist fashion: no higher degree, no particular education, training, or knowledge proved necessarily helpful. Arendt reduces the necessary equipment to act to a dialogicity, an inner dialogue, that is available to any person of any status and background. The main argument in this context-bound text is similar in structure to her treatment of natality: By virtue of being born, human beings are equipped to act.

---

[42] Hannah Arendt, *Responsibility and Judgment* (New York: Schocken Books, 2003), 44f.

[43] Christina Schües, *Philosophie des Geborenseins* (Freiburg: Karl Alber, 2008), 20.

[44] Kristeva, *Hannah Arendt* (2001), 5.

The philosophers Lisa Guenther and Anja Karnein have expressed concern over the future of women as giving birth in a rapidly developing world of assisted reproductive technologies.[45] Moreover, the Jewish and Christian ethics of assisted reproduction have been typically discussed in relation to research in genetics and prenatal diagnosis.[46] Philosophical and ethical reflections on genetic research are usually of a critical nature and often exhibit suspicion regarding future practices and their imagined implications. Women philosophers generally have expressed more concern than satisfaction over assisted reproduction. Feminists have typically emphasized the freedom of choice for ending, not for initiating, pregnancy. But Arendt's and Kristeva's miracle of birth is not endangered or relativized by the contemporary common practice of assisted reproduction. In the currently widespread use of assisted reproduction technologies (ART) like in vitro fertilization, assistance is given to the process of fertilization and the transfer of the embryo to the woman's uterus. The actual implantation of the embryo, its development, and eventual birth remain pure miracles of motherhood. Accordingly, women continue to be the "mothers of humanity" and they are irreplaceable as long as an artificial uterus is unthinkable.

My understanding of Arendt differs from Kristeva and others' astonishment at the key role Arendt assigns to the "mothers for humanity." First, it must be emphasized that Arendt's thought about natality is not about parenting. Rather, it is about being born. Having been born is the most common human denominator. I read Arendt's *The Human Condition*, with its emphasis on initiative and acting, together with Levinas' claim for ethics as first philosophy. Arendt and Levinas are sharply different philosophers, but they share a disappointment in the intellect's capacity to prevent Nazism or at least resist it ideologically. In both philosophers' works, the deed is accorded higher value than the thought. In Arendt's theory of the deed, everybody is well equipped to act. The person responsible for the capacity of each of us to act – and to do the right thing when needed – is each and everyone's mother: not by her good advice and education, not even by her role modeling, but by virtue of her having given birth to us. The very human condition, being born, accounts

---

[45] Lisa Guenther, *The Gift of the Other: Levinas and the Politics of Reproduction* (Albany: State University of New York Press, 2006); Anja Karnein, *A Theory of Unborn Life: From Abortion to Genetic Manipulation* (Oxford: Oxford University Press, 2012).

[46] See Elliot N. Dorff and Laurie Zoloth, eds., *Jews and Genes: The Genetic Future in Contemporary Jewish Thought* (Philadelphia: Jewish Publication Society [Lincoln, NE: University of Nebraska Press], 2015).

for acting, and acting in order to enhance the human as well as the humane.[47] Thus *vita activa*, living an active life, is not meant to be a piece of good advice against aging. Rather, active living is the proper response to having been born. It is not an ideal but the most appropriate human behavior. According to Arendt, the capability for initiative is rooted in the original *initium*, the Latin word for "beginning." It is not a "right" to work – let alone a right to parenthood or "birthright" – that qualifies the human condition, but birth alone. Arendt's "by birth alone" might even be understood to echo Luther's "by grace alone" (*sola gratia*). In both cases, additional qualifications and preparations for doing the right deed are declared not to be essential. But this parallel between Luther and Arendt consists only of their strong confidence in this initial prerequisite; Luther's approach to the deed in itself was contrary to Arendt's since it is secondary at best to belief.

One might also hear a distant echo of the debate between Luther and Calvin on what facilitates the right deed. Calvin, who agreed with Luther's doctrine of justification by faith alone, advocated orientation on how to act (law) for the faithful. Here too, Luther insisted on reliance on grace alone. Just as Arendt in her article on judgment presents only the capacity for inner dialogue – and not education, conviction, values, or law – as the prerequisite for resisting evil, having been born is itself the sole qualification for acting, in her view. In a Lutheran reading of Arendt, birth is pure grace. Grace might indeed be a helpful word to balance the discussions about assisted reproduction as well as parenthood, especially when dominated by the category of privilege and "right," as in contemporary Israeli discourse.

The Gospel narratives vary greatly in the importance they attribute to birth. Jesus' birth is not mentioned in the oldest text, the Gospel according to Mark, and densely summarized as "the word became flesh" in the youngest Gospel, that of John. Matthew and Luke both exhibit a detailed interest in Jesus' naissance, but their details cover entirely different aspects of Jesus' human origin: Matthew follows Jesus' patrilineal ancestry until Abraham,[48] while Luke tells the story of Mary giving birth in Bethlehem (Lk 2). Yet Jesus' actual birth comprises only three words in an otherwise fairly expansive narrative. Again, as in the case of Arendt, it was not a

---

[47] Thus I would say that *Vita activa* is not about the active life but activity as the core characteristic of living.

[48] The synoptic parallel in Luke presents Jesus as a direct descendant of Adam.

mother but a nun who called attention to the mother in labor here. The theologian Elisabeth Johnson has filled in what is missing in the story. As Johnson states,

No details are given. But the words 'she gave birth' evoke that event of almost cataclysmic stress by which women bring forth new life. The phrase recalls women's pain and strength involved in laboring, sweating, counting contractions, breathing deeply, crying out, dilating, pushing hard while riven to the very center of one's being with unimaginable bursts of pain, until slowly, slowly, the baby's head finally appears and with more pushing the little creature slips from the birth canal, to be followed by the discharge of the placenta, with much bleeding, and then deep fatigue, breasts swollen with milk, and unpredictable hormonal swings.[49]

Johnson's declared aim is a Mariology that enables us to see Mary as a person. Her filling in the details of the story could certainly constitute an anti-Docetic stance. Against the ancient Docetic heresy, which understood Jesus' humanity to be merely an illusion, Johnson here underscores holiness as lying precisely in the very human happening of birth: "Real blood was shed at this delivery, by a poor woman of peasant society far from home, laboring in childbirth for the first time. And it was holy." The notification "and she gave birth" – instead of "he was born" – keeps the memory of her, Mary, or Miriam, as subject of this birth.

While the birth of Jesus is narrated only in the gospel of Luke – and even there the birth itself is confined to just three words – it is the one fact of Jesus' biography that is mentioned in the Creed. Thus the birth of Jesus became the strongest scripture-based creed against Docetism. While questioning his human body and soul affected the notion of his true suffering and death, the notion of his humanity could always be supported with his having been born. Hannah Arendt's rooting the capacity of humans to act humanely in having been born also resonates with the early Church renunciation of Adoptionism, the declared heresy that Jesus was adopted as God's son at some time after his birth. The initiating moment of Jesus' messiahship and sonship was, on the contrary, his birth. He was messiah in every aspect and "the Son" from the moment he was born. He did not grow or develop into this status. Similarly, according to Arendt, by their

---

[49] Elizabeth A. Johnson, *Truly Our Sister: A Theology of Mary in the Communion of the Saints* (London: Bloomsbury, 2003), 274. Elizabeth Johnson is a feminist Catholic theologian, a professor of theology at the Jesuit Fordham University in New York, and a member of the Sisters of St. Joseph of Brentwood.

very birth people are fully equipped to act as human – and humane – beings.

When formulating the creeds, the church fathers expressed little interest in the details of Jesus' human life. In church tradition, his death gained overwhelming attention. In this light, the fact that the first ecumenical council (Nicaea 325) preserved the memory of his birth and turned it into dogma is truly remarkable. The last of the major Christological formulations (Chalcedon 451) reinforced the significance of his birth and explicated its twofold contexts according to the two proclaimed natures.

COVENANT CONTINUED: CIRCUMCISION

Jesus was circumcised (Luke 2:21: "And when eight days were accomplished for the circumcising of the child, his name was called Jesus"). If there is anything unambiguously historical about his biography in the Gospel, it is this fact. In contemporary Historical Jesus research, his circumcision is just one more fact illustrating his rootedness in Second Temple Judaism. But long before historical research emphasized context,[50] his circumcision was remembered in the Christian church as bearing theological value. This is a remarkable phenomenon. There is no doctrine of circumcision in any church, and no ecumenical dogma mentions the fact. Still, in church tradition it is not referred to as just another detail, but an occurrence worth remembering. The most fundamental testimony of this acknowledgment is found in church calendars. Liturgically, the first of January is marked as the day of Jesus' circumcision in all major traditional churches. The feast marks a rather late liturgical development, going back to the Council of Tours (567); but it was only later, in the ninth century that the memory of circumcision was added to the Roman feast of the octave of Jesus' birth. Without any obligation rooted in dogma or doctrine, this late remembering of Jesus' circumcision is a remarkable phenomenon. While in the late twentieth century, the Catholic Church re-dedicated the day to Mary, and Anglicans and Lutherans added the memory of the "name of Jesus" to the first of January, it is historically appropriate to speak of what I would call an "all Christian" memory. Jesus' circumcision is a common motif in Art

---

[50] As especially in the third quest of the Historical Jesus research that peaked at the end of the twentieth century.

History and may actually be the most visual account of Jesus being "under the law."

In his recent monograph on Jesus' circumcision, Andrew Jacobs argues that "the divine circumcision is that anomalous oddity that unfolds the deeper contradictions of Christian orthodoxy, revealing, within a discourse of theological purity, traces of 'otherness' that can never be fully expelled."[51] Jacobs derives from this a dialectic theory of incorporated "otherness." But his multifaceted account of Jesus' circumcision as it is found in a wide range of theological literary genres – polemic writings, bible commentaries, homilies etc. – can also be interpreted differently. The otherness of Christ's circumcision has not been completely incorporated into doctrine. Nor has it been assimilated. Jacobs comes to the conclusion that what "... varied treatments of Jesus' circumcision ... have in common is their desire to simultaneously reject and reincorporate the essence of 'the other'."[52] It is, of course, difficult to reconstruct the motivations of historical institutions. But even if one were to attribute "desire" to an institution like the Catholic Church, Jacobs's binary assessment of "rejection" and "reincorporation" cannot comprehend the astonishing prodigy of this Christian memory. The example of the Christian calendar involves neither rejection nor reincorporation, neither assimilation nor trivialization! Marking the day of Jesus' circumcision in a non-circumcising Church is actually a very complex phenomenon. A binary hermeneutics of interreligious relations that offers only hostility or integration as approaches to signs of otherness does not precisely describe the phenomenon.

My own analysis of the Churches' record of circumcision builds on treating the phenomenon as a memory, and more specifically as a "latent memory." This categorization takes into account the complexity of remembering that is often not in line with intention. Memory accounts for counter-memories and it is in the nature of memory to be something that is not completely controllable. We can think about this in relation to three historical facts in early and contemporary Christian history: (1) the circumcision of Jesus is not mentioned in early creeds; (2) the marking of Jesus' circumcision in Christian calendars occurs between the sixth and ninth century; and (3) the revision or renaming of the feast occurs only in the late twentieth century. The last of the three facts is remarkable in

---

[51] Andrew S. Jacobs, *Christ Circumcised: A Study in Early Christian History and Difference* (Philadelphia: University of Pennsylvania Press, 2012), 75.
[52] Ibid., 182.

itself. At a time when "Jesus the Jew" is becoming a mainstream topic in academic as well as popular Christianity, the most physical sign of his Jewishness has been removed from the Church calendar.

In his cultural account of circumcision, Boyarin clearly presupposes an alienated attitude to circumcision within Christianity. This account can be easily illustrated through recent public debates on circumcision in Western countries.[53] They show that the Christian memory of Jesus' circumcision is significantly weaker than the growing awareness of his Jewishness. In contemporary political debates – as in Canada or in North-European countries and especially in Germany – circumcision is typically described as an "archaic" rite, with those practicing it presented as forced to do so by some "ancient" law or custom. This is certainly a misrepresentation. Circumcision is also practiced by a majority of Jews affiliated with Reform Judaism who officially don't commit to Halakhah. In Israel, it is a common practice among secular, including outspokenly secular, Jews. The Israeli health-system is built on modern Western standards, and Israeli medical experts are well equipped to assess health risks and benefits of circumcision. Thus the contemporary Western tendency to discredit circumcision as an archaic rite today serves a certain cultural supersessionism that portrays Judaism as outdated. In interreligious perspective, the Western intent to prohibit circumcision as a medical impediment displays a general unfamiliarity with Halakhah that facilitates hostility. It is a view of Jewish Law that resembles anti-Jewish readings of Jesus as preserving spiritual life in contrast to the "carnal" and "materialistic" laws of Torah. But, as we learned, Halakhah has always held life holy – at the end of the Second Temple period as well as in Talmudic times and until the present. Health is not the main objective of Jewish Law, e.g. kashrut is not built on the sole rationale of proper nutrition. But if the practice of a certain historical commandment proved seriously unhealthy, let alone life-threatening, Halakhah tends to be adapted and interpreted so as to protect life. In our case, there is an ongoing debate about the preventive function of male circumcision regarding certain diseases. If the opposite were the case, if for example circumcision had increased the risk of HIV infection, Jewish religious lawmakers would likely have found

---

[53] Alfred Bodenheimer wrote his essay about circumcision in the context of the 2012 debate in Germany. See Alfred Bodenheimer, *Haut ab! Die Juden in der Beschneidungsdebatte* (Göttingen: Wallstein Verlag, 2012).

ways to avoid that risk. Halakhah upholds ample possibilities of interpretation, and problems can always be solved in order to save lives.[54]

Interestingly, intellectual and cultural discourse developed at great
distance from Western medical concerns and legal applications. Scholars
and philosophers like Derrida and Boyarin have referred to the phenomenon of circumcision as an occasion to discuss bodily aspects of difference.[55] In contrast, most of the newer non-supersessionist Christian
theologies have not included circumcision as a major topic of discussion.
This is remarkable insofar as the language of covenant has been truly
constitutive for post-supersessionist Christologies.[56]

Theologies of the covenant were until the twentieth century mainly
present in traditions connected with the Reform church theologies, going
back to Calvin. At the beginning of the twentieth century, Karl Barth
re-discovered "covenant" as a major theological category, later to be
picked up by theologians in Jewish–Christian dialogue. Paul van Buren
had written his dissertation about Calvin under the supervision of Karl
Barth. This was decades before he turned to a reformulation of Christian
theology in the context of renewed Jewish–Christian relations. But the
basic framework of his Christology *Christ in Context* shows the impact of
this Calvinist theological tradition. Van Buren further develops the adjective "covenantal" as a criterion for Christological thinking. A covenantal
Christology emphasizes the dynamics in the God–Human relationship.
Thus van Buren offers a covenantal interpretation of Easter and the
resurrection as God's answer to Jesus' tragic death.[57]

---

[54] Jewish feminists and scholars of Halakhah might consider in this light the many problems
still not resolved, most prominently the problem of women confronted with the refusal of
their ex-spouses to grant them the document required for divorce. My admittedly positive
account of the dynamics of Halakhah is not to be mistaken for idealization. I am aware of
deficits in halakhic practice and, like the late Yeshayahu Leibowitz, look forward to a
future with women authoring Halakhah. An excellent introduction to the philosophy of
halakhah has been written by Tamar Ross, *Expanding the Palace of Torah: Orthodoxy
and Feminism* (Waltham, MA: Brandeis University Press, 2004).

[55] Boyarin, *A Radical Jew: Paul and the Politics of Identity*, especially 106–135. Among the
many interpreters of Derrida, I find Elisabeth Weber most helpful. In her interview,
Derrida speaks of circumcision as a sign of humanity. See Elisabeth Weber, *Jüdisches
Denken in Frankreich* (Frankfurt: Suhrkamp, 1994), 65.

[56] Philip A. Cunningham and Didier Pollefeyt, "The Triune One, the Incarnate Logos, and
Israel's Covenantal Life." In Philip A. Cunningham, Joseph Sievers, Mary C. Boys, Hans
Hermann Henrix, and Jesper Svartvik, eds., *Christ Jesus and the Jewish People Today:
New Explorations of Theological Interrelationships* (Grand Rapids, MI and Cambridge:
William B. Eerdmans Publishing Company, 2011), 183–201.

[57] Van Buren, *Christ in Context*, 107–147.

Despite the tradition of substitution theology implied by such terms as the old and the new covenant, church declarations eventually expressed their acknowledgment of Judaism in a language of covenant. This is a fascinating development: covenant, the core category originally exploited to produce a grammar of "old and new," one that Christians sought to read back into the prophecies of Jeremiah (31:31), has today come to comprise the heart of a language of Christian respect for Judaism. Contemporary Christian statements about the relationship between God and the Jews usually describe the covenant of Israel as unrevoked. This is not a new theological insight but the adducing of an old one. Paul explicitly declared the faithfulness of Israel's God when contemplating the fact of a majority of Jews not following Jesus. Post-Shoah theologians obviously found the category of covenant helpful to describing the ongoing vitality of the Jewish people. Nevertheless, confessing the theological validity of Israel's covenant was never developed in all its implications. The recent Christian confesson of the unrevoked covenant makes a strong gesture toward interreligious thought, to be sure. But looking at Irving Greenberg's post-Shoah theology proves helpful in illustrating the disconnect at work here.[58] When Greenberg describes the current phase of the Israel covenant as under Israel's rather than God's lead, he focuses on the human aspect of the covenantal relationship. The recent Christian reinforcement of God's faithfulness was well intended, but nevertheless reflected a certain disregard for actual Jews by ignoring many Jews' ambivalent view of God's reliability in a post-Shoah perspective. Christian post-supersessionist covenant theologians have not at all been mistaken in reaffirming the ongoing covenant of Israel. But they have focused solely on God while neglecting the human side of the covenant. This is how they missed the ambivalences and disappointments expressed in some Jewish post-Shoah theologies such as Greenberg's, as well as the human bodily aspect of Israel's covenant that is traditionally connected to circumcision.

In fact, the connection between covenant and circumcision has been pointed out by very few Christian theologians – despite the fact that the knowledge of key Hebrew words is included in their basic theological training. In Hebrew, the same word *brit* means both covenant *and* circumcision. While the exact term for circumcision is *brit mila*, the

---

[58] Irving Greenberg, in Steven T. Katz, Shlomo Biderman, and Gershon Greenberg, eds., *Wrestling with God: Jewish Theological Responses during and after the Holocaust* (Oxford: Oxford University Press, 2007), 497–555.

Jewish rite of passage is commonly referred to as *brit* in Jewry worldwide. Among Christian theologians, the topic of circumcision has usually appeared within exegetical discussion, with the main question being Paul's approach. Traditionally, that was answered negatively, quoting his polemics against the continued practice of circumcision by non-Jewish members joining the Jesus movement. But Paul's theological stand is not best assessed with a list of his negative versus his positive views on circumcision.

Clearly, Paul rejects the practice of circumcision for non-Jews, which is not an unusual Jewish perspective. If Paul's view were to be understood within Jewish tradition, it would clearly uphold the value of circumcision rather than diminish it. Theologically, in Paul's writings circumcision belongs to the set of revelations declared as continuously valid as listed in Romans 9,1-4: "... to them belong God's adoption, and the glory, and the covenants, the giving of the law, the worship and the promises." Paul reinforces the fact that God's gifts are irrevocable (Romans 11,29) and circumcision is a sign of the trusted word (Romans 3,2). Last but not least, Paul refers to his own circumcision with pride (Philippians 3,5). In the letter to the Romans, circumcision is first of all discussed as the sign of the emerging religious "other" – even though Paul himself belongs to the group of the circumcised. That makes his deliberations shared in this epistle particularly interesting. Affirming circumcision here does not mean approving of a sign connecting the followers of Jesus. Rather, the validity of circumcision is here discussed as the remaining signature of Jews not joining the Jesus movement.

Shall Christians today then revive the January 1 Feast of Circumcision, as Philipp Cunningham suggests?[59] I certainly agree with the importance of this memory as a very strong signifier of Jesus' Jewishness. It might not need to be celebrated, but its remembrance may prove helpful for orientation in contemporary multicultural discourse. Christians have no reason to be indifferent toward circumcision. If in the Western sense of superiority circumcision is "westplained" as injury enforced by an "archaic" law, Christians are equipped as Christians to witness differently. From contemporary research on Jesus they can retrieve knowledge about the grammar and logic of Halakhah. As the main churches have affirmed the

---

[59] Philipp Cunningham, "Reviving the Catholic Observance of the Feast of the Circumcision of Jesus" In Celia Deutsch, Eugene J. Fisher, and A. James Rudin, eds., *Toward the Future: Essays on Catholic-Jewish Relations in Memory of Rabbi Leon Kleinicki* (Mahwah, NJ: Paulist Press, 2013), 129–146.

covenant of the Jewish people as ongoing and alive, they are informed to confirm as well one of the most profound signs of this covenant.[60] The combination of these three insights, that Jesus was under the law, that this law's interpretive continuation protects bodily integrity, and that Israel's covenant remains unrevoked, leads to a very fine "Christian circumfession" that need not include any particular idealization of what Jewish mothers (and, increasingly, fathers) experience as a rather uneasy moment of early parenthood! The future of the Jewish people, in biblical language, the future of the covenant, is properly and appropriately confessed in a Christian witness of Jewish circumcision.

LIKE US – BUT DIFFERENT: TWO-NATURES CHRISTOLOGY

It was typical for Christologies that appeared in the context of early Jewish–Christian dialogue to avoid references to the so-called Two-Natures Christology. Based on the Council of Chalcedon (454 CE), these Christologies sought to give equal attention and emphasis to both the divine and the human nature of Jesus Christ. During the 1970s, Christian theologians expressed a strong preference for Christologies that would either re-interpret the divinity of Christ or silence it altogether. This was connected to an intuitive urge to close the gap between Judaism and Christianity and linked to the suspicion that Christologies emphasizing divinity had been responsible for the Christian claim of religious superiority. Indeed, until quite recently the rediscovery of Jesus' Jewishness was discussed mainly with regard to the human nature of Jesus Christ. It is only in the last decade that an explicit effort has begun to describe the relevance of his Jewishness with regard to both humanity and divinity.[61]

Is the emphasis on Jesus' Jewishness compatible with Two-Natures Christologies? Looking at the tensions raised by this focus can offer new insights and raise fresh questions. How does the notion of Jewishness regarding both Jesus' human and divine nature connect Christology back

---

[60] See my article in the context of the debate in Germany: Barbara U. Meyer, "Was haben Christen heute mit der Beschneidung zu tun?" *Begegnungen: Zeitschrift für Kirche und Judentum* 1 (2013): 14–21.

[61] Barbara U. Meyer, "The Dogmatic Significance of Christ Being Jewish," in Philip A. Cunningham, Joseph Sievers, Mary C. Boys, Hans Hermann Henrix, and Jesper Svartvik, eds., *Christ Jesus and the Jewish People Today: New Explorations of Theological Interrelationships*, 144–156.

to theology, the doctrine of God? An inquiry into Christological questions leading to the language of two "natures" in the early church will also help us to understand the original questions that this doctrine was developed to answer. The questions leading to the formula of two natures in the early church have changed but in no way has the doctrine functioned as a magic formula to solve underlying problems, such as the question of suffering with regard to divinity and humanity.

In German theological literature on the topic, the phrase "the true human is truly a Jew" ("Der wahre Mensch ist wahrer Jude") became popular in the eighties. Generally, the few theologians who focused on the Jewishness of Jesus – Marquardt, John Pawlikowski, Roy Eckardt, van Buren – did not build their Christologies on the Two-Natures doctrine, as had Karl Barth and Paul Tillich most prominently. Recently, the Lutheran theologian Kayko Driedger Hesslein has tried to bring these two concerns together. Her monograph *Dual Citizenship: Two-Natures Christologies and the Jewish Jesus* appeared in 2015.[62] Driedger Hesslein seeks to connect the notion of Jewishness to both "Jesus' historical particularity and his divine universality."[63] Her core interest is to mediate between contemporary contextual Christologies and the Jewish identity of Jesus that she presents in distinctly non-supersessionist language. As she notes, "… his identifier as Jewish in this book serves as a reminder of his continuity and continued relationships within the historical and contemporary communities of the people Israel."[64]

Much to her credit, Driedger Hesslein tries to balance contemporary contextual theologies with an emphasis on Jesus' Jewishness that has often been in tension with theologies of liberation. In her view, "a new Christology … must establish a universal characteristic of humankind – a prerequisite for citizenship – that Jesus shares with all humans, while respecting the multiply-constituted singularity of each human individual."[65] Jesus' Jewishness is what describes his specific particularity, while particularity as such is presented as a universal human feature. Thus, although Driedger Hesslein explicitly opts for the preservation of difference against any kind of assimilation, she eventually does assimilate Jesus' Jewishness to the universal attribute of contextuality. For Driedger Hesslein, Jesus' specific identity, his Jewishness, is assimilating to particularity as a general human feature. His being both human and divine is offered as identification for

---

[62] Kayko Driedger Hesslein, *Dual Citizenship: Two-Natures Christologies and the Jewish Jesus* (Bloomsbury: T&T Clark, 2015).
[63] Hesslein, *Dual Citizenship*, 11.   [64] Ibid., 17.   [65] Ibid., 67.

believers who find themselves within a set of identities that are commonly viewed as in tension with each other. Driedger Hesslein's approach that "one can be this and another" and belong simultaneously to different groups seeks a validation of complex identities. But theologically, the most challenging aspect of Jesus' Jewishness is that this central aspect of his identity is not shared by his followers today. Most of Christian interpretational history has tried to undermine his Jewishness as something exterior or overcome, at least partly. In contrast, Driedger Hesslein emphasizes this particular belonging as compatible with universality.

She applies contemporary language of multicultural theory to describe Jesus' belonging to the Jewish people as a general human feature of rootedness and relatedness: "Jesus is constituted by his relationships with his Jewish disciples, his Jewish mother, his Jewish teachers, and also by his encounters with the Roman soldiers, the Samaritan woman, the taxpayers, and others."[66] With this highly unusual formulation, she actually suggests a "multicultural" rather than a predominantly Jewish context of the historical Jesus. This goes together with her criticism of what she calls "Jesus-the-Jew-Christologies": "In Jesus-the-Jew Christologies," claims Driedger Hesslein, "Jesus is entirely determined by the traditions (van Buren and Soulen would say covenants) of his faith. Jesus exhibits no personal agency, no divine agency, and is simply a body at the command of a religious tradition. Jesus, in this view, is totalized by his status as a Jew."[67] True, as Driedger Hesslein notes, van Buren would say "covenant" and not "Jewish religion." But he had also contemplated extensively the meaning of covenant, which is for him not simply a "religion." Nor for van Buren is being Jewish a "status." Driedger Hesslein's harsh criticism points to the lack of discussion that she invests in the topic of Jewishness, halakhic being, and covenantal existence. Her theory lacks an in-depth discussion of possible contents and questions of Jewish identity. I agree with her that Christologies committed to Jesus' Jewishness often prioritize Jewish majority over minority opinion. But in the case of van Buren, "context" is not at all presented in a one-dimensional manner, but rather explored as a textual, spiritual, halakhic, and historical framework. Although Driedger Hesslein's criticism does not do justice to the works of the aforementioned authors, her initial insight remains important. The designation "Jewish" should not be seen as comprising some clear and self-evident definition. Any Jewish person is

[66] Ibid., 75.   [67] Ibid., 56.

"more" than just Jewish. As Driedger Hesslein suggests, Jewish belonging does not determine interactions and communications with other Jews only. At the same time, other aspects of person and personality are present within Jewish relationships. Few New Testament texts shed light on the emotions of Jesus, such as anger, loneliness, or other emotional features that we do not learn about because the New Testament authors apparently were not interested in reporting about them. Do the few texts that do depict emotions present them as universal human expressions of anger and solitude? Jesus' anger in the Temple is due to an intra-Jewish dispute and in his loneliness he is quoted as speaking the language of the Psalms. An in-depth discussion of Jewishness, its manifold implications and expressions, could have helped here – not in order to find a closing answer but rather to broaden the horizon of the discussion. "Jewish identity" is vague in itself and requires deeper analysis to account for its range and complexity, for all Jews in Jesus' time as well as for Jesus himself.

Driedger Hesslein's theoretical frame of reference is multicultural theory. It is a theoretical framework too small for the phenomenon of Jewish identity with its national, religious, textual, and cultural dimension.[68] Driedger Hesslein's criticism of being Jewish as a "status" and the conception of Judaism as an all-commanding religion are likely driven by her alternative view of Judaism's compatibility with any other national or religious identity. This question of compatibility is indeed worth discussing. When deliberating on the impact of Jesus' Judaism, it is necessary to reflect on Jewishness and Judaism as categories. As we have seen, Judaism is best described in historical terms. Arguing against the contemporary post-modern Jewish self-description of Jewishness as a mere construct, I have laid out a perspective of the continuity of textual reference (see Chapter 2). This understanding is not essentialist but capable of taking a Jewish self-understanding of continuity seriously. A complex view of Jewishness and Judaism that is developed in conversation with both traditional and contemporary Jewish self-reflection is necessary to discuss the impact of Jewishness on a complicated Christian discussion as Two-Natures Christology. Both his human and his divine nature connect with the textual and spiritual canon of Israel. This explains how Jewishness is not just one of many features, but the overall frame of reference. Within that context, Jewishness is not an isolating component, neither textually

---

[68] As Boyarin noted: "Jewishness disrupts the very categories of identity." See his *A Radical Jew*, 244.

nor spiritually. The texts of Israel never presented Israel alone in the world or the God of Israel as limited geographically. Jewish identity is not an isolated matter, and according to the text of Genesis, the God of Israel is the God of creation. Both natures point to the manifold expressions of Judaism, and both also transcend Jewishness.

Driedger Hesslein finds Two-Natures Christology helpful to mediating between contemporary contextual Christologies and non-supersessionist Christologies emphasizing the Jewishness of Jesus. The relationship between these two Christological directions is important since they have increasingly grown apart since the last third of the twentieth century. In a way, they resemble a growing alienation between what is perceived and presented as "West" and "East" or "First" and "Third" World theologies. The tension that is relevant here is of a special kind, however. It is not the tension between the Western tradition with its sense of superiority versus Third World Christianity developing its own cultural orientation, as one might describe traditional Western churches meeting liberation theologies in the sixties and seventies. Rather, the dispute regarding the centrality of Jesus' Jewishness divides theologians highly critical of the overall supersessionist tradition on the one side, and on the other, Western as well as non-Western theologians who mistake the supersessionist version of Christianity for an original truth.

Remarkably, Driedger Hesslein comes to the conclusion that all Christologies – even those committed to other and further contexts of belonging and liberation – still need to consider Jesus, the Jew.[69] Within her theoretical framework of multicultural theory, Driedger Hesslein finds the Christian tradition of non-exclusive thought constructive and helpful to expressing integrity in situations of multiple belonging. But her translation of Two-Natures Christology to multicultural language bears the touch of a "Two-Natures idealism." We need to remember that this doctrine was formulated as an attempt to solve obvious problems, and that its peak was an entirely negative formulation. According to the council of Chalcedon, the divine and the human natures of the one person Jesus Christ are not dissolved and not distinguished, not mixed and not held apart. Maybe this negative conceit that the truth about Jesus Christ's divinity and humanity cannot be stated positively remains the most adequate corrective to Christological theory-building.

---

[69] Driedger Hesslein, *Dual Citizenship*, 186.

This corresponds to Dietrich Ritschl's Christological ideas in his early work *Memory and Hope*: "Jesus Christ is not the answer, however paradoxical, to our Christological questions, but he is the calling into question of our questions, presuppositions and answers."[70] Driedger Hesslein's attempt to reconnect and rethink Jesus' historical Jewishness with the dogmatic tradition of Two-Natures Christology is important. But it must be remembered that the Two-Natures Christology was originally not a harmonizing doctrine. It is, in fact, far from the comforting idea that "you can be this *and* the other." The idea of one person's two natures is a doctrinal answer to a problem regarding conceptions of the personhood of Jesus Christ. It was forged in a particular historical context and does not readily lend itself to reinterpretation as a theory of or analogue to multiculturalism. Two-Natures Christology is not a model either for complex identities or personality empowerment. The challenge of Jewish particularity here is, rather, a different one: The Jewishness of Jesus is not one particularity equivalent to and thus potentially exchangeable with some other particularity. Instead, framed in Christian language, Jesus Christ connects all other particularities to this one specific particularity. Contemporary contextual Christologies, whether they emphasize ethnic belonging, gender, or another feature constitutive for identity, must not forego Judaism as the context of Jesus. Some particularities are more compatible with this specific context than others.

It is important to resist nonsensical talk about a "Jewish God." After refuting Marcion, the God Christians pray to is reaffirmed as the God of Israel. Christ's divine nature corresponds to – is in communication, in communion with – the God of Israel, not a universal deity. This God, according to the first chapters of the Bible, also created the world. Two-Natures Christology was developed to ensure Jesus' humanity against an overriding divinization. And, like almost every early church dogmatic discourse, the objective was to avoid idolatry. Later doctrines were developed to hold the natures together. At the same time, they display the intellectual difficulties inherent in the concept.

This is obviously the case with the teaching of the "exchange of properties" known typically under the Latin designation "*communicatio idiomatum*." This teaching provides a framework for the discussion of an exchange of both natures' respective characteristics. As is sometimes the case with further developments of doctrine, the explanatory character is almost drowned out by subsequent debates and disagreements. Basically,

[70] Dietrich Ritschl, *Memory and Hope*, 204.

the teaching of *communicatio idiomatum* underlines the integrity of Jesus Christ's person, as the idiomata, the properties, belong to the whole person and not merely to just one of the two natures. The various interactions between the two natures were named according to perspective and direction. That the *idiomata* of the divine are present in the human was called *genus majestaticum* (a formulation rejected by the Reformed Church). The other direction, that the *idiomata* of human nature were also the *idiomata* of divine nature, was called "*tapeinotikon*," and was usually denied by the church. Indeed, it is remarkable that this idea was conceptualized at all, since it significantly uplifted the human! The *tapeinotikon* would actually make it easier to think of the divine nature as Jewish. On the whole, the controversial teachings about the *idiomata* further show the difficulties of thinking of personhood in terms of both humanity and divinity. For this reason, the Christological concept of the *communicatio idiomatum* is often seen as a not particularly helpful extension of doctrine. I would suggest a new perspective here. Rather than limiting the discussion to decisive statements about the *majestaticum* or the *tapeinotikon*, we may welcome the mental freedom necessary to think of the divine impacting the human and the human configuring the divine, as expressed in thinking in terms of the exchange of properties. The discussion helps to keep in mind the original complexity of talking about two natures in one person. Instead of understanding the *idiomata* as "properties," I suggest translating them as "expressions." Divinity may be well expressed in human language, while the human may address the divine.

Two-Natures Christology was historically meant to reinforce and ensure Jesus' humanity. His humanity refers back to geography, culture, and the history of his life, today called "context." The Jewishness of his context shines through New Testament texts and is manifest in latent memories of the Church, as we have seen. But it is also this most human Jewishness that maintains the reference to the God of Jesus, the God of the Bible. In this sense, the historical Jewishness of Jesus, primarily informing Christological discourse, is highly relevant for the core of theology, the question of God par excellence. "Truly divine" means union with the God of the Jews. This is the Christological reason for Jesus' Jewishness anchoring Christianity in the God of Israel – rather than in some universal transcendent principle. Thus a Christology pointing out the Jewishness of Jesus is constitutive for theology in the narrow sense of the word, ensuring the continued identity of God speaking through both parts of the Christian canon.

5

After and Against Suffering

It is precisely the memory of Jesus' Jewishness that could lead – and for several key thinkers has led – to a critical approach to suffering in Christian theology. Remembering Jesus as a Jew who suffered enables today's Christians to understand his suffering primarily as the suffering of an Other. It is exactly the suffering of the Other that holds a central place in the philosophies of Emmanuel Levinas and Adi Ophir, two Jewish thinkers who help to illuminate the place of suffering in our analysis of the Jewish Jesus. It is the suffering of the Other that calls for a response and is situated in the heart of their moral theory. And it is the suffering of the Other that is not for us to interpret, as both philosophers state. The memory of Jesus the Jew's suffering can help Christian ethical discourse come to terms with philosophical insights that connect critical understandings of suffering and moral theory.

AGAINST "PATHODICY": AFTER LEVINAS

Thinking about suffering has never been the same since the publication of Levinas' 1982 essay "Useless Suffering."[1] The title of his essay might be understood to imply that there could be such a thing as "useful" suffering. But this is not what Levinas is suggesting. On the contrary, he emphasizes that there is a kind of suffering that needs to be regarded as not bearing

---

[1] The French original appeared in 1982. Quotes here follow the English translation: Emmanuel Levinas, "Useless Suffering," in Robert Bernasconi and David Wood, eds., *The Provocation of Levinas: Rethinking the Other* (London and New York: Routledge, 1988), 156–167.

any meaning at all. This has certainly become clear after the Shoah. Levinas knows of the rich and varied Jewish tradition of interpreting the suffering of the Jewish people. In his view, the Shoah cuts through this tradition of interpretation. "The disproportion between suffering and every theodicy was shown at Auschwitz with a glaring, obvious clarity," concludes Levinas.[2] Here the "end of theodicy" is proclaimed not with a theological statement but with an attempt to express the inconceivable dimensions of suffering in the Shoah and other atrocities of the twentieth century. "Perhaps the most revolutionary fact of our twentieth-century consciousness – but it is also an event in Sacred History – is that of the destruction of all balance between the explicit and the implicit theodicy of Western thought and the forms which suffering and its evil take in the very unfolding of this century."[3]

Levinas here closely connects the themes of theodicy and suffering. Since the initial publication of this essay in 1982, both topics have been taken on in different, even separate, discourses. Jewish post-Shoah thinkers have developed an impressive intellectual creativity in seeking to avoid any defense of God. Zachary Braiterman calls this approach "anti-theodicy" and presents it as the central feature of Jewish post-Shoah thought.[4] On the other hand, Levinas' notion of superfluous suffering has also exerted a strong impact on the Israeli philosopher Adi Ophir, who built his moral theory on the distinctions between unavoidable and preventable suffering. Ophir's focus is entirely on reducible and preventable suffering. The notion of preventability entails the moral commandment to try to prevent and limit other people's suffering. While Levinas presents his reflections on suffering as part of the discussion of theodicy, he actually shifts the conversation to moral theory, that is, theory concerned with human interrelationships. "It is in the inter-human perspective of *my* responsibility for the other person without concern for reciprocity, in my call to help him gratuitously, in the asymmetry of the relation of *one* to the *other*, that we have tried to analyze the phenomenon of useless suffering."[5] One might find meaning in one's own suffering – Levinas does not negate the possibility of this kind of self-reflection. But it is only "meaningful in me, useless in the Other."[6]

---

[2] Levinas, "Useless Suffering," 162.   [3] Ibid., 161.
[4] Zachary Braiterman, *(God) after Auschwitz: Tradition and Change in Post-Holocaust Jewish Thought* (Princeton, NJ: Princeton University Press, 1999), 31.
[5] Levinas, "Useless Suffering," 165.   [6] Ibid., 164.

Attributing meaninglessness to human suffering here acquires a moral dimension. Jewish post-Shoah theologians have expressed their empathy and solidarity with the victims of the Shoah via a profound reproach to theodicy, the term that Levinas also refers to here. After the Shoah, any attempt to defend or justify God must come to an end. But Levinas' path-breaking essay is less about God and more about humanity. His unique contribution to thinking about suffering after the Shoah would be more precisely described as a fundamental, comprehensive critique of the justification of human suffering. I would call this the "end of pathodicy," that is, a refusal to justify human suffering. Levinas connects this view to the overwhelming suffering of the Shoah, but interestingly he formulates his moral conclusion philosophically and not as something embedded in any particular religious tradition. Thus, perhaps the most notable sentence of this essay does not describe morality but immorality: "... the justification of the neighbor's suffering is certainly the source of all immorality."[7]

Levinas' interconnection of suffering and theodicy transforms the end of theodicy, which some twenty years later will be proclaimed as the heart of Jewish post-Shoah thought, into much more than a theological topic. Now, it is not simply that defending God is inadequate, but that defending suffering as something meaningful is problematic. Interpreting the Other's suffering has now come under moral scrutiny. This philosophical post-Shoah approach transcends religion. The changing attitude to suffering, facilitated by the irreconcilable human suffering of the Shoah, applies to humankind as a whole.

For Christians, the age that I here call "after pathodicy" has only partly begun. Strikingly, though seldom noticed, the notion of suffering does not belong to the key topics that have been revised in conversation with Jews. Even among the numerous Christian thinkers who have attempted to conceptualize Jewish–Christian relations anew, the topic of suffering is not perceived as something in urgent need of rethinking. There are multiple reasons for this perception. The topic is not viewed as falling across a typical Jewish–Christian divide. The biblical account of suffering, shared by Jews and Christians, includes a variety of basic views commonly held by both. The book of Job invites a broad spectrum of interpretations and questions recognized by both interpreting communities as difficult if not impossible to answer. Both Jews and Christians know of suffering, ask about the suffering of the innocent, and pray for an

---

[7] Ibid., 163.

end of suffering. The theme is often perceived by Christians as pertaining to all humanity rather than as fundamentally structuring Christian–Jewish discourse.

Another reason why the topic of suffering has attracted at best secondary attention as a topic requiring Christian reformulation may be that it is not generally regarded as an obstacle to Christian pluralism or tolerance. The far-reaching moral implications entailed by concepts of suffering have not appeared obvious to Christian theologians, and only a small number of thinkers have developed alternatives to the traditional embrace of Jesus' as well as Christian suffering. Nevertheless, the Christian thinkers who *have* managed to break through thick traditions and habits of theology eventually showed that embracing suffering is not a theological necessity of Christianity and certainly not dogma. Coming from different denominations and theological backgrounds, these path-breaking Christian thinkers share a common feature: They are deeply touched and shaken by the Shoah and have allowed this sense of upheaval to disturb their inherited theological thought traditions.

Still, even among the numerous Christian theologians engaged in rethinking Christianity in relation to Judaism, only a few have dared to initiate a reevaluation of suffering. Outstanding in their rigorous critiques of their own traditions we find especially the German Catholic Johann Baptist Metz, the German-born American Lutheran Dorothee Soelle, the American Anglican Paul van Buren, and the American Methodist Alice Eckardt. It is all the more impressive that these few Christian thinkers from quite different backgrounds and denominations have expressed comparable concerns about Christianity's traditional approaches to suffering. Still, the critiques so far have been only partial or nascent. There is still no full-fledged Christian post-Shoah theory of suffering. In fact, the few writings in this pioneering field share a certain fragmentary style, one that underscores stylistically what is true regarding the content, that is, uncertainty.

THE CROSS AND JEWISH SUFFERING

Since the middle of the twentieth century, Christian thinkers have critically confronted theological traditions that explicitly embrace human suffering. For instance, the spiritualization and idealization of poverty was effectively discredited by classical Latin American liberation theologians.[8] The theologian Dorothee Soelle subsequently drew attention to the connection between the understanding of Jesus' suffering and attitudes to general human suffering.[9] Her criticism of the cruel portrayal of the "Father" killing the "Son" in some German Protestant theologies was widely adopted by feminist Christian interpretations of "the cross." Soelle confronted the Christologies that she diagnosed as "sadist" with spiritual depictions of the cross that she found among disadvantaged and poor Christian communities. Far from idealizing agony and misery, she identifies spiritual traditions that view suffering as at times unavoidable but rejects exploiting political and social circumstances to rationalize oppression. Building on those mainly Latin American traditions, Soelle developed her own spiritual approach of resistance to oppression that neither avoids nor praises suffering. By the end of the twentieth century, Christian theologians had generally come to refrain from idealizations of human suffering, let alone its divinization. Still, most Christologies have retained a notion of the proximity and relatedness to divinity that is particularly manifest in suffering. While no longer praising suffering itself, a certain embrace of it remains common, one that typically sees God's presence in afflictions and atrocities and assumes God's being "on the side" of those who suffer.[10] In such cases suffering is not exalted, but God is viewed as present where suffering is manifest.

Thinking of suffering as bearing a redemptive quality is deeply rooted in Christological tradition. But typically overlooked is the fact that the early Christian creeds themselves do not include interpretations of Jesus' suffering. The Nicene Creed (325) notes almost laconically that "he suffered"; but that the objective of this suffering was "for our sins" is a rationale that was only added later. (In the creeds, "for us" is related to the crucifixion). Especially for the Greek Fathers, noting that Jesus had suffered was important mainly as an anti-Docetic statement, manifesting his true humanity – which is no less dogma than his divinity, and apparently by the fourth century the more contested aspect of his being. Suffering is thus essential to Jesus' humanity. In this early dogmatic

---

[8] Gustavo Guitierrez, *A Theology of Liberation: History, Politics, and Salvation* (Maryknoll, NY: Orbis Books, 1973).

[9] Dorothee Soelle, *Suffering* (Philadelphia: Fortress Press, 1975).

[10] Although a marginal voice among Jewish post-Shoah thinkers, the notion of transcendence as present in Auschwitz has also been voiced, for instance, in Melissa Raphael, *The Female Face of God in Auschwitz: A Jewish Feminist Theology of the Holocaust* (London and New York: Routledge, 2003).

discourse, then, the capacity to suffer marks the core characteristic of the human being.

The Christian discourse on suffering has traditionally been intertwined with Christology. Thus, it is no coincidence that post-Shoah Christologies trace contemporary approaches to suffering back to formulations about Jesus and the symbol of the cross. But have all concepts of redemptive suffering, which is generally considered a core concept of Christian thought, become problematic after the Shoah? Paul van Buren tried to express the benefit of the Christ event in language that barred salvific suffering. Van Buren emphasizes that neither the Council of Nicaea (325) nor Chalcedon (451) offer theological interpretations of the crucifixion that employ the words "for our sake."[11] Also typically overlooked by systematic theologians, the Council of Chalcedon, in fact, "contains no reference to the cross at all." Thus, concludes van Buren, "no ecumenical council formulated a dogma concerning the effects of the death of Jesus on the cross."[12] Van Buren here draws attention to the fact that the Church Fathers were very hesitant to inscribe in dogma a certain inter-pretation of what was accomplished with Jesus' death. He presents this original hesitance as appropriate, both spiritually and – in the post-Shoah era – ethically as well.

The trigger for van Buren's rethinking of the cross is found in Jesus' Jewishness, which he expresses in the language of election: "whatever the Church may say as to the unique role of that one Jew – and for the Gentile Church at the least he is surely unique – it cannot be forgotten that each and every one of the six million was one of God's elect, one of God's own people Israel."[13] Van Buren links Jesus and twentieth-century Jewry closely together as God's covenant partners: "God is hurt by any loss to the covenant partner," he comments.[14] And in convergence with his covenantal thinking, but still unusual for contemporary theology, van Buren suggests a method for thinking about Jesus' suffering in the terms of post-Shoah language: "We shall learn to speak of Auschwitz from the perspective of the cross, then, by first learning to speak of the cross from the perspective of Auschwitz." He continues by formulating a "rule" – and rule should be understood here as a frame of reference, a reminder of proportions, or maybe, as I would call it, a hermeneutics of memory. "[T]he death of one Jew, no matter whom or what he was in God's purposes, should not be spoken of so as to lessen the significance and

---

[11] Paul van Buren, *Christ in Context* (San Francisco: Harper&Row, 1988), 158.
[12] Ibid.   [13] Ibid., 158f.   [14] Ibid., 63.

the pain of the death of any human being, least of all that of six million other Jews."[15]

The formulation of such a "rule" is not only unusual but even unheard of in dogmatic discourse. But it should be noted that van Buren is rooted in the Anglican tradition that is deeply connected to early dogmatic discourse. In Chalcedon, we find a formulation about Jesus' full humanity and divinity that is very similar in structure to van Buren's: His full humanity should not to be understood as lessening his divinity, and his full divinity is not to be understood so as to lessen his humanity. While van Buren's rethinking the Christian language of crucifixion is unusual, he does make sure to remain within the margins of Christian dogmatic discourse, even when he stretches them, for instance, by suggesting that "the death of God's faithful son Jesus must have hurt God."[16]

But this formulation directly follows from van Buren's declared decision to speak about the cross from a post-Shoah perspective. Despite some ultra-Orthodox Jewish readings of the Shoah as an expression of divine punishment, there is a consensus in religious post-Shoah thought that God stands with his people Israel against killing. Still, Christian theologians usually hesitate to apply this understanding to Jesus' own suffering and death as well. Van Buren, in contrast, does not hesitate to describe Jesus' death as "tragic."[17] Constitutive for van Buren's thinking here is a Jewish victimhood that, in the framework of the covenant, cannot be an expression of God's will. This is quite remarkable. Van Buren regards it as theologically intolerable to imply that God favored Jewish suffering in the Shoah. Consequently, it is also intolerable to suggest that God favored Jesus' suffering on the cross. In this manner, any interpretation of "the cross" needs to be referred back to Jewish suffering, and, more specifically, to the recent tragic climax of Jewish suffering, the Shoah. Taking Jewish suffering seriously and taking the covenant seriously prevents van Buren from seeing God as acting on behalf of – or in favor of – suffering. If God is with the Jewish people in the Shoah – and seldom would a Christian theologian today suggest otherwise[18] – and God is against the suffering of his chosen ones, it makes sense to say that God stood opposed to Jesus' suffering too. Thus, both

---

[15] Ibid., 165.   [16] Ibid., 166.   [17] Ibid., 169.

[18] Like Propst Gruber, whose depiction of God torturing his people led Richard Rubinstein to proclaim God's death. See Richard L. Rubenstein, *After Auschwitz: History, Theology and Contemporary Judaism* (Baltimore: John Hopkins University Press, 1992 [1966]).

cases of suffering are seen as caused by other humans. Van Buren's suggestion that "we shall learn to speak of Auschwitz from the perspective of the cross ... by first learning to speak of the cross from the perspective of Auschwitz" thereby works in two directions.

The memory of the Shoah shakes Christians up and hinders a language oblivious to pain and agony. Dorothee Soelle has found that Christian theologians had not just become unaware of how painful pain actually is but had even indulged in imagining the excessive violence the God-Father's inflicted on the Son. Had Christian theologians gotten used to referring to death and suffering as not only God-caused but even God-promoted? While Soelle's main positive references are to contemporaneously suffering Christians, her critique was written in a context of questioning the former generation of German Protestant theologians in the late 1960s. This lends support to Levinas's contention that it is the disproportionate agony of the Shoah that has lead to a paradigm shift in thinking about suffering.

From a historical standpoint it is astonishing that attributing meaning to suffering came to be seen as one of the core foundations of Christianity. As mentioned, van Buren's examination of the early dogmatic discourse shows that only the pure fact of Jesus' suffering, but not one definitive interpretation of his suffering, is mentioned in the Ecumenical creeds. For the Christology of the various creeds was built on Jesus Christ being both human and divine, not on his suffering. Remarkably, some of the most outspoken recent critics of Christian approaches to suffering present themselves as speaking against the Christian thought tradition without acknowledging the fact that while attributing meaning to suffering is a strong tradition, in dogmatic perspective it need not be seen as an inherent part of the Christian creed. For instance, in their highly personal account, *Proverbs of Ashes: Violence, Redemptive Suffering and the Search for What Saves Us*, the feminist theologians Rita Nakashima Brock and Rebecca Ann Parker remark in connection with their own suffering, "Neither Jesus' death on the cross nor our own acts of self-sacrifice had saved us."[19] And in her introduction to *Cross Examinations*, which treats the "meanings of the cross today," Marit Trelstad quotes womanist and feminist theologians as having criticized the impact of "the cross" in

---

[19] Rita Nakashima Brock and Rebecca Ann Parker, *Proverbs of Ashes: Violence, Redemptive Suffering and the Search for What Saves Us* (Boston: Beacon Press, 2001), 7.

general terms: "the cross reinforces both victim passivity and violent oppression."[20] One might almost speak of a consensus among feminist theologians criticizing the impact of "the cross" on women's lives and calling for an end to the glorification of passive suffering. This ethical critique should take a more dogmatic turn, reclaiming the early church's hesitance over interpreting the cross.

"Jesus suffered." Between his being born and having died, this is the only information about his life shared in the Creed of Nicaea. That he really suffered and felt pain was of great importance to the Church Fathers. As mentioned, this is precisely what makes him a full human being – rather than a divinized person immune to suffering and incapable of pain. In histories of dogma, this vulnerable "humanness" is typically explained as a prerequisite for an economy of salvation: Humanity can be saved only by the savior who is truly human. It is the capacity to suffer that is important to the Church Fathers – one might call it Jesus' "sufferability." Sufferability then becomes the *chiffre* of true humanity in dogmatic discourse. It is not the same as Martha Nussbaum's notion of fragility, but it might be closer to contemporary Jewish women philosophers' thinking than to the type of sadistic Christian theology cited by Soelle.[21]

While van Buren's formulations sound radical, he is thus closer to the spirit of early church dogmatic discourse than one might think. The early creeds mention Jesus' suffering but barely interpret it. It is important as a fact. What might be even more significant for a critique of later theologies could be formulated as "the suffering is of Jesus." He suffered. The cause of his suffering is not divine, is not rationalized in terms of divine bloodthirstiness or of theodicy. The creeds do not portray the Father of the Son as the perpetrator. The suffering of the Son is indeed important. It is not stated as divine, however, but rather as purposeful. Still, there is no purpose and divinity attributed to a violent intention on the part of God to cause suffering. I would even dare to say, in more contemporary phrasing, that in the early creeds Jesus' suffering is portrayed in "victim-centered" language. It seems that later interpretational traditions of Jesus' suffering have not been attuned to any other human suffering. And one might understand Metz's theology as even drawing a direct line between

---

[20] Marit Trelstad, ed., *Cross Examinations: Readings on the Meanings of the Cross Today* (Minneapolis, MN: Augsburg Fortress, 2006), 1, 6.

[21] See Martha Nussbaum, *The Fragility of Goodness: Luck and Ethics in Greek Tragedy and Ethics* (Cambridge: Cambridge University Press, 2001).

the concept of Jesus' overbearing suffering and the deafening effects of traditional vernaculars of salvation.

THE SUFFERING OF THE OTHER

Johann Baptist Metz shares with Levinas a central focus on differentiating between one's own and the other's suffering. It is a fundamental difference, shaping his discussion of theodicy: One cannot refer the Other who is asking about his or her suffering to God's mystery, declares Metz.[22] Characteristic for Metz is the emphasis on "foreign" suffering (*fremdes Leid*).[23] The term "foreign suffering" sounds a little awkward, not only in the English translation but even in the German original. "*Fremdes Leid*" is an unusual idiom both within and outside of Church language. Metz has a very good sense for critical language and frequently creates his own combinations of words. My suggestion in this case is that by saying "foreign" – instead of "Other" – Metz deliberately wants to challenge the traditional Christian term "neighbor," the Hebrew *re'a*, typically translated with the German "Nächster," which literally means "the next." Metz, over against the closeness implied in German "der Nächste," aims instead to stretch the distance to the person further away whose suffering we should be concerned with. It is not my suffering that lies at the center, nor just the suffering of those close to me. Rather, the suffering that is distant from and unknown to me is what requires my attention, and, as Metz emphasizes, my compassion. His use of the Latinized word "compassion" instead of the more common "empathy" is meant to accord the emotion-based term a more political sense as with the act of siding with those who suffer. Metz also speaks of the "authority" of the sufferers, thus underlining the need to listen to suffering people and support their cause. Here he explicitly interprets Levinas's ethics theologically and claims the authority of the sufferers as God's sole authority manifest in the world.

[22] Metz mentions this example in criticism of his teacher Karl Rahner. See Johann Baptist Metz, *Memoria Passionis: Ein provozierendes Gedächtnis in pluralistischer Gesellschaft* (Freiburg im Breisgau: Herder, 2006), 26.

[23] Metz, "*Im Eingedenken fremden Leids*," in Johann Baptist Metz, Johann Reikerstorfer, and Jürgen Werbick, eds., *Gottesrede* (Münster: LIT, 2001), 3–20, 12.

Metz adds an impressive thought and identifies what we usually call "God's voice" with our own reaction to this "foreign" suffering.[24] This theological adaptation of Levinas's ethics is remarkable, as Metz does not look for religious equivalents to Levinas's human wording, e.g. the "face." He does not find God's voice in the Other's call for help, but in one's reaction to this call. Thus, it is not the call to help that is divinized but responding to the call.

Memoria passionis is the title of Metz's book from 2006.[25] He uses this Latin term in a way that broadens its narrow traditional meaning of referring back to Jesus' suffering. Obviously, it means more than its literal translation, the memory of suffering. In a collection of articles from 1967–1997, Metz describes the *memoria passionis* as the connecting thread (*"roter Faden"*) of his theological biography.[26] The Latin word for suffering, *passio*, is in German *Passion* and is used exclusively with regard to Jesus' suffering in the past and to the seven weeks leading up to Easter in the liturgical calendar. Remarkably, Metz hardly mentions the connotation of Jesus' suffering that would be obvious to the German-speaker. Instead, he concentrates on what is highly unusual in the German theological context: the calling to mind of "foreign suffering" that he puts forward as a theological category. The critical theodicy question should not be silenced with a message of "salvation." As with Levinas, for whom theodicy and human suffering are closely intertwined and connected with the concept of theodicy, Metz coined another term, *leidempfindlich*, meaning sensitive to suffering. Theodicy discourse, like monotheism as a whole, should be sensitive, perceptive, and attentive to suffering.[27] This plea should not be underestimated in its critical force. Of course, one might assume that every Christian and every person should be sensitive to suffering. In Metz's phrasing, though, making *Leidempfindlichkeit* a component of theodicy makes for a profound critique of the theological tradition. What it implies, although Metz does not spell it out, is that the Catholic language of salvation tends to be too loud to hear the human cry

[24] This remarkable formulation is worth quoting in the original: "... was wir seine Stimme nennen, ist unsere Reaktion auf die Heimsuchung durch dieses fremde Leid." Metz, "Im Eingedenken fremden Leids," in Johann Baptist Metz, Johann Reikerstorfer, and Jürgen Werbick, eds., *Gottesrede* (Münster: LIT, 2001), 3–20,13.

[25] Johann Baptist Metz, *Memoria Passionis: Ein provozierendes Gedächtnis in pluralistischer Gesellschaft* (Freiburg im Breisgau: Herder, 2006).

[26] Johann Baptist Metz, *Zum Begriff der neuen Politischen Theologie: 1967–1997* (Mainz: Matthias Grünewald Verlag, 1997), 210.

[27] Metz, *Memoria passionis*, 162.

of suffering. His call for compassion instead of apathy is meant as a broad theological-political critique, following his general diagnosis of the Christian teaching of salvation as having dramatized sin and relativized suffering.[28] A theological language that is overly invested in explaining "salvation" is not sensitive to human voices expressing agony and pain.

Notably, Metz does not present, as had liberation theologians, an alternative understanding of salvation, one that connects salvation to the spirituality expressed in the resistance to oppressive regimes. Instead, for Metz salvation remains a word not owned by people who suffer but something that is spoken over the heads of the sufferers if not turned against them. What, one might ask, would a theology built as *leidempfindlich* look and sound like? Unfortunately, this question must remain open since Metz never wrote a comprehensive theology and never turned his theological, social, and political critique into a complete and comprehensive theory. He clearly prefers a prophetic style of short, intense, programmatic, and critical texts. There may be further good reasons for Metz not offering a theological-political alternative to doctrinal talk about salvation. Sounds of suffering, Metz might be saying, need to be heard from the suffering person.

How then does one write a theory on suffering that is not deaf to people who suffer? What might giving suffering people a voice sound like in a theory? These are difficult methodological questions, not just for theologians but also for philosophers. Among contemporary philosophers, Adi Ophir has picked up this challenge in his path-breaking moral theory *The Order of Evil*, a work that focuses on the victim and the harmed person.[29] Levinas's essay "Useless Suffering" finds an echo as well as a philosophical platform in Adi Ophir's comprehensive study of suffering as a core component of his theory of evil. Not all suffering is equally evil but rather its preventability is the ultimate criterion: "Suffering that is not prevented or relieved is an evil."[30] To identify suffering that can be prevented or reduced is constitutive for Ophir's moral philosophy since the preventable entails the imperative to prevent. Thus, differentiating between suffering that cannot be prevented and suffering that can be reduced or even prevented becomes constitutive for

---

[28] Metz, *Memoria passionis*, 164.
[29] Adi Ophir, *The Order of Evils: Toward an Ontology of Morals* (New York: Zone Books, 2005).
[30] Ibid., 24.

moral theory. "Moral interest is an interest in an other who is (or might be) in distress, in his suffering and welfare." Ophir presents this understanding of moral interest as indebted to Levinas.[31] "What counts are the needs of others."[32] The echo of Levinas is clearly heard in this prioritizing of the Other over oneself. Slightly differently accentuated, Ophir explains that the concrete needs of concrete others establish the moral situation. In this situation, the moral task is precisely to answer a call. Again, with Levinas this call describes one's most universal encounter with the Other, while for Ophir there are various others with changing needs. Ophir describes the situation of being called to attend to someone's suffering as a general, universal situation. I would take this idea further and describe this situation of being called to help by a suffering person as the human situation par excellence. Independently of Ophir, Metz identified responding to the call of the suffering as hearing God's voice!

According to Ophir, the only way out of the situation demanding that one respond to a call of a suffering person – in Levinas's language, to take responsibility – is through indifference. "Indifference to someone who suffers superfluous evils is the end of moral interest and of the moral matter ... [I]ndifference to superfluous suffering and loss excludes one from the moral domain."[33] Remarkably, there is no way not to be addressed, as Ophir details. One cannot avoid being called; one can only decline to respond. Here too, Ophir and Levinas are closer than their very different philosophical languages might make them appear. For Levinas, this moment of responsibility for the Other establishes the subject. Ophir does not employ this same formulation, but one could say that he concretizes the encounter between the suffering Other and the addressee who is called to help. In both cases, priority is given to the Other in need, while the responding person, the "I" or "me," is characterized precisely in her or "my" being responsible, being called and needed.

Ophir's meticulous study of suffering lies at the heart of his theory of evil. Evil is examined according to its effects on a harmed and suffering person. It is not the perpetrators who receive Ophir's attention, but the people affected by evil. Thus Ophir explores and analyzes "the way in which an evil is suffered, experienced, assigned expression or compensation; the way it addresses a call, invites response, opens up a gap in someone's existence, institutes duties, and creates obligations."[34] Ophir's initial explanation of suffering as "caused in an encounter with casualties

---

[31] Ibid., 15.   [32] Ibid., 27.   [33] Ibid., 12.   [34] Ibid., 27f.

in which one refrains or is refrained from disengaging" highlights a situation of uninvited intensity and the lack of opportunity to distance oneself.[35] This is a strikingly physical description, but the definition also works for suffering that is not limited to the body. Acknowledging the suffering of somebody then means to acknowledge the suffering person's longing for disentanglement. "The sufferer suffers because she cannot disengage, or because she chose not to disengage in order to prevent more suffering (for her or for others). But to acknowledge her as the one who suffers means to acknowledge her as the one who is yearning, begging, craving, aching to disengage."[36] The addressee, the person who could help to reduce or end a certain superfluous suffering, plays a crucial role in this concept. "In any occurrence of suffering, some one is posited as the addressee of a call to disengage."[37] This is a remarkable feature of a moral theory of suffering. The suffering person is clearly at the center. Yet in any situation of a person suffering superfluous, reducible suffering, there is someone appointed who could help to reduce the suffering. Anybody can turn into a suffering person at a certain moment in his or her life. But almost every adult human is also a potential addressee of a suffering person's call at any given time.

How does one become the addressee of another's suffering and cry for help? Interestingly, here Ophir does not engage in narrow definitions. There is not even a need to be present in order to be the addressee of an utterance of suffering.[38] Nor is such an "utterance" limited to speech, nor, moreover, does it need to be explicit. Thus, Ophir speaks of a "call."[39] Although Ophir emphasizes that his concept of morality is built on the needs of concrete others rather than a comprehensive responsibility for the Other, as with Levinas, both philosophers appear closer than Ophir might admit. Although the "utterances" of suffering relate to concrete situations, considering oneself "called" by a suffering person seems to be essentially as general a human situation as being responsible for the Other.

Ophir makes an extensive effort to describe the suffering person as possessing a range of options and possibilities, perhaps best described as multi-leveled agency. One can, for instance, choose to communicate and express one's own suffering, ask for compensation, or even give up – but one cannot do this with the other's suffering. Thus, regarding the presentation of agony and misery, the difference between one's own and the

---

[35] Ibid., 257.   [36] Ibid., 261.   [37] Ibid., 259.   [38] Ibid., 262.   [39] Ibid., 261.

other's suffering is key. Can one avoid the call of the other's suffering? Ophir offers an interesting answer to this question, one that again brings him close to Levinas's concept of unlimited responsibility for the Other. "To censor, to repress, to remove, to prevent access to communication channels, to communicate in a way that neutralizes the cry – all these are responses in the face of the suffering of the other, in my ring of communication, but each response can only be made once I have already been the addressee of this suffering."[40] Clearly, being the addressee is not my choice – just as with Levinas, responsibility precedes one's decision to take responsibility.[41]

These are compelling philosophical ideas. As we have seen, in early Christology the human (Jesus Christ's humanity) was constituted by the capacity to suffer. In Ophir's moral philosophy, any human is called by the suffering of an Other. To understand oneself as an addressee makes the human subject humane. Metz, having Levinas in mind but without having read Ophir, hears God's voice in the reaction to the suffering's call.

How does Adi Ophir's study of suffering as part of his theory of evil translate to Christology? First, applying philosophical thinking to theology is rarely an obvious undertaking. Ophir did not write his philosophy about evil and suffering to help Christian theologians reframe their language about the cross. On the other hand, Ophir explicitly invites his readers to draw freely from his theoretical work and apply his ideas and findings to other fields.[42] Levinas's philosophy has been exported widely to other disciplines, even to the extent that some Levinasians fear a resulting oversimplification, one that indeed seems almost unavoidable in such trans-disciplinary re-orderings. But Ophir's methodology more readily enables applications to other fields, since he works with almost no presuppositions. Ironically, although he demonstratively situates his philosophy in the Israeli political context, his observations and reflections on suffering are universally human. Ophir's philosophy readily invites importations and adaptations into significantly different contexts.

At the same time, just as with Levinas, so too with Ophir's moral theory – it cannot be stretched to do anything. There are methodological lines that commit both reader and interpreter. Ophir's moral theory

---

[40] Ibid., 268.
[41] Levinas, *Otherwise than Being, or, Beyond Essence* translated by Alphonso Lingus (Pittsburgh, PA: Duquesne University Press, 1998 [1974]).
[42] Ophir, *The Order of Evils*, 313.

cannot be used to mystify suffering and evil since his work treats both suffering and evil as part of the human experience – in his language as "part of that which is."[43] More direct and more explicit than with Levinas is Ophir's commitment to preventing preventable suffering, limiting limitable agony, and reducing reducible misery. Christian thought traditions do not sufficiently emphasize this commitment insofar as they do not underscore the necessity of differentiating between preventable and non-preventable suffering.[44] Is the basic Christian notion of redemptive suffering, then, to blame for this lack of decisive commitment to confront suffering?

AGAINST REDEMPTIVE SUFFERING

Alice Eckardt has come to precisely this conclusion. Eckardt has directly taken on this most problematic tradition and unambiguously denied to suffering any redeeming quality. Alice Eckardt, who took part from the beginning (the 1940s) in her husband Roy Eckardt's pioneering studies of Jewish–Christian relations, and in the 1980s made her own groundbreaking examinations of survivors' testimonies, came to view traditional praise for the endurance of suffering as a form of moral distortion. All attributions of spiritual value to suffering, in her view, distract from the evil that lies behind it, which must be confronted.[45] In her decisive formulation, she identifies a proportional relation between embracing suffering and remaining passive toward evil. "As long as we try to comfort ourselves or others with ideas about the positive effects of suffering – including a redemptive function – the less we will be inclined to reject it as the evil it is, and the less we may be inclined to fight against it."[46]

---

[43] Ibid., 35.

[44] In a time when catastrophes of nature are increasingly linked to failed human behavior that, e.g., contributes to climate change, the axis of the preventable and non-preventable will need to be re-examined.

[45] Alice L. Eckardt, "Leiden – Herausforderung des Glaubens – Herausforderung Gottes," in Reinhold Boschki and Dagmar Mensink, eds., *Kultur allein ist nicht genug: Das Werk von Elie Wiesel – Herausforderung für Religion und Gesellschaft* (Münster: Lit Verlag, 1998), 245–261. An English version of this text can be found on the website of the International Council of Christians and Jews: www.jcrelations.net/Suffering__Challenge_to_ Faith__Challenge_to_God.3077.0.html?id=720&L=3&searchText=Eckardt&searchFilter= %2A&page=1.

[46] Alice Eckardt, "Suffering, Theology and the Shoah," in Steven L. Jacobs, ed., *Contemporary Christian Religious Responses to the Shoah* (Lanham, MD: University Press of America, 1993), 34–57.

Eckardt developed her distinctive views on suffering and evil after decades of comprehensive and intensive study of Elie Wiesel's books and numerous other accounts of Shoah survivors. This has made her approach quite unique. While she does not owe her ideas to Levinas, she exhibits comparable notions to Levinas's proclaimed "end of theodicy" as well as what I have called the end of "pathodicy." Deeply immersed in survivors' literature, she is well aware that not every survivor's thinking can be summed up as "anti-theodicy," as Braiterman has labeled the Jewish religious refusal to justify God despite the Shoah. Still, what survivors of the Shoah think and have thought matters to her greatly. "But even if some of those who perished and some of those who survived the Kingdom of Night are willing to accept the traditional answers, are we permitted to evade the difficult questions?"[47] She comes to a conclusion that is both mindful of survivors and still committed to radical rethinking: "Perhaps only the survivors, those who have already experienced the worst [that] can be dealt out, have the right to cling to the older answers."

Outstanding among Christian thinkers, Alice Eckardt draws a clear line between Christian theological concepts, such as vicarious suffering, and the undermining of human responsibility.[48] In her efforts to revise an approach to suffering that fosters responsibility, she also quotes contemporary "victims of oppression," such as "Blacks, women, Hispanics, poor, tortured." Remarkably, she finds that the very different contexts and levels of suffering do not lead to fundamentally different estimations. It is worth citing her full statement on the dangers of viewing suffering as inherently redemptive that I mentioned earlier:

Along with survivors of the death camps, these victims of oppression insist that suffering does not ennoble, does not provide moral stature or spiritual depth or refined sensibility. It does not make a person superior or more authentic than a non-sufferer. These people tell us that as long as we try to comfort ourselves or others with ideas about the positive effects of suffering – including a redemptive function – the less we will be inclined to reject it as the evil it is, and the less we may be inclined to fight against it.[49]

Unlike Levinas and Ophir, the distinction between one's own and the Other's suffering is not constitutive for Alice Eckardt. Nevertheless, she honed her remarkable insight and sharp judgment not by reflecting on her

---

[47] Ibid., 35.   [48] Ibid., 54.   [49] Ibid., 55.

own suffering but, as noted, after decades of reading survivors' testimonies and literature. Eckardt draws a direct line between the acceptance
of suffering and a lack of resistance to its causes. Emphasizing this
causality of suffering is rare even in explicit critiques of traditional Christian approaches to suffering.

Levinas, Metz, Soelle, Ophir, and Eckardt concur in their concern
about interpretations of suffering. Levinas sees the justification of the
Other's suffering as key to immorality, while Ophir states that "one can
never appropriate an other's suffering."[50] Ophir, like Eckardt, emphasizes the sufferer's preference for action over theory: "The one who cries
for help has no time to give meaning; she is interested in relief, not
interpretation."[51] Likewise, Eckardt and Ophir support an analysis of
the conditions that lead to the suffering in order to prevent and reduce
what can be prevented and reduced.

Both Alice Eckardt and Adi Ophir seek to take suffering seriously and
side with the suffering person. This is best expressed by their commitment
to analyzing the sources and mechanisms of suffering, and to fighting,
resisting, and minimizing the harm caused by human-made evil. My
highlighting of Eckardt's claim, that rationalizing suffering promotes
indifference to or acceptance of the evil sources causing it, is not intended
to discredit the undoubted achievements in Christian-based practices that
seek to ease the lot of sufferers. There are numerous Christian traditions
and practices of accompanying the sick and the dying, for instance, whose
worthiness is undeniable.

Still, Eckardt's radical stand that suffering is generally to be rejected as
an admirable or desirable situation and is never attributed to divine will
or "God's wish" but exclusively to the effect of evil constitutes a powerful
challenge to Christian tradition.

Remembering Jesus as a Jew helps Christians to remember his suffering
as the suffering of an Other. This notion may shape Christian interpretations of that specific *memoria passionis*, the memory of Jesus' suffering
that is evoked in the liturgy of the Eucharist. Yet Levinas's path-breaking
distinction in interpreting suffering as "meaningful in me, useless in the
other" provides an important moral compass here. Picking up on Eckardt's claim, a Christology less invested in interpreting suffering, with less

---

[50] Ophir, *Order of Evils*, 262.   [51] Ibid., 265.

of a stake in claiming it as a theological "possession," may engage with taking the Other's suffering more seriously and develop a language capable of expressing a commitment to prevent the suffering that is preventable.

It is fascinating that the philosopher Adi Ophir and the theologian Johann Baptist Metz, while evidently not aware of each other's work, have both followed Levinas in two specific steps. The first is that of siding with the suffering person, which Ophir employs in his methodology as a whole and which Metz describes as the authority of those who suffer. In the second step, that of not idealizing victims and not divinizing victimhood, the decisive moment is identified as reacting to the call of the suffering person. This notion of the addressee receives ample attention in Ophir's philosophy and is described by him in considerable detail. Metz simply and briefly identifies it as the manifestation of God's voice. Metz does not identify the sufferer as one abandoned by God. But he is far from simply seeing the presence of God within suffering, as numerous theologians have done. The true divine moment that Metz finds manifest lies in an individual's responding to rescue the sufferer. Christologically, Metz can be seen as walking back from Christ to Jesus. Thus, he describes Jesus as attentive to the suffering of others and claims that for Jesus sin was the refusal to respond to others' suffering.[52]

Compared to the achievements of New Testament scholars in changing the Historical Jesus research or Pauline studies, the necessity of rethinking traditional Christian suffering has received far less recognition. One possible reason for the lacuna is that there seems to be no direct Pauline quote that may lend authority to a uselessness of suffering – comparable to the quote from Romans manifesting the ongoing validity of Israel's covenant (Rom. 11:1) – or that affirms the holiness of the Torah and the commandments (Rom. 7,12). The ideal quote, we might wishfully imagine, would be something along the lines of Paul saying, in his characteristic rhetorical style, "Are we then turning suffering into salvation? By no means!" is unfortunately not to be found. There is good reason why Paul never uttered such a sentence limiting the spiritual value of suffering; namely, his focus in earlier writings on "the cross." And so, his

---

[52] Metz, "Im Eingedenken fremden Leids," in Johann Baptist Metz, Johann Reikerstorfer, and Jürgen Werbick, eds., *Gottesrede* (Münster: LIT, 2001), 3–20,11.

formulation in Corinthians 1:23, "But we preach Christ crucified, unto the Jews a stumbling block, and unto the Greeks foolishness," presents the idea of "Christ crucified" as a challenge to all. At the same time, it is not yet here a fully developed notion. The New Testament scholar John Gager views the contrast between polemics in Galatians and affirmative thought in Romans – regarding topics like the law – as a self-corrective development. Following this line of analysis, Paul would not have self-corrected his thoughts on "the cross," because "the cross" did not yet present for him an established category.

Metz chooses a different New Testament text corpus for proof-reading the Gospels. Without quoting specific verses, he simply recalls Jesus as primarily directing himself to others' suffering. Jesus' turning to the marginalized and the sick presents a most obvious account of the gospel. It could be added that most New Testament stories do not just report Jesus' care and concern but his actual helping and healing. In this light – in the light of Jesus answering the call of the Other's suffering – it is subsequent Christianity's *embrace* of suffering that seems far afield of the New Testament text.

In academic Christian theological contexts, the emphasis on Jesus as a teacher and ethical "model" is typically regarded as something that reduces him. Historically, this was the criticism directed at the eighteenth-century Enlightenment's depictions of Jesus as a sort of exemplary and perfected human being, a human role model of virtue. In more contemporary history, theologies of liberation had to defend themselves against the charge of reducing Jesus to the image of a reformer, liberator, or freedom fighter. But the continuous suspicion leveled by Christian traditionalists of memories of Jesus that emphasize his active help in treating the suffering of others clearly lacks a Christo-logical as well as a biblical foundation. For, if we take the model of a Two-Natures Christology seriously, then a socially active Jesus who alleviates suffering is simply part of the fleshing out of his fully human nature.

Post-Shoah Christology on the whole has focused on reformulating the thought traditions rather than the practices of the churches. This is an important phenomenon, though not at all an obvious one. The conviction that a profound revision of harmful Church traditions needs to be argued in the framework of dogmatic rather than ethical discourse is in itself an expression of the traditional hierarchy of faith and deeds. Although Jesus lived prior to rabbinic times, it may still be appropriate for us to describe him as a "halakhic man." He is a man who cares and acts, a man of deeds. In Soloveitchik's words, "halakhic man's religious viewpoint is highly exoteric. His face is turned toward the people."[53] The memory of Jesus the halakhic Jew would support Metz's Christology that focuses on a Jesus who responds to the sufferer's call.

[53] Joseph B. Soloveitchik, *Halakhic Man* (Philadelphia: The Jewish Publication Society, 1983), 42.

6

Between Jesus, the Jew, and the Other

We have seen that the different temporal modes of Jesus the Jew highlight different sets of questions. The framework of memory refers to different modes of time and helps to shape their respective critical discourses. When connected to the past, memory both sharpens and blurs lines of historical research and historiography. With regard to the present, memory frames the search for continuities and schemes of transmission. Directed to the future, memory leads to reflections on responsibility for generations to come. The memory of Jesus the Jew connects these different modes, revives the historical Jesus, refines the contemporary quest for continuity, and deepens the commitment to future humanity. All these interconnections involve interreligious relationships.

This chapter focuses on interreligious interactions between Jesus the Jew and the Other. I will first introduce and discuss "otherness" as a category for Christological discourse, both in continuity with and in contrast to its central role in twentieth-century theology. Jesus the Jew remains an Other for contemporary Christians with regard to his embodiment of Torah and bodily practice of the commandments. His otherness thus increases with an intensified memory of his Jewishness. Then I will discuss recent reflections on Christ and Torah in conversation with contemporary Pauline studies that has taken a dramatic turn, appreciating more fully Paul's complex attitude toward Torah law. I will then turn to a discussion of Jesus the Jew in recent Islamic theological outreach to Christianity. Contrary to what is generally believed, Muslim theologians are well informed about Jesus' Jewishness. In my interpretation of the path-breaking statement of Muslim scholars "A Common Word," I expect that many readers will be surprised at the notion of Muslims reminding

Christians of Jesus' Jewishness. Finally, I develop an interreligious theory of mainly Jewish but also Muslim interlocutors shining a light through the cracks of the various theological systems. I do this through conversation with the philosopher Martha Nussbaum whose notion of vulnerability I introduce as a creative and apposite tool for dogmatic thinking.

"Otherness" is neither a traditional theological category nor a central term in Christian narratives or self-reflections. The concept, though, has gained significant relevance in the twentieth century. While the overall affirmative connotation of otherness is a more recent philosophical phenomenon, talking about God as Other was constitutive for early twentieth-century Protestant theology, especially the thinking of Karl Barth.[1] The radical otherness of God over a spiritual synthesis with nature or culture was first shaped in the context of World War I and the striking nationalism of "liberal" German Protestant theologians. As a theological criterion, radical otherness eventually also enabled critical political judgment. Because Barth could not identify God with any current cultural, natural, or spiritual event, God, in his view, could also not be assimilated to the Zeitgeist of the Nazi-movement.[2] Barth's theology is present in theologies committed to post-war Jewish–Christian reconciliation mainly through the works of some of his students.[3] For Friedrich-Wilhelm Marquardt, it was not a theological coincidence that the understanding of God as radical Other helped strengthen intellectual resistance in Nazi

---

[1] Samuel Moyn recently argued that Levinas was influenced by Karl Barth's intensive use of the language of "the Other." Samuel Moyn, *Origins of the Other: Emmanuel Levinas between Revelation and Ethics* (Ithaca, NY: Cornell University Press, 2005).

[2] The Barmen Declaration, the founding document of the Confessing Church, is famous for its Christo-centrism. Barth's insistence on Christ as "the only Word" has been criticized as not leaving space for Judaism. I suggest we remember that it was, with Bonhoeffer, the only pronounced form of Protestant theological resistance. All anti-Barthian German Protestant theologians need to ask themselves why their predecessors (e.g. in liberal theology) had nothing theological or Christological to say to counter the so-called German Christians.

[3] In the German sense of "Schüler": These theologians went to study with Barth in Basel, wrote their dissertations under his supervision, and developed their own theological profiles in conversation and dispute with him. The case of Karl Barth is special since his students divide into "Barthians" and "Barth-students." While the "Barthians" basically followed his theological model, his "students" built on his revival of Old Testament themes for systematic theology – for example, the covenant – but added a revival of the reality of those themes, meaning an understanding of the Israel covenant as alive. Thus, it is no coincidence that the leading systematic theologians of Jewish–Christian relations in the late twentieth century were Barth students: Friedrich-Wilhelm Marquardt, Paul van Buren, and in the younger generation, Bertold Klappert. Dietrich Ritschl also belongs to this group, although his main focus is ecumenical theology.

Germany. He took it on himself to further develop the theology of God as Other, not assimilated to culture or nature, in the post-Shoah context. The notion of otherness, then, becomes central in Marquardt's post-Shoah theological thought.[4] As "Auschwitz" stands for the attempt to annihilate otherness, God is believed to take the side of otherness.[5]

Marquardt did not explicitly introduce otherness as a major category in his Christology of Jesus, the Jew.[6] Only with the radical change of thought facilitated by Levinas could otherness be understood as something desirable and enriching, something that could express deeper dimensions of the divine. But this theological Levinas-reception occurred only in the nineties, while most of the Christologies emphasizing Jesus' Jewishness, including Marquardt's, were written in the 1980s.[7]

OTHERNESS AS A CHRISTOLOGICAL CATEGORY

Christologies written in the context of reframing Jewish–Christian relations usually pictured the Jewishness of Jesus as a bridge between Judaism and Christianity. Difference as a structuring principle of Christology had been traditionally bound to a negative account of Judaism, with Jesus pictured as different and thus detached from his Jewish environment. "Different," in this Christian thought tradition, always meant better or higher, possessing deeper truth and imbued with greater spirituality. Difference, when stated positively, was used to underline Jesus' uniqueness that was likewise synonymous with superiority.[8] Yet, seldom has "otherness" been made a central category to a Christology committed to

---

[4] Barbara U. Meyer, "Applying for Otherness," in R. Burggraeve, J. Hansel, M.-A. Lescourret, J.-F. Rey, and J.-M. Salanskis, eds., *Recherches Levinassiennes*, Bibliotheque *Philosophique du Louvain* 82 (Louvain: Peeters, 2012), 437–449.

[5] Marquardt, *Eschatologie I*, 184.

[6] The concept of otherness is increasingly central to Marquardt's dogmatics due to his growing interest in and acquaintance with Levinas's philosophy. Thus otherness is of formative importance to Marquardt's works on eschatology (1993; 1994; 1996) but not to his works on Christology (1991;1992).

[7] Marquardt later shaped his doctrine of Trinity through the notion of otherness, while Philipp Cunningham has developed a Catholic language of otherness. Cunningham described the Christian study of Judaism as a "sacrament of otherness." See Philipp A. Cunningham, "Celebrating Judaism as a 'Sacrament of Every Otherness'." In Kristen Colberg and Robert Krieg, eds., *The Theology of Cardinal Walter Kasper: Speaking Truth in Love* (St. John's, MN: Liturgical Press, 2014), 223–240.

[8] This resembles Sanders' key argument against the term in Jesus research. See E. P. Sanders, *The Question of Uniqueness in the Teaching of Jesus* (London: The University of London, 1990).

renewed Jewish–Christian dialogue, and seldom has the developing language of otherness been applied to talk about Jesus' Jewishness – both probably due to the previous prevailing effort of Christian theologians to embrace Jesus' Jewishness as primarily a bridge to Jews and Judaism.

Kayko Driedger Hesslein has recently picked up Levinas's notion of the responsibility for the otherness of the Other and applied it to the Jewishness of Jesus: "The Jewish Jesus is that particular Other for whom Christians are particularly obligated to assume theological responsibility and by whom Christians must allow themselves to be formed."[9] This formulation is remarkable in its bringing together of Jewishness and otherness. Levinas's notion of the otherness of the Other, which has become an idiom of its own, is appropriately here referred to in relation to his ethics. According to Levinas, the otherness of the Other represents not only a value in itself but entails an unlimited responsibility. This responsibility constitutes the subject and precedes even the decision to take responsibility.[10] Driedger Hesslein here applies this most central Levinasian idea in a particularly daring way. Jesus the Jew is marked as the Other for whom Christians are responsible. The idea that Christians bear responsibility for the Jewishness of Jesus resembles Marquardt's call to take responsibility for Jesus as committed to Torah – against a traditional depiction of Jesus whose most prominent feature is his stand against the law. Marquardt had found that more than any other version, it was the antinomian Jesus who had been exported to non-Christian cultures.[11] Similarly to Driedger Hesslein, but with more concrete content, Marquardt saw Christians as responsible for their understanding of Jesus the Jew. A Jesus who is first of all opposed to "the" law will sooner or later be translated into a Jesus who is presented as estranged from Torah. We see this exemplified in Paul Tillich's Christology that lies at the heart of his comprehensive Systematic Theology.[12] Tillich did not disregard Judaism theologically nor did he explicitly promote Christian superiority; on the contrary, late in his life he even engaged in dialogue surrounding world religions. But his apparent disregard of Jesus' Jewishness appears together with his presentation of an antinomian Jesus, a combination that clearly implies a theological inadequacy of religious law. This is why

---

[9] Driedger Hesslein, *Dual Citizenship*, 188.

[10] Emmanuel Levinas, *Otherwise than Being or Beyond Essence* (Pittsburgh: Duquesne University Press, 1998), 10.

[11] Marquardt, *Christologie I*, 92.

[12] Paul Tillich, *Systematic Theology: Three Volumes in One* (Chicago: University of Chicago Press, 1967).

Tillich's Christology offers a good example of the close connection between representations of Jesus' belonging and theological approaches to Torah. Described in existentialist terms that are characteristic for Tillich, Jesus as the Christ presents the "New Being," a term unique to this theology, that enables "essential being" under the otherwise estranging conditions of existence. "The New Being is new in so far as it is the undistorted manifestation of essential being within and under the conditions of existence," Tillich writes. "It is new in two respects: it is new in contrast to the mere potential character of essential being; and it is new over against the estranged character of existential being."[13] Tillich then proceeds to describe "the same idea" in more biblical terms:

The New Being is new in so far as it is the conquest of the situation under the law – which is the old situation. The law is man's essential being standing against his existence, commanding and judging it. In so far as his essential being is taken into his existence and actualized in it, the law has ceased to be law for him. Where there is New Being, there is no commandment and no judgment. If, therefore we call Jesus as the Christ the New Being, we say with Paul that Christ is the end of the law.[14]

Contra Tillich, taking responsibility for the Jew Jesus as Other means to see Jesus as committed to Torah rather than assimilating him to antinomian fashion. Driedger Hesslein does exactly this in her naming of the Jewish Jesus as the particular Other for whom Christians must take responsibility, a path-breaking Christological reception of Levinasian philosophy. It is especially illuminating as Hesslein's main intellectual effort is directed at mediating between contemporary contextual Christologies that often subordinate Jesus' Jewishness to his humanity, on the one hand, and declared non-supersessionist Christologies that typically emphasize Jesus' Jewishness, on the other. In the midst of this very difficult mediation, the Levinasian philosophy of an ethics of otherness proves helpful.

Clearly, naming the Jewish Jesus as *the* Other for all contemporary Christian followers of Jesus from whatever contexts challenges our current discourse on otherness. While any difference and identity marker of a marginalized group or minority deserves respect, Levinas did not foster a concept of groups promoting themselves as Others – in regard to their minority status, marginalization, or disadvantages. On the contrary, with

---

[13] Tillich, *Systematic Theology*, Vol. II, *Existence and the Christ* (Chicago: University of Chicago Press, 1957), 119.
[14] Tillich, *Existence and the Christ*, 119.

Levinas the Other is always the Other! While explicitly respecting variable particularities expressed in various contextual Christologies, Driedger Hesslein maintains the Jew Jesus as a non-exchangeable Other for whom all Christians are responsible.

Karl Barth's theology of God as the Other emphasized "vertical" revelation over such "horizontal" dimensions as nature and culture. His epistemology was clearly unidirectional: God has spoken to humankind. The highlighted sovereignty of God functioned as a Christian self-critique, preventing and resisting the domestication of God or the identifying of divinity with history in general or with the Zeitgeist in particular. Continuing the Barthian theological tradition, the radical otherness of God leads to a critical understanding not just of God but also of humanity's proceedings. As radical Other, not identified with any force of nature or history, God can be seen as standing over or even criticizing history.[15] The idea of God as critiquing human history offers an alternative to the helpless repetitions of theodicy, both classically defending God or more temporarily declaring God as powerless or not in charge. How then does Jesus the Jew as the Other relate to God the radical Other? With Jesus Christ, otherness needs to be outlined differently. God, the radical Other as proclaimed in Barth's theology, is not a theological matter to be simply exported to Christology, nor can the otherness of Jesus Christ be simply described as an extension of God's radical otherness. In this regard, one of Marquardt's outstanding ideas about God and the Other expresses an interesting dynamic: God upholds the otherness of the Other.[16] This wording is close to the Levinasian notion of otherness as something that is not to be dissolved. In theological terms, Godself withstands dissolving otherness, according to Marquardt. One could interpret this idea Christologically as well: If God is the subject of the Christ story – as Paul van Buren claims[17] – then God upholds Christ's otherness. In this Christological interpretation, otherness is expressed within the dynamics of humanity trying to be close to Jesus and God pushing back against this assimilation. In this case, otherness with regard to Jesus Christ would be far from presenting a certain property or feature of his person. Rather,

---

[15] Dietrich Ritschl, who was also a student of Karl Barth, developed this idea. Dietrich Ritschl, "Praising God as Interpreter and Critic of History." In David S. Cunningham, Ralph Del Colle, and Lucas Lamadrid, eds., *Ecumenical Theology in Worship, Doctrine and Life: Essays Presented to Geoffrey Wainright on His Sixtieth Birthday* (Oxford: Oxford University Press, 1999), 69–77.
[16] Marquardt, *Eschatologie I*, 186.   [17] Paul van Buren, *Christ in Context*, xviii.

otherness would be an aspect of the God–Christ–Christians relationship, mainly reflecting a vivid dynamic of distancing and appropriating.

The otherness and Jewishness of Jesus are not to be generally considered identical, although they may at times interpret each other. There is a tendency in contemporary philosophical discourse to reduce otherness to Jewishness and idealize Jewishness as inherent otherness. But otherness, in the Levinasian sense, cannot be defined as a certain identity – in Levinasian language that would be turning a "saying" into a "said," determining and thus neutralizing the otherwise vivid and inventive model. The relationship between Jewishness and otherness is typically assumed and seldom critically analyzed. Does this synthesis primarily work within Jewish diaspora thought? Boyarin's straightforward identification of Jewishness with difference – he abstains from using the wording "otherness," it should be noted – might very well point that way. In Levinas's philosophy, otherness is not simply a value, and it is not suggested as an ideal. In an adaptation of Levinasian language, not only vocabulary but also grammar need to be considered. Driedger Hesslein's impressive articulation of Christians' responsibility for Jesus as the Jew and thus their primary Other is illuminating in this regard. Could it serve as a model as well for the formulation of otherness within Jesus Christ? Historically, the church fathers were strongly concerned about anchoring Jesus' full humanity within the Christian creed. One could say that they took responsibility for the Son's true humanity as an otherness of the divine.

Otherness and Jewishness may be seen as interpreting each other with regard to Jesus Christ but this mutual interpretation is no simple matter. The interconnection between Jewishness and otherness belongs to a Christology of Gentiles only – but then, Gentiles are the ones in need of Christology. The early Jewish followers of the Jew Jesus did not need theoretical deliberations about their fellowship. Later non-Jewish followers of Jesus Christ practice the formulation of their belonging as an act of belief and commitment. Marquardt's key sentence about the dynamics of contemporary Jewish–Christian relations may be helpful here. Without dissolving the tension between the Christian urge to reestablish closeness and the Jewish preference for disentanglement, he states that after 2,000 years of ignorance, Christians have a duty to reconnect, while Jews own the right to distance.[18] This idea of disparate but complementary

---

[18] Marquardt, *Eschatologie II*, 164.

dynamics of closeness may be read together with the statement of Marquardt about God as protector of otherness.[19] Combining the notion of appropriately differing urges for distance in a relationship and God's siding with otherness, I would venture this interpretation of the 451 Council of Chalcedon with its famous confirmation that Jesus Christ is "like us" regarding his human nature. Christians are meant to identify with Jesus, as he is proclaimed and confessed to be "like us." But God sides with the otherness of Christ and continues to protect him from our efforts to domesticate him. In this dynamic, otherness needs God's protection but also protects the vitality of Jesus Christ. The human urge to approach Jesus – in devout fellowship as well as in historical scholarship – is appropriate for the Christian. Looking for Jesus in history and coveting his closeness in the present are Christian intellectual and spiritual practices. That Jesus Christ will not be defined (Mark 8,29 ≈ Matthew 16,15: "Who do you say I am?"), however, is an expression of God opting for Christ's ongoing otherness. In this interpretation, otherness can function as a Christological category, sustaining the uniqueness of Jesus Christ in accordance with the early Christian creed.

Dissolving Jesus' Jewishness leads to Marcionism, and dissolving his otherness as both human and divine leads to either Docetism or Arianism. Thus otherness is an important notion for both natures of Jesus Christ. As Driedger Hesslein has formulated it, for Christians, the Jew Jesus is the concrete Other. One may state further that Christians are responsible for the Jewish humanity of Jesus. Historically, the Church Fathers took responsibility for Jesus' humanity and anchored it in dogma. The otherness of his divine nature is in communication with God's radical otherness. Otherness is thus prone to serve as a Christological category in correspondence with a theology of God as radical Other.

Neither the word "Other" nor the concept "otherness" belong to the immediate vocabulary of the Church Fathers. But early Christian intellectual discourse was all about developing wordings of difference and closeness, togetherness and particularity, uniqueness and unity. In fact, the dispute that led to the first articulation of the Christian faith in Nicaea was characterized by the need for precision in the language of similarity and difference. The Greek term "homo-ousios," translated as "the same regarding the essence," exemplifies the attempt to express maximal

---

[19] Marquardt, *Eschatologie I*, 191.

proximity while avoiding identification. "Homo-ousia" was an entirely new wording with no biblical base, but it served the intellectual theological effort of avoiding idolatry.

Karl Barth's introducing God as the radical Other was similarly motivated by the need to safeguard God's sovereignty over domestication. One might make the distinction that while "homo-ousia" protected primarily Christ's humanity, radical otherness was meant to shield God's unambiguous divinity. In both cases, language is stretched and expanded to prevent idolatry. While "otherness" is not an original or even early Christological term, a case can be made for the concept as appropriate to and much-needed for the twenty-first-century precision of Gentile Christian belonging and commitment to Jesus Christ, the Jew.

AFTER THE "END OF THE LAW": THE *TELOS* OF TORAH

Jesus the Jew is contemporary Christians' Other mainly in the sense of his Jewish life. His being Jewish is expressed by a certain perception of time and belonging, by structuring the year according to the major feasts and pilgrimages to Jerusalem, by discussing, performing, and interpreting commandments, by knowing and studying the texts of the Pentateuch and the Prophets. All together this can be called a Torah-bound life. Christians today do not share this life of Torah, they do not share its rhythm of the year, the month, or the week, they do not practice discussion of religious laws, and they generally regard study as a secondary religious practice. Still, today's Christians are not disconnected from Torah. They know of Jesus' bond with Torah and they consider the written Torah as a part of their own holy book. Christians live with the traits of a Torah-bound life; certain texts and certain laws, such as the Ten Commandments, are central to the Christian faith. The promises of God's covenantal care as expressed in the covenant of Noah and Abraham represent core stories of the Christian heritage. Most of all, Christians know that the Torah is from God; this they know from Paul.

It has often been stated that Paul did not exhibit any deep interest in Jesus' biography. But the almost theological statement that Paul did not care about Jesus' actual life is anachronistic in itself. The stories told of Jesus' life were most probably vividly remembered when he wrote his epistles (in the middle of the first century, CE), while their incorporation into the new literary form of gospels would take another generation. Paul, who may be called the first theologian of what will emerge as

Christianity, was definitely the first "Christologian" – he was asking about the meaning of Jesus' story as a whole.[20] His grappling with the events of Jesus' life and death as part of God's story with Israel became the foundation of later Christian theological thought. This is why Pauline exegesis always played a constitutive role for Christian theology. Certainly, the thought systems built in later systematic theology went far beyond Pauline ideas. But, remarkably, Paul has maintained his authority throughout the Christian centuries. Moreover, since the second half of the twentieth century, the developing critique of Christian supersessionist thought traditions has been mainly argued through a re-reading of Paul – both in Catholic and in Protestant Christianity. For example, supersessionism, the idea that Christianity had superseded Judaism, had been inferred by some Church Fathers from certain readings of New Testament texts, and even more so by contrasting Old and New Testament in terms of an imputed obsolete versus a vital faith.[21] But those who sought to repudiate supersessionism were able to quote no less an authority than Paul, who explicitly insisted that the gifts of God are irrevocable (Romans 11,28), and among the "gifts" to the people Israel are the covenant, the calling, prophecy, and Torah (Romans 9, 1–4).

Most twentieth-century ecclesial documents revoking supersessionism – both in the Catholic and Protestant churches – employ mainly the language of "covenant." This is interesting, as "covenant" – other than in the Calvinist, Reformed thought tradition – had not previously been a central theological category in Christian thought. Although covenantal language used to be uncommon, it has proved to be a helpful biblical concept for expressing interreligious affirmation. The transformation of covenant-talk reflects the various stages of twentieth-century Jewish–Christian dialogue, starting initially with the critiquing of the new–old binary by means of suggesting the existence of a single covenant as a theological category encompassing both Christianity and Judaism, to the more recent emphasis on the unilateral Christian affirmation of Israel, the Jewish People's ongoing covenant with the one God.

---

[20] Corinthians 2:2 can serve as a "prooftext" here (not in the sense of proving my argument as the correct interpretation but as a reading engaging with Paul's thinking), where Paul says, "for I determined not to know anything but Jesus Christ and Christ crucified." Paul does not speak of knowing only "Christ crucified" but both, "Jesus Christ and Christ crucified."

[21] Soulen Kendall, *The God of Israel and Christian Theology* (Minneapolis: Augsburg Fortress, 1996).

At the same time, this profound change in Pauline studies has not yet led to a similar revision of Torah-theology. Here, the effort at redefinition may be more complicated, as the subordination of law under faith has been manifest in further theological conceptions. Protestant theology faces more challenges in this regard than the Catholic tradition, since the Reformation-based doctrine of justification indeed maintains the "secondary-ness" of law and even "works." The critical memory of the Jewish Jesus can be helpful to highlight and face these challenges. What does the Jewish Jesus have to do with the doctrine of justification? Today, Lutherans, both in Europe and the United States, are committed to a general revision of Lutheran misreadings of Jewish tradition and have forcefully repudiated the anti-Semitic writings of Luther. At the same time, the doctrine of justification has not ordinarily been among the concepts viewed as in need of revision.[22] At first sight, this Reformation hypothesis informs Christians of their primary path in relation to God – which is faith. That justification occurs by faith alone is the affirmative content of the concept. However, the rub is that the solely positive wording is not comprehensible in itself and, at second sight, lacks a self-explanatory capacity. "Justification by faith alone" – this acclamation needs a contrasting statement to make sense. In the Reformation account of the Augsburg Confession (1530), as well as the Pauline text used to support it (Romans 3:28: "a man is justified by faith without the deeds of the law"), faith is contrasted to the works of the law. A binary concept of law and gospel has been constitutive for Lutheran hermeneutics of the Bible and the God–Human relationship.[23] Law, in this view, is presented as a divine demand that humans lack the capacity adequately to fulfill. Accordingly, law, as a directive of works and deeds, cannot be efficacious as the means to winning God's approval.

The consequences and implications of this doctrine are considerable. It treats any directive of human practice as secondary for God–Human relations (secondary, at best – in fact, the binary concept of law and gospel tends to lend a slightly negative connotation to the function of law for the believer). This is most apparent in the Lutheran tradition

---

[22] In contrast, in many systematic theologies as well as theories of homiletics and didactics, the doctrine of justification has seemingly taken on a life of its own. For a critique of isolated doctrinal statements, see Dietrich Ritschl, *The Logic of Theology*, 79–82.

[23] For a critique, see Barbara U. Meyer, "Mose – Their Rabbi or Our Rabbi? Lutheran Hermeneutics Re-Visited." (Hebrew) In Moshe Hallamish, Hanoch Ben-Pazi, and Hannah Kasher, eds., *Moses the Man – Master of the Prophets* (Ramat Gan: Bar Ilan University Press, 2010), 320–329.

where reliance on "works of the law" is seen as potentially leading a person to misapprehend the sole efficacy of grace, which is on the contrary depicted as the correct and only way to and with God.

The understanding of law inherent in the doctrine of justification entails two major problems, one intra-Christian, the other interreligious. As for the Christian conceptualization, one might ask, what is the problem with favoring belief over everything else? Why does making law secondary prove deeply problematic? Marquardt came to the conclusion that a motivated approach to good works and deeds requires a relationship with law.[24] Independently, the American New Testament scholar Lloyd Gaston reached similar conclusions. He sees justification as a language rather than a doctrine.[25] Gaston was one of the first New Testament scholars to point out Christian hostility toward law as a major structural problem of Christian thought.[26] He qualified this hostility as a leftover of the heresy of Marcionism with its call to separate Jesus from Israel's Scriptures and Israel's God. In Gaston's striking historical analysis, the church's successful refutation of Marcion eventually went together with a sliding adaptation to Marcionite hermeneutics. The canon now consisted of both the Hebrew Bible and the Apostolic Writings, called by Christians the "Old" and "New" Testaments.[27] Gaston claims that the decision against Marcion did not halt a neo-Marcionite hermeneutics of the canon, and he even seems to suggest that a general Marcionite perspective of antithesis "compensated" for the refutation of Marcion.[28] Gaston shows how this view of New Testament superiority over Old Testament text and content was extended to a very specific (mis)reading of the Gospels and Paul. We should note that Gaston's critique of the "antitheses" as a general approach was originally voiced by the strongest opponent of Marcion among the Latin Fathers, Tertullian (c.155– c.240 CE): "For it is certain that the whole aim at which he has strenuously labored even in the drawing up of his Antitheses centres in

[24] Marquardt, *Eschatologie I*, 241.
[25] See Lloyd Gaston, *Paul and the Torah* (Eugene, OR: Wipf and Stock, 1987).
[26] See especially his article "Legicide," at www.jcrelations.net/Legicide.2192.0.html?id= 720&L=3&searchText=Gaston&searchFilter=%2A.
[27] Lloyd Gaston, like other Christian theologians committing to renewed Jewish–Christian relations, saw the terms "old" and "new" as implying the superiority of the latter and preferred alternatives terms like "Hebrew Scriptures" and "Apostolic Writings." The search for a language that would explicitly withstand supersessionist understandings was characteristic for this group of Christian scholars in the 1980s.
[28] According to Tertullian, "Antitheses" was the title of Marcion's main writing, describing also his approach of juxtaposing Gospel and Torah in one word.

this, that he may establish a diversity between the Old and the New Testaments, so that his own Christ may be separate from the Creator, as belonging to this rival god, *and* as alien from the law and the prophets."[29]

Most interestingly, Gaston sees this theology of displacement as focusing on law, which leads him to use the striking term "Legicide." The term sounds dramatic, but the claim can be well supported with statements of Rudolf Bultmann, prominent scholar of New Testament and Gnosis studies of the mid-twentieth century. Bultmann reads Paul's preference of a "righteousness by faith" over a "righteousness of law"[30] as an indictment of both Judaism and the law: "... Judaism is vanquished and the law is disqualified as the means of winning acceptance in God's sight by one's own achievements."[31] Two components are important here: Judaism with law, or with a positive, optimistic attitude to law that is declared to be Jewish. In this sense, Gaston's use of the term legicide to describe extreme Protestant interpretations of Paul as fully negating the Jewish path to God through fulfillment of the law is not exaggerated; it is rather an indictment of a longstanding Protestant misinterpretation.

Indeed, Bultmann's method, to seek information about Judaism from a juxtaposition attributed to Paul, was criticized by James Parkes as early as 1936: "the Church worked from his [Paul's] conception of Law to that conception of the Jewish people which originally created anti-Semitism."[32] But in the post-war period, E. P. Sanders became the most influential New Testament scholar to break up the exegetical supersessionism of Christ substituting for "law." Perhaps Sanders remarkable long-term success – today leading exegetes agree with his position that was still regarded as far-fetched at best in the 1980s – has to do with the openness he attributes to Paul. Rather than juxtapose an unambiguously positive account of Paul's view of the law with the traditional supersessionist interpretation of the Apostle, Sanders acknowledges that for Paul the Torah–Christ relationship was difficult to describe: "He knew

---

[29] Tertullian, *Ante Nizene Fathers*, Vol. III. Quoted in Adolf von Harnack, *Marcion: The Gospel of the Alien God* (Eugene, OR: Wipf and Stock, 2007), 151, n. 4.

[30] "... not having my own righteousness, which is of the law, but that which is through the faith of Christ, the righteousness which is of God by faith" (Phil. 3.7–9).

[31] Rudolf Bultmann, "Christ the End of the Law." In Bultmann, *Essays: Philosophical and Theological* (New York: Macmillan, 1955), 36–66, 60.

[32] James Parkes, *Jesus, Paul and the Jews* (London: Student Christian Movement Press, 1936). Parkes was an Anglican theologian and a pioneer in the study of Christian antisemitism.

that righteousness is only by faith in Christ, but he still tried repeatedly to find a place for the law in God's plan."[33]

The modern Jewish approach of embracing Jesus and keeping a distance from Paul, whose classic expression was the work of the Zionist literary scholar Joseph Klausner, finds a certain echo in contemporary Israeli scholarship.[34] In Israeli academic discourse that crosses disciplines of legal, Jewish, and historical studies, Paul is still basically the "old" Paul. The otherwise widely acknowledged "new perspectives" on Paul are typically ignored or dismissed as momentary "political correctness." This is not, however, to deny the fascinating research being conducted by Ishay Rosen-Zvi, who offers an illuminating and innovative method of looking at the interreligious exchange of concepts and ideas.[35] He describes his method of intertextual study as searching for "problematization": Rather than relying only on explicit quotes, he sees the Rabbis' reinforcements of certain Jewish concepts as an indication that these ideas were taken into consideration. This, as Rosen-Zvi claims, is precisely what happened with regard to Paul's most polemical writings when he characterized the works of the law as under a curse (Galatians 3,10). Rosen-Zvi sees these polemical writings as reflected in early rabbinic literature in the very reassurances the rabbis provide there of the life-giving capacities of commandments.[36]

Yet, however intriguing this hypothesis, it remains the case that Rosen-Zvi shares the disregard for the new perspectives in Pauline studies that he sees as an expression of "post-Holocaust" sensitivities. He disagrees that anti-legalism begins with Luther, and refers post-supersessionist Christian exegetes back to Paul himself, whose innovative thinking he finds to be underestimated by them.[37] The intertextual method of "problematization" appears to me to be a very sophisticated way to track the communication of ideas and needs to be taken seriously. Still, I do not think that a rabbinic reaction to a Pauline theme is sufficient to determine that Paul's polemics in Galatians should be taken as representative of Paul's theology as a whole. Taking Rosen-Zvi's findings seriously means assuming that there was an early rabbinic reaction to Paul's most negative views of Torah. It makes

---

[33] E.P. Sanders, *Paul, the Law, and the Jewish People* (Philadelphia: Fortress Press, 1983), 199.

[34] Joseph Klausner, *Jesus of Nazareth: His Life, Times and Teaching* (London: Allen and Unwin, 1925); Joseph Klausner, *From Jesus to Paul* (New York: Macmillan, 1943).

[35] Ishay Rosen-Zvi, "Pauline Traditions and the Rabbis: Three Case Studies." *Harvard Theological Review* 110:2 (2017): 169–194.

[36] Ibid., 182.   [37] Ibid., 177.

sense that extreme ideas, such as the works of the law being under a curse, would have led to critical reactions. But even if correct this finding would not provide a hermeneutics for the study of the letter to the Romans, where law is discussed in an entirely different tone. My thesis is that Paul's polemics in Galatians against the law caused questions that led him to treat the subject very differently in Romans, the non-polemical letter he wrote later. Thus, I do not think that "new-perspective" Paul-scholars are proven wrong in their critique of Protestant anti-Jewish hermeneutics.

The disconnect between contemporary Jewish and Christian readings of Paul is nevertheless fascinating. It is also perplexing, given that the pioneers of revised Pauline exegesis, E. P. Sanders and Lloyd Gaston, originally developed their new perspective through their studies at the Hebrew University. Others working in the same direction, such as Krister Stendahl and Peter van der Osten-Sacken, gained new exegetical insight through academic Jewish–Christian dialogue and cooperation. All these New Testament scholars developed fresh understandings of Paul that called into question traditional assumptions about his anti-Judaism. Decades later, these pioneering views have become the leading voices in New Testament scholarship, especially in English-speaking academia. In his 2002 book, *Reinventing Paul*, the respected historian of late antiquity John Gager presented an overview and a largely positive evaluation of this emerging new approach.[38] His well-structured presentation of the main exegetes focuses on historical and not on moral arguments, explaining how much of the anti-Jewish reading of Paul is actually anachronistic, since Judaism and Christianity did not yet exist as opposite viewpoints.

While for the most part, the new Pauline exegesis has yet to be translated into the conceptual language of systematic theology, Paul van Buren represents a remarkable exception. Different from theologians overly identifying with Paul's alleged positions, van Buren adopts a more detached stance. Paul, in his view, should have only the first word. The last word, according to van Buren, is what describes contemporary Christians' responsibility.[39] He almost certainly learned this textual approach from his Jewish colleagues at the Hartman Institute, the Modern Orthodox Bet Midrash in Jerusalem, where he studied in the eighties.

[38] Gager shows how most of the "old" view was actually based on anachronism, projecting onto Paul "Christian" views in criticism of "Judaism" – but Christianity did not yet exist. John Gager, *Reinventing Paul* (Oxford: Oxford University Press, 2002).
[39] Van Buren, *A Theology of the People Israel*, 283.

Interpretational freedom is a traditional Jewish approach, strongly emphasized by Modern Orthodox thinkers. Interestingly, when it comes to Paul, the suggestion here is often to read the text "as is." This creates an ironic situation: The "old" Paul has been criticized by Christian scholars as an anti-Jewish projection of Protestant tradition, while their "new" Paul, who knows of the Jewish people as loved by God, is typically viewed by Israeli scholars as a projection of political correctness. So, does the contemporary Israeli reading of Paul represent freedom from "political correctness" that a Christian exegete cannot possibly adopt, or is it a mere repetition of old Protestant views based on initial anachronism that pictured Paul as a severe critic of Judaism?

One way to answer this question might be to translate "nomos" back to "Torah" and see how this re-translation makes sense with regard to the "historical Paul," another Jew of the Second Temple period.

Far from the almost stereotypical reiteration of Paul's disinterest in Jesus' real life, we come to the conclusion – as I shall now argue – that Jesus' Jewish life actually serves as a cornerstone of Pauline Christology. It is precisely Jesus' halakhically oriented life, his life rooted in Torah, that is called "nomos" in theological summary and reflection. As discussed earlier, Halakhah and Torah are not identical in the Second Temple period, in rabbinic times, or even today. But there clearly are several threads connecting halakhic discussion and Torah interpretation from the first through the twenty-first centuries. For Jesus' generation as for observant Jews today, halakhah structures daily life, the week and the year, and it includes reflection and discussion over the right deed in a specific situation. A life rooted in Torah meant in the past as it means today a life shaped by the memories embedded and reflected in the Tanakh (Torah, Prophets, and Writings) as well as in the ongoing rabbinic corpus that authoritatively interprets them.

Translating the Greek word "nomos" back to Torah, it comprises all of this: the texts called Torah in the broader sense (Pentateuch and books of the Prophets and Writings), in the liturgical sense (Pentateuch and numerous other works of Prophets and Writings, like Lamentations and Psalms), the written as well as the oral Torah (Mishnah, Midrash, Talmudim, etc.), and thus all the biblical texts and their interpretations. Torah includes narrative and jurisprudence and the interconnection of both in memory. For example, both the commandment to keep Shabbat holy (Deuteronomy 5:14) and the commandment to love the stranger (Leviticus 19:34) are supported with reference to the Exodus narrative ("because you were slaves/foreigners in the Land of Egypt"). Of course, historically, living according to the Torah means different things in different epochs of Jewish history, and interpretations are continuously added. But certain texts, memories, and commandments have not been subtracted from Torah from the first compositions of these early, multi-layered texts until the present. Among them are the categories that Paul lists as unrevoked and in fact irrevocable, such as sonship, the covenants, and the giving of the law (Romans 9,4). Torah thus comprises the narrative, the promise, the practice, and the memory of the God–Israel relationship with all its legal components.

Torah life means all of this: the text together with its various readings, as well as the sense of belonging to that text as a reader connected to the many generations that had been engaged in its transmission; as well as the stories and their interpretations, the legal texts, and their reasoning. Paul explicitly indicates his commitment to this generationally transmitted Torah reception. His belonging to the interpreting chain of generations is expressed in terms of Torah; "... circumcised on the 8th day, of the nation of Israel, of the tribe of Benjamin." This autobiographical positioning shows that Paul thinks within Torah-fellowship, out of a Torah-bound identity. True, he may open the borders of the Torah community up for discussion. And his theological thinking may not focus on Torah, but on Jesus Christ. But it still makes an immense difference that even the question of the relevance of Torah is not at all discussed from a neutral, outsider position. I would describe this as the central meaning of Paul *being* Jewish – not a certain attitude toward Halakhah but rather a basic self-understanding of being part of the chain of generations living in the light of Torah and transmitting it.

The question of whether Paul was transgressing the borders of "Judaism" has been described as anachronistic; historically, we need to maintain that anything that Jesus and Paul say is said within the "borders" of Judaism, while the concept of a "border" is in itself not the most helpful construct. This is why, in discussing the Judaism of the historical Jesus, I have preferred to look at the contemporaneous Jewish texts as a "frame of reference." As in the case of the historical Jesus, not every saying of Paul may have been representative of mainstream or majority vote – but then, one main characteristic of the emerging rabbinic tradition would be an astonishing respect for minority opinion, reflected in the practice of quoting and thus transmitting them alongside the majority view. As stated in BT Eruvin 13b: *elu ve-elu divre elohim ha'im* (these two conflicting statements are equally the words of the living God). Until the canonization of the Mishnah (about 150 years after Paul's writing of his epistles), what would be agreed and what will be in future quoted as minority opinion remained open.

Paul's *nomos*, when identified as Torah, can be described as a theological signifier of the ongoing relationship between the Jewish People and God. The twofold change in Pauline exegesis consists of both identifying *nomos* as Torah and recognizing Torah as one of the irrevocable gifts of God. The combination of these two interpretational insights enables an entirely new perspective on the Torah–Christ connection. Clearly, Paul's explicit theological qualifications of the *nomos* in the Epistle to the Romans 7:12, "the law is holy and the commandment holy, righteous and good," and 3:31, "do we then make void the law through faith? Yeah, God forbid, we establish the law!," have been key to new attempts to understand the ongoing significance of *nomos* for Christians.[40] These verses outweigh Paul's sometimes polemical stand on law (as in the letter to the Galatians), for the simple historical reason that Paul wrote them later than his polemics, and for the theological reason that they fit with his understanding of God who is faithful and does not take back promises, gifts, and blessings. Far from not being interested in Jesus' life, as Paul was typically described by scholars until the twentieth century, Jesus' life as structured and shaped by the narratives, the rhythms, rites of passage, and obligations compiled in the concept of "Torah" was actually constitutive of Paul's theological thinking.

As pointed out by E. P. Sanders, for Paul, Jesus Christ and Torah did not exclude each other but belonged together. The precise formulation of this belonging, however, remains an open theological task. The Vatican's profound affirmation of *Nostra Aetate* in 2015, "The Gifts and the Calling of God Are Irrevocable," also offers a new interpretation of the Torah–Christ relation: "Christians affirm that Jesus Christ can be considered as 'the living Torah of God'. Torah and Christ are the Word of God, his revelation for us human beings as his testimony of his boundless love."[41] This theological statement is very impressive. It follows a detailed

---

[40] See Barbara U. Meyer, "Welches Gesetz ist heilig, gerecht und gut und für wen? Christliche Umkehr zum Gesetz." In Andreas Pangritz, ed., *Biblische Radikalitäten: Judentum, Sozialismus und Recht in der Theologie Friedrich-Wilhelm Marquardts* (Würzburg: Ergon Verlag, 2010), 129–140.

[41] Philipp Cunningham, "The Sources Behind 'The Gifts and the Calling of God Are Irrevocable' (Rom 11:29): A Reflection on Theological Questions Pertaining to Catholic-Jewish Relations on the Occasion of the 50th Anniversary of *Nostra Aetate*," (No4), Commission of the Holy See for Religious Relations with the Jews, December 10, 2015, in: *SCJR* 12:1 (2017): 1–19, 19 (paragraph 26 of the document).

description of Jewish understandings of Torah as the Word of God and Christian theologies of Christ as the Word of God. The paralleling of Torah and Christ (parallel and moving in the same direction, but not identical) would in itself have addressed the needs of the post-supersessionist approach as well as of comparative theology. But the instruction to consider Jesus Christ as "the living Torah of God" marks an entirely new stage of what I would describe as interreligious thinking. The encounter in theological language connects Judaism and Christianity by affirming the validity of Judaism's difference as well as belonging to the same God. It is astonishing to find this kind of creative Christological thought in a Church document – but perhaps *Nostra Aetate* inspired Catholic theologians to continue the search for Christian language affirming God's love of Israel, or as Cardinal Bea put it, "to follow Christ in his love for this people."[42]

Torah is intrinsic to Christ. There is no Christ without Torah, which means that it does not make any sense to counter-position Torah and Christ in systematic theology. Torah was the form as well as the content of the connection between the historical Jesus and the God of Israel, comprising a set of narratives, memories, and reflections on these memories, rituals, commandments, and their discussion. Torah is the comprehensive name of the texts and legal traditions shaping Jesus' life and his perspective on God and Israel. What, then, happened to the Torah–Christ connection with the parting of the ways?[43] Torah observers would no more see themselves as potential followers of Christ, while the followers of Christ would not recognize a relationship to Torah. The Torah changed, developed legally, intensified philosophically, and increased textually. The term would now comprise the written Torah (the biblical books) and the oral Torah (the Mishnah and its voluminous discussions, the Talmud). Christians would seldom use the term, but they maintained a strong relationship to the written Torah under the name "Old Testament."

Between the Historical Jesus and the parting of the ways (whether dated in the third or the fourth century) stood Paul. His rootedness in and reflections about Torah lay the groundwork for what I call

---

[42] Cf. Augustin Bea, *Die Kirche und das jüdische Volk* (Freiburg: Herder Verlag, 1966), 146.

[43] For more recent research on the question of dating the separation of Judaism and Christianity, see Adam H. Becker and Annette Yoshiko Reed, eds., *The Ways That Never Parted: Jews and Christians in Late Antiquity and the Early Middle Ages* (Minneapolis: Fortress Press, 2007).

"Interreligious Christology" – Christological reasoning that acknowledges the Other's different way with God while also opening up to the
idea of re-connecting.

JESUS, THE JEW, AND ISLAM

A most remarkable Muslim statement about Jesus the Jew was published
in 2007 by the Jordan Royal Institute for Islamic Thought in a document
authored by the Jordanian Prince Ghazi bin Muhammad and launched as
a letter to Church leaders.[44] The document is entitled "A Common
Word," quoting a Koranic verse about the interconnectedness of the three
book religions: "O People of the Scripture! Come to a common word
between us and you: that we shall worship none but God, and that we
shall ascribe no partner unto Him, and that none of us shall take others
for lords beside God." (Aal Imran 3:64) The document's stated aim is to
enhance Christian–Muslim understanding, and it bears the signature
of numerous Muslim scholars. In the years following the declaration,
"A Common Word" has received a great deal of attention, provoking
Christian responses and Muslim endorsements, although Jewish commentaries remained scarce. In line with addresser and addressee, theological
feedback has tended to focus on matters of Christian–Muslim relations,
whereas the unusual portrait of Jesus in this Muslim text has been widely
overlooked.

Thematically, the text of "A Common Word" is structured according
to two commonalities between Islam and Christianity, the love for God
and love of the neighbor, exploring both themes in both scriptural traditions. The central quote from the New Testament is Mark 12:28–31:
"Hear, O Israel, the Lord our God, the Lord is One. And you shall love
the Lord your God with all your heart, with all your soul, with all your
mind, and with all your strength. This is the first commandment. And the
second, like it, is this: you shall love your neighbour as yourself. There is
no other commandment greater than that." The use in a Muslim text of
these New Testament verses to represent Jesus is remarkable, especially in
synoptic comparison. According to the Gospel of Matthew, Jesus gives
the same answer to the question about the greatest commandment,
though there he omits the verse, "Hear, O Israel the Lord our God, the

---

[44] "A Common Word between Us and You." *Sophia: The Journal of Traditional Studies*
14:2 (2008/9): 16–38. Endorsements of and reactions to the document can be found at
the website https://www.acommonword.com.

Lord is One."[45] This verse, quoted in Mark 12:28 as based on Deuteronomy 6:4, goes to the very heart of Jewish liturgy. The decision of the Muslim authors to quote Jesus' approach to the love of God according to Mark and thereby to include the *"Hear Israel"* is extraordinary. The Jesus presented in this contemporary Muslim document is the most outspokenly Jewish Jesus one could possibly find in a New Testament text! This is especially striking since Deuteronomy 6:4–9, colloquially referred to as the *"Shma,"* the Hebrew word meaning "Hear!," is the opening statement in one of the two central prayers in Judaism and is famous as the faith affirmation of rabbinic martyrs. Although Deuteronomy 6:4–9 as a biblical text is part of the Old Testament, Christians as well as Jews would most probably identify this text as particularly important to the Jewish tradition. The name "Israel" as addressee of the verse strongly underlines this reading.

The document "A Common Word," issued by the Royal Aal al-Bayt Institute for Islamic Thought, has been typically received as an expression of outreach on the part of moderate Islam, emphasizing what Islam and Christianity share in common. But reading the text as an effort to accentuate Islamic tolerance and Muslim–Christian scriptural convergence would be a superficial reading. The original intention of the authors may have been apologetic rather than critical, but there are very good reasons to read this document as a highly sophisticated text, one from which Christians can learn a great deal. The language of love that structures "A Common Word" actually displays a very different grammar from traditional Christian treatises on the subject. The love of God presented in "A Common Word" is not God's love of humans nor Christians' love for Jesus, but rather the Gospel's text presenting Jesus as calling on believers to love God. Dietrich Ritschl has emphasized this original, biblical call of Jesus to love God over a pious and Pietist tradition to love Jesus.[46] Since Augustine, especially in Western Christianity, the notion of love has been

---

[45] Matthew 22,36–40: "Love the Lord your God with all your heart and with all your soul and with all your mind. This is the first and greatest commandment. And the second is like it: Love your neighbor as yourself. All the Law and the Prophets hang on these two commandments." In synoptic reading, comparing the older version of Mark with the younger gospel of Matthew, this would be evaluated as an intentional omission. Presumably, the verse "Hear Israel" was too particular even for the redaction behind the Gospel of Matthew!

[46] Dietrich Ritschl, *The Logic of Theology*, 177.

dominated by the idea of the God who loves.[47] Love, in this case, has often been synonymous with forgiveness, and thus doctrinally connected to the need to be forgiven and juxtaposed to sin.

Jesus, quoting the Torah's directive to love God, uses the same term but speaks a language that today's Christians are less acquainted with. Presenting the Christian tradition with the commandment to love God as attributed to Jesus in the Gospel of Mark has notable theological implications. Quoting Jesus' call to love God implies the oneness of God in Islam and Christianity. The connecting thread though is clearly that of Judaism. Introducing the commandment to love God with "Hear, Israel" points unmistakably to the God of Israel. It is this God that Christians are to love – and it is the same one that Muslims refer to as God. With the rejection of Marcion, Christians made explicit that they pray to none other than the God of Israel, who also created heaven and earth. But this historical theological fact is usually not emphasized in Christian–Muslim dialogue.

Since the second half of the twentieth century, in numerous Church declarations, Christians have emphasized the fact of their praying to the same God as Jews. Rarely, however, was this reciprocated, the key exception being the outstanding Jewish affirmation of the Christian worship's addressee in the document from the year 2000, "Dabru Emet," with its famous opening statement "Jews and Christians worship the same God."[48] Here, the extraordinary Jewish affirmation of Christians belonging to the same God ironically underlines the fact that this is not a general assumption of most Jews today. At the same time, while Christians have recently strongly emphasized their belonging to the same God as Jews, conservative as well as liberal Christians remain hesitant to make such claims with regard to Muslims. What is remarkable then about "A Common Word" is that the identity of the one God of the peoples of the Scriptures is stated unequivocally. Quoting Mark 12:28 connects the identity of God "in common" to the God of Israel. Again, this may not

---

[47] Many Christian responses to "A Common Word" emphasized the Christian understanding of God as love. See especially Miroslav Wolf, "God Is Love: Biblical and Theological Reflections on a Foundational Christian Claim." In Miroslav Wolf, Ghazi bin Muhammad, and Melissa Yarrington, eds., *A Common Word: Muslims and Christians on Loving God and Neighbor* (Grand Rapids, MI: William B. Eerdmans, 2010), 125–142.

[48] Andrew S Jacobs, "A Jewish Statement on Christians and Christianity." In Tikva Frymer-Kensky, David Novak, Peter Ochs, David Fox Sandmel, and Michael A. Signer, eds., *Christianity in Jewish Terms* (Boulder, CO: Westview Press, 2000), xv–xviii.

have been the main intention of the authors. But it is certainly a strong interpretational option of "A Common Word" from the perspective of interreligious theology.

Theological statements on Christian–Muslim relations have been scarce compared to the rich body of Jewish–Christian dialogue in the twentieth century. The Second Vatican Council's *Nostra Aetate* statement on Islam is not well-known and had little apparent impact in comparison with the church's deeply invested declaration on Judaism. Still, the paragraph on Islam, with its core statement implying the identity of God in the three Abrahamic faiths, stands out as the most profound theological statement to date of a Christian church regarding Islam. "A Common Word" can be seen as a direct response to this fundamental affirmation of the oneness of God.

The 2015 Vatican interpretation on *Nostra Aetate* included an impressive portrait of Christ and Torah as the Word of God. The Vatican text also supports the paralleling of Christ and Torah with a famous text from the early rabbinic midrashic commentary *Bereshit Raba* that pictures the Torah as God's guidebook for creation. In the Vatican document, the notion of the Torah helping to structure creation is viewed in relation to the gospel notion of the preexistent Logos: "For Christians, the preexistence of Christ as the Word and Son of the Father is a fundamental doctrine, and according to rabbinical tradition the Torah and the name of the Messiah exist already before creation (cf. Genesis Rabbah 1,1)."[49] At first sight, the Vatican document just mentions two different ideas of extra-Godly preexistence. But linking together the preexistence of the Logos and the Torah can be understood as an effort to reach much further. As outlined with regard to Pauline exegesis, this "thinking together" of concepts goes far beyond mere comparison. The parallel reading underlines the notion that Torah is not just a text and not just law. In a move that I here call interreligious theological thinking, Christ is presented as an affirmation of the Torah. This encourages appreciation for the Torah among contemporary followers of Christ and certainly leaves no space for disrespect of Jewish religious law. One of the significant differences between the comparative and the interreligious theological method might be that the interreligious orientation is not limited to the discovery of parallels in thought patterns and does not call for reciprocity.

---

[49] Cunningham, "The Gifts and the Calling," 19 (paragraph 26).

Islamic thought developed a similar notion of the Koran as preexistent. In his in-depth study *Repercussions of the Kalam in Jewish Philosophy*, Harry Austryn Wolfson (1887–1974), a pioneer in interreligious scholarly research, described the dynamics between the concepts of preexistent "words" in a detailed manner.[50] He introduces his chapter on "the pre-existent Koran and the pre-existent Law" with the following conjecture: "When the Jews in Arabic-speaking countries learned of the Muslim belief in a pre-existent uncreated Koran called the Word of God and when from Christian literature they also learned of the Christian belief in a pre-existent Christ called also the Word of God, they must have reminded themselves of their own Word of God which was the Torah."[51] As Isidore Twersky points out, the term "repercussions" reflects a multi-faceted view of the history of ideas.[52] Instead of depicting an "influence" of one over the other, Wolfson discovers a set of complex dynamics. As he writes, "Beliefs and ideas are indeed contagious, and the history of beliefs and ideas is often a history of imitation by contagion. But for the contagiousness of a belief or an idea to take effect, there must be a predisposition and susceptibility on the part of those who are to be affected by it."[53]

Our reflection on the preexistent Koran, the Torah, and the Son may echo this respectful account of their historical interdependence. A synopsis of preexistent Words of God might help to develop a more appreciative approach to Islamic thought altogether. The debate about the createdness versus an uncreatedness of the Koran goes back to the ninth century and is usually depicted as reflecting a broader debate about the authority of the Koran. At times, this historical dispute is depicted in terms of Islam's shift toward fundamentalism, but surely that is a superficial reading. Rather, "interreligious recognition" might pose something along the following progression linking Jewish–Christian and Christian–Muslim relations: first, through reconsidering Paul's writings, Christians learn to recognize Torah as theologically valid; second, the study of midrashic literature depicting the Torah as the blueprint God studies to create the world underscores the notion of preexistence as a philosophical and imaginative rather than a fundamentalist concept; finally, when the

---

[50] Harry Austryn Wolfson, *Repercussions of the Kalam in Jewish Philosophy* (Cambridge, MA: Harvard University Press, 1979).

[51] Wolfson, *Repercussions of the Kalam in Jewish Philosophy*, 85.

[52] Isidore Twersky, Foreword to *Repercussions of the Kalam in Jewish Philosophy*, viii.

[53] Harry Austryn Wolfson, *The Philosophy of the Kalam* (Cambridge, MA: Harvard University Press, 1976), 70.

preexistence of the Logos and of the Torah in their respective and very different narrative settings are recognized as philosophy-based, the dispute about the uncreatedness of the Koran can be understood more as a philosophical notion than fundamentalist reversion.

Interreligious thought will never be independent of contemporaneous power relations. But "power" and "need" appear in highly variable forms. Christianity was in great need of repairing its basic traditions as well as its academic theology, both of which had been distorted by supersessionism. Christian theologians did not always know how to even begin their revisions and looked for guidance from Jewish philosophers and historians, rabbis, and scholars of rabbinical literature to help them re-read texts. In academic Jewish–Christian discourse, a dynamics of Christian listening and Jewish teaching was developed, similar to the undercurrents of Jewish–Christian interfaith dialogue. These dynamics were later questioned and Christian insecurity at times ridiculed, but they were nevertheless appropriate for the first decades of Christian self-critical scrutiny.

In stark contrast, Christians have rarely looked up to Islamic thought in the twentieth century. Islam has not held a position Christians asked to learn from. Even if Islam's critique of Christological thought might have been similar to the traditional Jewish view, the former was never respected as a valuable form of criticism.

"A Common Word" offers Christians the opportunity to reverse this legacy of condescension. Muslim scholars now remind Christians of the Jewish Jesus and even reconnect him to the Hebrew Bible. Both scriptural quotes, Mark 12:28 and Deuteronomy 6:4, are distinct signifiers of the God of Israel, who is identified in the early church creed as well as in the *Nostra Aetate* statement about Islam as the creator of heaven and earth. David Ford stands out among systematic theologians in his eagerness to address "A Common Word" within the framework of Christian theology proper, rather than simply as a specialized topic regarding relations with Muslims. Thus he incorporates his reflections on two contemporary interfaith documents – the Muslim declaration "A Common Word" and the Jewish statement "Dabru Emet" – as integral to his study on *The Future of Christian Theology*.[54] Here "Dabru Emet," the Jewish response to decades of Jewish–Christian discourse, along with the path-breaking Muslim initiative "A Common Word," are discussed in terms of the

[54] David F. Ford, *The Future of Christian Theology* (Malden, MA: Wiley-Blackwell, 2011).

spiritual enrichment of Christianity. Ford sees them as blessings to Christian theological thought. He develops the deliberately biblical concept of "blessing" as a "leading theological category for relating across differences."[55] "Interfaith-Blessing" thus becomes a central feature of contemporary – and future – Christian thought.

VULNERABILITY IN DOGMA AND HISTORY

The notion of vulnerability has always been central to Martha Nussbaum's impressive body of philosophical work. While "fragility" was the focus of her early work on Greek tragedy and philosophy,[56] more recently, the related concept of vulnerability lies at the core of her innovative understanding of emotions as intelligible forms of judgment.[57] One of her major insights is that fragility goes together with attachment, most of all the attachment to other people. Thus fragility lies at the opposite pole of the idea – or rather, the fiction – of self-sufficiency.[58] Vulnerability is intensified by relationships that involve trust.[59] Far from constituting an impediment, Nussbaum argues that "part of the peculiar beauty of *human* excellence just *is* its vulnerability."[60] Nussbaum originally derived her notions about fragility from Greek tragedy that exhibits a strong preference for control over one's fate and independence from others. I would like to apply her insights to Christianity and interpret the Jewish Jesus as the major signifier of Christian vulnerability rooted in its dogma and history.

Christianity's vulnerability is first of all manifest in its narrative not being independent from history. One may read the Historical Jesus research as an attempt to gain control over the attachment to Jesus in the face of historical doubt, most pointedly as in the case of Bultmann's short-lived claim that it does not even matter whether Jesus had actually lived at all. Historically, the first attempt to avoid vulnerability and attachment was Marcionism. Marcionism bore the promise of a new

---

[55] Ibid., 130.

[56] Martha Nussbaum, *The Fragility of Goodness: Luck and Ethics in Greek Tragedy and Philosophy*, second revised edition (Cambridge: Cambridge University Press, 2001).

[57] Martha Nussbaum, *Upheavals of Thought: The Intelligence of Emotions* (New York: Cambridge University Press, 2001), 136.

[58] Nussbaum, *The Fragility of Goodness*, 3.

[59] Martha Nussbaum, *Anger and Forgiveness: Resentment, Generosity, Justice* (New York: Oxford University Press, 2016), 94.

[60] Nussbaum, *The Fragility of Goodness*, 2.

religion that would be immune to previous revelations and other peoples' sacred histories – even the problematics of creation would not disturb its mindset since Marcionism suggested that the good God was not responsible for it. No theodicy questions disturbed the Marcionites! But Marcionism did not persevere – apparently an un-attached Christianity could not hold. The Christian story remained connected to the God of Israel and the story of Israel and thus to another text community, with tensions of interpretation over many of the texts held in common. This vulnerability was long rejected and thus turned into pure aggression – in the thought tradition of supersessionism and anti-Jewish exegesis.[61] Following the refutation of supersessionism and the churches' declared intent to jettison their invented but deeply internalized notion of superiority, Christianity now has a chance to retrieve this vulnerability that would match its particular and initial nature as a community of interpretation that is inherently interconnected. In her revised edition of the *Fragility of Goodness*, Nussbaum notes that vulnerability is not a value in itself.[62] Rather, it is the constituency of connected life, one might say, or "lived life." With regard to the Christian community, its connectedness makes it at the same time more alive and more vulnerable.

Caring about vulnerability describes the Church Fathers' strong commitment to Jesus' full humanity against concepts that would depict him as immune from injury, pain, and suffering. That he truly suffered was clearly a central matter that early Christians cared deeply about. It is almost as if "full humanity" was understood as the capacity for affliction. I would also interpret the Two-Natures model as expressed in the Chalcedonian Creed as part of a "vulnerable dogma," since there the interconnection between the two natures within the one person is expressed only in negative terms. Christ's divine and human natures are not consolidated by means of a positive definition. Building on this foundation, we can see how the notion of vulnerability might also be developed as a helpful framework for interreligious relations. For fragility is part of just being alive, and in this sense Christianity's vitality also increases with the fragility that comes with the risk of attachment.

---

[61] It is not my intention to explain the multifaceted, violent phenomenon of anti-Judaism in terms of the rejection of vulnerability. Rather, I am exploring the many dimensions of vulnerability while trying to avoid an idealization of the matter.

[62] On the contrary, extreme exposure can enhance physical injury; see Nussbaum, *Fragility of Goodness*, xxx.

As the description of an academic discipline, the term "Interreligious Theology" is relatively new. Self-evidently, interreligious theology engages in thinking that crosses the traditional borders of religion.[63] Other than that, however, no specific methodology has yet been developed to intellectually guide this kind of crossing of thought traditions. Nor has its relationship to such approaches as "pluralist theology" and "theology of religions" yet been clearly defined. In fact, in a recent volume, the term "Interreligious Theology" was connected to "religious pluralism," and several theologians identify with both concepts.[64] In German publications, Interreligious Theology seems to continue the sub-discipline of the theology of religions.[65] Whether the move to interreligious theology represents a fundamental change in method or just a shift in nuance is further complicated when one considers that Jewish scholars deploy the term very differently from Christian ones; so, for example, Ephraim Meir's most recent book also uses the title *Interreligious Theology* but it derives its intellectual outline from Emmanuel Levinas.[66]

At the same time, interreligious theology has not typically been employed by Christian theologians engaged in revising Jewish–Christian relations. There may, in fact, be good reasons for this. First of all, most theologians of Jewish–Christian reconciliation view the Jewish–Christian connection as a unique type of interreligious relationship.[67] This is well expressed in the title of Paul van Buren's *Theology of the Jewish-Christian Reality.* The unusual term "reality" here signifies that for the Christian side interconnectedness with Jews is not a matter of choice but a theological given. To deny it would be to engage in dangerous fantasy. This points to another characteristic of Christian theologies committed to the Jewish–Christian relationship. Whether Anglican, Lutheran, Methodist,

---

[63] Rosenzweig's philosophy could be described with this term. On his presentations of Judaism and Christianity, see Barbara U. Meyer, "Walking the Way of the Star: Paul van Buren," in Yehoyada Amir, Joseph Turner, and Martin Brasser, eds., *Faith, Truth and Reason: New Perspectives on Franz Rosenzweig's "Star of Redemption"* (Freiburg i. Br.: Karl Alber, 2012), 409–421.

[64] Perry Schmidt-Leukel, *Religious Pluralism and Interreligious Theology* (Maryknoll, NY: Orbis Books, 2017).

[65] Reinhold Bernhardt, Perry Schmidt-Leukel, eds., *Interreligiöse Theologie: Chancen und Probleme* (Zürich: TVZ, 2013).

[66] See Ephraim Meir, *Interreligious Theology: Its Value and Mooring in Modern Jewish Philosophy* (Oldenbourg: De Gruyter, 2015).

[67] This has sometimes been expressed in the title, as was the case with Paul van Burens' *Theology of the Jewish-Christian Reality.*

Reform, or Catholic, all show the mark of highly self-critical examination of both explicit and, though more difficult to detect, implicitly anti-Jewish traditions. Pluralist theologies originated from radical criticism of the traditional assumption of Christian superiority and uniqueness. But unlike theologies within Jewish–Christian dialogue that continued to scrutinize and examine every detail within their traditions, pluralist theologians often underwent a different process. Their emphasis on accepting as equally valid other faith traditions quite logically led to general Christian self-acceptance rather than continued self-critique. These tendencies do not disqualify the respective methodologies. But it is important to continue the discussion about implied understandings of "difference." Christian theologies building on Jewish–Christian dialogue in the seventies and eighties emphasized what Judaism and Christianity have in common. Emphasizing the one God or shared scripture was a constructive step in sorting out anti-Jewish distortions and Christian truths that had gotten intertwined over time. The appropriate reaction to this emphasis on shared texts and traditions was a call for respecting different and distinct interpretations. But this call for difference was presented by sharply contrasting groups: on one hand, by Jewish scholars, who saw the disparity between Jewish and Christian traditions of thought misrepresented, and on the other hand, by Christian theologians who had not welcomed the Christian self-critique as part of renewed Jewish–Christian relations in the first place.

The emphasis on criticizing Christianity in relation to Judaism led to the impression that these theologies were relativist. This was not how they understood themselves – indeed, quite the contrary. Roy Eckardt, the first theologian to systematically rethink Jewish–Christian relations in the twentieth century – his first book *Christianity and the Children of Israel* appeared in 1948 – positioned himself as the true Christian.[68] In the introduction to *Elder and Younger Brothers* from 1967 he explains:

My own views on the Jewish-Christian relationship are sometimes identified as "radical." Beyond the truth that the use of this term, like the use of "conservative," is always relative to a given historical situation and to the perspective of the evaluator, I can only say that I do not think of my position as anything but orthodox Christian. My point of view may be "radical" in contrast to one or another claim that has become entrenched in the churches, but it is "conservative"

---

[68] Roy Eckardt, *Christianity and the Children of Israel* (New York: King's Crown Press, 1948).

from the perspective of the enduring Covenant between the only God and his people, and of the essential solidarity of Israel and the church.[69]

Apparently, pluralist theologians had to overcome a serious problem with the Christian faith tradition, namely, its propensity to self-ascribed absolute truth. Without understating the effort required, this appeared doable![70] In contrast, theologians invested in Jewish–Christian relations seemed to confront a Christian tradition with more failures than feats.

Christologies committed to renewed Jewish–Christian relations appeared reductionist to some critics. But this general prejudice was connected to the prejudgment that Jesus the Jew is somewhat "less Christian" than Jesus "with his Jewishness not mentioned." But it was precisely the Christologies written in the context of renewing Jewish–Christian relations that would try to formulate the specifics of Christian identity. Thus in 1967, shortly after the Second Vatican Council and two decades before Marquardt's and van Buren's Christologies, Roy Eckardt stated that the Christian "knows that were it not for a certain Jewish Man, he would be without hope. That Man is the Christian's risen Lord. Christianity is the religion of the upstart who is granted an odd chance to find out what faith is. That chance comes to him whenever he fills a lowly seat in his hidden Father's house, the only seat proper to a younger brother."[71] Eckardt's language of the "younger brother" was later accepted in mainstream Catholicism. But some Protestants suspected a certain subordination of the Christian faith. Indeed, in theologies committed to repairing Jewish–Christian relations, we often find a language of "secondariness." But these are usually terms expressing an original and ongoing connection, as typically manifested in family metaphors.

Jesus' Jewishness is the most apparent signifier of Christianity's vulnerability. With Jesus the Jew at its heart, the Christian faith cannot succeed in isolation but holds an inbuilt connection to Judaism and Jews. After overcoming the aggression of rejecting this bond, Christians have the chance to experience the blessings of connectedness. Vulnerability is increased by attachment, but so is the vitality of the Christian community.

---

[69] A. Roy Eckardt, *Elder and Younger Brothers* (New York: Schocken Books, 1973), xix f.

[70] Reinhold Bernhardt has successfully and comprehensively undertaken this task. See Reinhold Bernhardt, *Der Absolutheitsanspruch im Christentum. Von der Aufklärung bis zur pluralistischen Religionstheologie*, second edition (Gütersloh: Gütersloher Verlagshaus Mohn, 1993).

[71] Eckardt, *Elder and Younger Brothers*, 162.

I would go as far as to connect the vitality of Christ himself to the Christian attachment to the people of Israel.

In the meantime, Jesus the Jew need not be limited to a certain time or a certain faith-tradition. His Jewishness qualifies him to transcend such limitations. The Jewish Christ seems to be most alive in the "betweens": between one and the Other, between the Torah and the Koran, and any day, often surprisingly, between the communities of interpretation, especially between the lines they write to each other.

Conclusion

The memory of Jesus the Jew has proven helpful to developing a Christian language for contemporary interreligious thought. Jesus the Jew is the key signifier of Christianity's inherently interreligious dimension, highlighting what is nonnegotiable in Christian thought – the God shared with the people of the book and the sharing of their book. Memory demonstrates the horizons of this sharing of thought traditions and narratives. With this twofold decision against Marcion, this interreligious dimension of Christianity became a fact, a challenge, a responsibility, and a chance.

As interpreting communities that share texts, Christianity and Judaism refer to each other, though not in reciprocal manner. Memory as a framework for discussing Jewish–Christian relations also helps protect against the risk of losing sight of a history of violence in interpretation.[1] Distinguishing between polemics as an integral part of interreligious communication, on the one hand, and de-evaluating the other's interpretation and its community, on the other hand, remains crucial. This difference between criticism and defamation is especially important when negative depictions of the other community are regarded as more "authentic" than affirmations, as we still see in interreligious scholarship, such as Pauline studies. Thus, far from simply promoting interreligious harmony, the framework of memory reveals the Jewishness of Jesus to be

---

[1] For a systematic account of patterns of violence in Christian Thought, see Barbara U. Meyer, "Structures of Violence and the Denigration of Law in Christian Thought." *Studies in Christian-Jewish Relations* (SCJR) 13:1 (2018): 1–21.

the most important factor connecting Christianity to Judaism while also exposing the vulnerability and danger of delegitimization caused by such proximity.

The quest for a concept of Christian memory led to a complex and multilayered discovery. Most textual memories Christians refer to are shared with Jews. Interpretations of narratives differ, and the commitments developed toward legal texts often even reflect entirely different readings. Still, in the Christian scriptures, the textual foundations of memories, as well as of their summaries and interpretations, are largely shared. Regarding interpretational traditions, the recent formulation of "the ways that never parted" seems more appropriate than the former "parting of the ways." It is impossible to express the whole history of communication and miscommunication over Bible interpretation in any single phrase. For the Christian side, this history passed through stages of replacement thought, disregard, and, more recently, curiosity. Jews developed an entirely different culture of interpretation and a unique literary genre of discussing Halakhah. Until the late twentieth century, Christians did not refer much to rabbinic literature, apart from in polemic and Christian Hebraist contexts. Remembering that Jesus belonged to Second Temple Judaism – a historical fact that was not unknown to earlier scholars but needed to be recovered from countless layers of academic anti-Judaism – led to an unprecedented interest in the early halakhic discourse that would eventually be codified in the Mishnah two centuries after Jesus. Today most scholars agree that the historical Jesus had participated in some of the early stages of those types of discussions that were later compiled in the Mishnah. This is how the memory of Jesus' Jewishness has led to a new interest in the mishnaic world of reflecting on laws concerning all areas of life, property, family, agriculture, etc. Historical Jesus research underwent nothing short of a complete reversal, from interpreting Jesus in contrast to Second Temple Judaism to understanding him as deeply rooted in that context. Here, memory functioned in a fashion complementary to historical research.

What made sense in Jewish memory, namely a Second Temple Jew being part of Second Temple Judaism, proved to be of higher historical probability than a Second Temple Jew entirely estranged from Second Temple Judaism. In the mid- and later twentieth century, a paradoxical gap still existed between Jewish and Christian historians of the period. Ironically, while Christian New Testament scholars, confronting serious difficulties to affirm Jesus' authentic sayings, expressed a broad skepticism regarding his historicity, Jewish scholars did not see any reason to question the existence of a Jewish man named Jesus in that period of history. He was sometimes "remembered" more strongly and clearly by a community of scholars not named after him and questioned or doubted by scholars defined as his followers. His Jewishness evidently made him familiar and thus historically probable to most Jewish scholars.

Beginning in the 1980s and peaking only in the nineties, Christian scholars increasingly came to share the view of their Jewish academic colleagues. Now Jesus the Jew gained greater presence, color, and shape, emerging as a true human being belonging to a particular tradition at a certain time. But the memory of Jesus the Jew also worked as a reminder of the one God Jesus knew, the God who created the world, took Israel out of Egypt, initiated covenants, and gave the Torah. It was awareness of this God, and the biblically recorded acts of this God, that shaped Jesus' memory, his understanding of the world. Much has been speculated about Jesus' self-understanding, in popular as well as academic Christian (and recently even Jewish) writing. But in line with a concept of text-based memory, Jesus lived in active remembrance of the Exodus, the covenant, and the Torah. As little as we know about the Historical Jesus, we know the textual traditions he referred to in his teaching, his speeches, discussions, meals, and feast days. Describing Jesus' life with such terms as "identity," "culture," and "context" always risks problems of anachronism. Still, one could say that the Pentateuch, the written Torah, helped form the basis of his identity in the sense of a general outlook on life. When this historical finding, the textual-cultural context of Jesus, is taken seriously, one can say that the Torah presents the key memory of Jesus the Jew.

Yet once Jesus is inseparably connected to Torah, historical as well as Christological statements contrasting him to "law" become less plausible. This textual memory of Jesus' Jewishness will then necessarily function critically toward antinomian tendencies in Christian theology. The impact of this corrective can hardly be overstated. On a most basic level, an interconnectedness of Jesus and Torah counteracts Christian anti-Judaism that has often taken on antinomian language. But the horizons of this corrective memory reach much further. If antinomian approaches can be counteracted on a larger interreligious scale, a core element of islamophobia might also be addressed, since Islam is also a nomian faith-tradition. Beyond religions, antinomian attitudes in intellectual culture typically disregard or at least diminish the importance of ethics as reflecting on praxis. In contrast, a re-evaluation of religious law may help us to re-appreciate justice as a core biblical principle – one that is central today mainly for theologies in contexts of oppression.

Remembering Jesus as observant of Torah-commandments also has a distancing effect on Christians. Following Jesus – in German expressed with the term "Nachfolge"[2] – is not simply imitating him (the "imitatio Christi" traditionally meant adopting his way of life as, for instance, poverty, practiced by a monastic minority rather than Christian families and larger communities). By not following in Jesus' footsteps and observing commandments as he did, the dominant Christian practice at least from the fourth century on, Christian identity is established in distinction to the person remembered as the heart and inception of the Christian way of life. What has changed through Historical Jesus research is that this difference has been powerfully reinforced as the memory of Jesus' observance has become supported by solid scholarly testimony. In this sense, the critical memory of Jesus the Jew increases awareness of the distance between Jesus and his followers today.

At the same time, contemporary observant Jews actually share significant aspects of daily, and especially weekly, life with Jesus, such as the weekly rhythm shaped by Shabbat. In this way, the memory of Jesus' Jewishness holds an additional challenge for Christians, namely, seeking affirmation of a different practice from a viewpoint of distance. The understanding that Jews who do not search for or cherish closeness to Jesus have more in common with him than do his followers creates an interesting paradox. New Testament scholars had resolved the problem until the middle of the twentieth century by contrasting Jesus with his environment. As we have noted, Historical Jesus research has undergone nothing less than a complete reversal since then. Since the so-called Third Quest for the Historical Jesus, context has become the core criterion for historical probability. Moreover, in the field of Historical Jesus research, memory has become an important category, and searching for the "earthly," the "real," and the "true" Jesus has been complemented with the "remembered" and the "historic" Jesus. Understanding the Jewishness of Jesus as a critical memory helps to connect historical research with contemporary Christological discourse. Memory as such is a category that reaches out to all temporal modes. Reading the Gospels as witness to the remembered Jesus (as Stegemann and Tilley do) facilitates an approach appropriate to the remembering communities that had collected, composed, and redacted these texts.

---

[2] The title of Bonhoeffer's powerful book; see Dietrich Bonhoeffer, *Nachfolge* (Munich: Kaiser 1937); translated into English as *The Cost of Discipleship*, translated by Reginald H. Fuller (New York: Macmillan, 1959).

The memory of Jesus the Jew presents an additional challenge when remembering is recognized as an activity of the present. When Jewishness is attributed to Jesus Christ in the present, the question of a continuity and connection between Jewishness in the first and the twenty-first century opens anew. Looking at various answers by Jewish scholars who have either tried to formulate an essence of Judaism or otherwise deride any such attempt as an artificial "construct," I have developed a theory of Jewish continuity as a continuous frame of textual reference. Of course, texts were added in Jewish history, and what is understood as Judaism and Jewishness never ceases to change. But the basic biblical texts of the Pentateuch and the Prophets were never given up as primary texts of the Jewish people. The Sages, connecting between Second Temple and today's Judaisms, understood their discussions as interpretations of this written Torah. These texts, the Pentateuch and the Prophets, contained the narratives and laws Jesus knew of and referred to. In this view, Jesus' Jewishness is described mainly through a content of textual meaning. The Historical Jesus lived and acted in the horizon of these stories and their interpretations, in knowledge of biblical laws and their contemporaneous discussions. Jesus then is understood as someone who heard, read, quoted, and interpreted these texts, a Jew who knows the stories and remembers their summaries and translations into commandments, such as the exodus-story and the prohibition on oppressing a stranger as derived from the experience of being foreigners (e.g. Exodus 23,9; Leviticus 19,33). Jesus the Jew is shaped by these texts and is part of the text-transmitting community, however divided it was into different factions with differing priorities.

This understanding of the Jewish as referring to certain textual traditions proved vital to my discussion of African American and Palestinian theologians. My examination of James Cone's black theology showed that the memory of Jewishness reinforces the blackness of Jesus as one who took the side of the oppressed. In Palestinian theologies, similarly, Jesus' Jewishness has become integrated as a commitment to the prophetic tradition and the principle of justice. My surprising finding shows that the memory of Jesus the Jew signifies for both African Americans and Palestinians that Jesus is close and is one of them. Jewishness here becomes the signature of taking sides with the disadvantaged. The memory of Jesus the Jew opens for contemporary Christians a new realm of otherness in the midst of their spirituality. Jesus the Jew connects them strongly to Jews today, and especially to Jewish artists, scholars, and writers expressing their knowledge of and views on Jesus. This connection is not primarily defined by closeness, but rather by curiosity. To Christian communities experiencing othering, discrimination, and dislocation, the memory of his Jewishness shifts Jesus to their side.

While I have questioned James Cone's understanding of "Jewish" and "black" as entirely identified with the side of the oppressed and thus fixing blackness and Jewishness as powerlessness, identifying suffering as Jewish did function as a turning point with regard to the understanding of Jesus' suffering. It was only when post-Shoah theologians identified Jesus' suffering as Jewish suffering that they could begin to critique Christian traditions of embracing agony and distress. As Jewish suffering, Jesus' affliction for today's Christians is the suffering of an Other, and thus, according to Levinas, something not to be interpreted. Levinas declared justifying the Other's suffering as immoral, even as the source of immorality. Taking this apodictic statement seriously would indict all Christian theological explanations of the suffering of Jesus the Jew. The few Christian theologians who have engaged in a sweeping rethinking of Jesus' suffering have not argued their case through Levinas, however. Identifying Jesus' suffering as Jewish and thus as the suffering of an Other is part of my own contribution to this analysis. But as for Levinas, so with Soelle, van Buren, and Metz, it was the disproportionate, immeasurable suffering in the Shoah that made it impossible for them to continue talking about suffering in an accepting tone.

It is precisely this decisive change in tone that they shared in common. These daring Christian thinkers have all expressed a strong need to distance themselves from a language that reconciles God and human suffering. To my knowledge, only Alice Eckardt has gone as far as to reject the attribution of any meaning whatsoever to human suffering. Her key argument is that reconciling oneself to unnecessary suffering diverts our focus away from confronting suffering. Although not made explicit, she clearly speaks about preventable suffering that is intentionally caused by evil people. Preventable suffering, in her view, is mainly produced by evil. And evil cannot be effectively fought as long as suffering is accepted, or even just tolerated.

In principle, many ideas in Christian post-Shoah theology could have been conceptualized prior to the Shoah – and indeed were often articulated by Jewish thinkers – for example, the critique of Christianity as replacing Judaism or of Christian missionary attitudes toward Jews. But a profound change of view regarding suffering was unlikely to have been formulated by Christian theologians independently from the Shoah. The Christian thought-tradition connecting suffering with a special divine presence has been very powerful, and even many scholars view Christianity as a belief system that inherently embraces suffering.[3] It is all the more remarkable that independently from one another, the Lutheran Soelle, the Anglican van Buren, the Catholic Metz, and the Methodist Eckardt each came to the conclusion that the Christian language of suffering needs profound change.

Among these thinkers, Metz alone identified Levinas as an important interlocutor in terms of referring to the Other's suffering. Levinas did not explicitly address Christians in his essay "Useless Suffering," and Christians rarely refer to this extraordinary text when discussing theodicy. We saw that even post-Shoah theologians hesitate to state an end of theodicy. They do not fully join in their Jewish colleagues' expressions of disappointment of God, which I explained with regard to the impossibility of the Christian casting God aside yet still remaining Christian. Still, post-supersessionist Christians who affirm the covenant of the Jewish people as eternally in place need to find ways to express this affirmation in a way that leaves space for such disappointment. Otherwise they risk losing sight of the one God. However Christian theologians formulate their idea of covenant, whether they see themselves as part of it or whether they use a different theological category to describe the specific Christian belonging to God, they are necessarily affected by the communication and lack of communication between the first covenant partner Israel and Israel's God, who is their only professed God too. Jesus the Jew is the strongest reminder of the identity and continuity of this one God. But the God Christians claim as theirs through Jesus Christ becomes lifeless when approval is reiterated without human anger, or at least without a feeling of solidarity with the other covenant partner's disappointment. Paradoxically, this questioning of God can make God come alive. Israel's covenant is acutely alive with its broad spectrum of criticizing and ignoring God, announcing God's irrelevance or simply preferring the Torah over God.[4] Christian theologians who are eager to affirm the unrevoked covenant risk adding even the affirmation of the Other to their list of unshaken Christian positive assessments. Emil Fackenheim did explicitly turn to Christians with his question of whether

---

[3] Leora Batnitzky, "On the Suffering of God's Chosen: Christian Views in Jewish Terms," in Tikva Frymer-Kensky, David Novak, Peter Ochs, David Fox Sandmel, and Michael A. Signer, eds., *Christianity in Jewish Terms* (Boulder, CO: Westview Press, 2000), 203–220, 203.

[4] Emmanuel Levinas, "Loving the Torah more than God," in *Difficult Freedom: Essays on Judaism* (Baltimore: John Hopkins University Press, 1990), 142–145.

Good Friday has overturned Easter Sunday. His question has not been frequently engaged by Christian thinkers, but it deserved to be. An answer defending the Christian message of Easter is less important here, just as an answer to the theodicy question does not hit the mark. Rather, the important thing is, in Metz's terms, to develop a Christian language that is sensitive to suffering instead of one that claims salvation. Christologically, that means making space to express what has not been achieved in Christ instead of simply asserting reconciliation with God as something that has mainly already occurred. The corrective memory of Jesus the Jew can help to formulate the Christ-message more in terms of what needs to be done and less in claims of what has been achieved.

The memory of Jesus the Jew keeps Christianity vulnerable. This vulnerability, without seeking to idealize it, can help Christians stay in touch with the needs of an unredeemed and deeply wounded world. Christianity is not feasible in itself; in fact, Christianity never existed by itself, neither historically nor dogmatically. Since the decision of mainstream churches to define themselves positively and not as the negation of others, the most adequate Christian way to think about beliefs and deeds (ethics and dogmatics) is in conversation with non-Christians who know Jesus in ways Christians do not.

Postscript

Interreligious Christology

"Interreligious Christology" seems like a contradiction in terms. Christology frames a specifically Christian discourse about the questions and tensions between the name "Jesus," the profession "Christ," and the proclaimed "Jesus Christ." One might think that these questions are best discussed by scholars and intellectuals who are also committed to this specific name and naming. Interreligious theory, however, develops in the space between such clearly distinguished ideas and owned concepts.

At a prior stage, interreligious dialogue would sort out the similar and the different. At the beginnings of redefining Jewish–Christian relations in the mid-twentieth century, Christians focused on what they had in common with Judaism – most of all Godself and the first half of Scripture. At that time, Jesus' impact was often described in the paradoxical terms of "uniting and dividing" Christians and Jews. These kinds of formulations echoed a Christian wish for unity as well as Jewish reminders of difference and the preference for distance. From a traditional Christian perspective, the relationship to Jesus marks the original difference between that which is Jewish and that which is Christian. Still, this alignment remains in the domain of transmitted traditional thinking. Intellectually and culturally, differences other than any particular component of belief, such as differences over what is important in life and what is secondary, what should be discussed and what needs to be remembered and how, may be far more fundamental to the disparity between contemporary Jewish and Christian perspectives.

Interreligious thinking describes a discourse beyond the binary categories of "mine" and "yours," beyond the sole alternatives of similarities and differences. As a historically oriented discipline, "Interreligious

Studies" focuses on the dynamics between the religions, on the exchange and reinterpretation of ideas, or on "repercussions," as Harry Austryn Wolfson put it. "Interreligious Theology," on the other hand, describes the activity of reinterpreting, importing, and exporting theological ideas in the present. The case of Christology is a particularly challenging model for this way of theory-building. In the interreligious Christological perspective, Jesus Christ need not be Christian property, enclosed with a set of properties, administrated by the community that owes her name to his profession.

In contrast, Interreligious Christology, as presented here, offers a framework for ongoing discussions about Jesus Christ that include the search for the historical Jesus, as well as new arguments surrounding old Christological debates and the effort to reconnect concepts from the realms of historical research and dogmatic discourse. Modern Christology has been mainly a discipline of Christian scholars – just as the philosophy of Halakhah is typically the domain of Jewish philosophers. In contrast, questions about God, humanity, and ethics generally serve as thematic frameworks for interreligious intellectual engagement. But there are good reasons to open up the Christological discourse to scholars and intellectuals who are not themselves committed to Christ. These reasons become most obvious when looking at historical research and comparative legal literature. Experts on rabbinic literature and early halakhic discourse have contributed tremendously to New Testament studies and Historical Jesus research. Some major shifts, like interest in Second Temple Judaism manifest in the Third Quest, would be unthinkable without this interdisciplinary discussion. While some path-breaking insights regarding Jesus' placement in halakhic discourse were pioneered by Jewish scholars, the academic landscape today shows a diverse mix of opinions and methods that often do not fit into any predictable alignment with a given scholar's religious affiliation. So, for instance, Daniel Boyarin speaks of the "Jewish Christ," while E. P. Sanders denies the claim of Jesus' uniqueness.[1] Of course, non-Christian intellectuals are less inclined to contribute directly to Christological questions of the present. It seems appropriate, then, to leave the classical question "Who is Jesus Christ for us today?" to those immediately implicated by this "us," and there are

[1] Daniel Boyarin, *The Jewish Gospels: The Story of the Jewish Christ* (New York: The New Press, 2012); E. P. Sanders, *The Question of Uniqueness in the Teaching of Jesus* (London: The University of London Press, 1990).

always important new internal disputes about what Jesus was and is, for example, in Black Theology and Womanist Christology.

But just like Christianity as such, Christological thinking has never been an island. The first reflections on the meaning of Jesus Christ having been sent happened within an intertextual setting – not yet an interreligious one, but already one engaged in translating concepts such as *logos* and *nomos* between languages and thought traditions. The rootedness of Jesus in Judaism – in Torah and prophecy, in practices and discussions – provided Christology from the beginning with an inherently interreligious dimension. To speak in Nicaean language: There was no time when Christology was not interreligious. Historically, of course, there was a pre-Christian period of the solely Jewish fellowship of Jesus. But there was never Christianity without Jewish texts, memories, promises, and hopes, as there was never Christianity without the God of Israel (only the idea of such a "non-God-of-Israel Christianity," namely, Marcionism). In that sense, it is not novel to formulate Christological thoughts in an interreligious perspective. What is new methodologically, however, is first of all the appreciation for Jewish interlocutors. This has been the overall approach in post-supersessionist Christology, often described positively as Christology in the context of Jewish–Christian dialogue. This dialogue was mainly seen as a source and resource to combat anti-Judaism and repair a wounded history between Christians and Jews. My approach to interreligious theory builds on this dialogue, especially in its academic and scholarly versions. But I do not limit the time of scholarly interreligious dialogue to the obvious need for refuting supersessionism.

Post-supersessionist Christology is at its best when it is interrupted by outsiders to the Christian tradition, perhaps especially those who may be insiders to halakhic thinking. At this point, many New Testament scholars have mastered the knowledge of Aramaic as well as Hebrew, studied Talmud, and gained basic knowledge of halakhic literature. But they will not replace Jewish scholars and philosophers of Halakhah as interlocutors in Christian theology. The study of the Other's text is important, but even the most profound knowledge of the Other's interpretations will be different from the Other's own voice. Moreover, in solely academic discourse the concrete Other's observations cannot be skipped. Finally, it is to be hoped that the discourse here named Interreligious Christology will also draw in additional circles, including Muslim philosophers and scholars of Abrahamic Thought.

My claim is that an embeddedness in dialogue is inherent to Christological reasoning. Roy Eckardt and Marquardt would have basically agreed with this view. As representatives of the first generation of anti-supersessionist systematic theologians, they needed to defend every new Christological formulation as based on scripture. Van Buren already used the new Christian affirmation of Israel's covenant for his argumentation. All three pioneers of systematic theology revising Jewish–Christian relations saw Christianity as inherently connected and in need of conversation with Jews. Our situation today is substantively different from Marquardt's in 1990, when his Christology first appeared. Back then, in other religions as well as ideologies, he found only antinomian portraits of Jesus – apart from the Jewish voices that were entirely different. The Muslim scholars' document "A Common Word" contributed to changing this binary map profoundly. Dialogically oriented Muslim theologians were now holding up a different mirror of Jesus. The Jesus they remind Christians of is a Jesus intertextually woven into Israel's covenant. This Muslim Jesus says: Hear, Israel, God is One!

REVISITING THE JEWISHNESS OF JESUS

The Jewishness of Jesus is not a dogma, nor the basis of any doctrine. The notion of him being Jewish is not an answer to a theological question, not even to the famous Christological question "Who is Jesus Christ for us today?" In this book, Jesus' Jewishness has served as a prism for looking at central themes reflecting what we today understand as "Jewish" and "Christian." Still, "prism" might be an understatement, as Judaism was never a variable in Jesus' life. The category of "memory" proved helpful to reflecting on the Jewish Jesus in various temporal modes. At first glance, memory seems to be mainly connected to history. But the act of remembering is an act that intensifies the present. Perhaps, then, Phil Cunningham is right and the church should re-enact the feast of circumcision on January 1 to be reminded of Jesus' Jewishness. It is no coincidence that the biblical tradition presents constitutive memories as commanded.

In Jewish tradition, the commandment to remember the exodus is most famously made manifest in the Passover Haggadah and is thus part of the Jewish liturgy that Jews recite annually.[2] The intensity with which the

---

[2] Even many nonobservant Jews worldwide and almost all secular Jews in Israel celebrate the Seder evening, with the Haggadah, the liturgical text framing the evening, being read at least minimally. The Haggadah text emphasizes the commandment to remember the exodus, offers rationales for and interpretations of that memory, as well as general reflection and celebration.

obligation to remember is expressed in the text, including rhetorical questions asking about the importance of telling the story, imply that biblical memory is not at all an easy task. Nostalgia, the longing for an idealized golden age or the glorification of a grand national foundation myth, is certainly commonplace in many cultures. But the biblical story of the exodus is unusual in that it deliberately evokes uneasy memories of humiliation, fear, and danger. Of course, the main message when remembering the exodus at the Seder is one of rescue and freedom. Still, it remains a challenging memory since the accompanying hardships are not eliminated. To remember the Jewishness of Jesus, admittedly, does not recall hardship in the sense of slavery in Egypt. But I still find memory a helpful term for grasping the complexity and the challenge that Jesus' Jewishness presents for Christians in the present. As I pointed out in my discussion of contemporary contextual theologies, there is no immediate empowerment to expect from a savior who is not just "like us" but also different. In continuation of the discussion with contextual Christologies, my point is that confidence in belonging need not be seen as promoted by identification alone. Just as Marquardt found in distance a strong form of relatedness, difference may also prove a strong factor in structuring a committed and devoted connection.

Van Buren drew a direct line between Christological reflection and the "behavior" of the church. "As the Church understands the things concerning Jesus of Nazareth, so it understands God and itself before God, and so it behaves."[3] Taking Jesus' Jewishness seriously as a memory informing dogmatic discourse, it is not Jesus' past that determines the behavior of the church, but how his past is conceived of in the present.

Meaningful memory transcends communities of interpretation but also creates new communities of discourse. Critical memories spark discussions across well-defined academic disciplines and open new channels for creative interference. One may hope that an unfolding inter-religious community will continue to reinterpret and discuss the memory of Jesus the Jew.

---

[3] Van Buren, *Christ in Context*, 23.

Bibliography

Adler, Rachel. *Engendering Judaism: An Inclusive Theology and Ethics*. Boston: Beacon Press, 1999.

Agamben, Giorgio. *Remnants of Auschwitz: The Witness and the Archive*. Brooklyn, NY: Zone Books, 1999.

Altmann, Alexander. *Moses Mendelssohn: A Biographical Study*. London: Litman Library, 1998.

Anderson, Benedict. *Imagined Communities: Reflections on the Origin and Spread of Nationalism*. London: Verso, 1983.

Anderson, Joel. "Translator's Note." In Axel Honneth, *The Struggle for Recognition: The Moral Grammar of Social Conflicts*. Cambridge, MA: MIT, 1996.

Anidjar, Gil. *The Jew, the Arab: A History of the Enemy*. Stanford, CA: Stanford University Press, 2003.

Arendt, Hannah. *The Human Condition*. Chicago: University of Chicago Press, 1958.

The Life of the Mind. New York: Harcourt, Brace, Jovanovitch, 1978.

Responsibility and Judgment. New York: Schocken Books, 2003.

Assmann, Aleida. *Erinnerungsräume: Formen und Wandlungen des kulturellen Gedächtnisses*. Munich: Beck, 1999.

Assmann, Jan. *Das kulturelle Gedächtnis: Schrift, Erinnerung und politische Identität in frühen Hochkulturen*. Second edition. Munich: Beck, 1999.

Ateek, Naim Stifan. *Justice and Only Justice: A Palestinian Theology of Liberation*. Maryknoll, NY: Orbis Books, 1989.

Bantum, Brian. *Redeeming Mulatto/a: Theology of Race and Christian Hybridity*. Waco, TX: Baylor University Press, 2010.

Bar-Asher Siegal, Michal. *Early Christian Monastic Literature and the Babylonian Talmud*. Cambridge: Cambridge University Press, 2013.

Barth, Karl. *Dogmatics in Outline*. New York: Harper & Row, 1959.

Batnitzky, Leora. *How Judaism Became a Religion: An Introduction to Modern Jewish Thought*. Princeton, NJ: Princeton University Press, 2011.

"On the Suffering of God's Chosen: Christian Views in Jewish Terms." In Tikva Frymer-Kensky, David Novak, Peter Ochs, David Fox Sandmel, and Michael A. Signer, eds., *Christianity in Jewish Terms*. Boulder, CO: Westview Press, 2000. 203–220.

Baumgarten, Elisheva. *Practicing Piety in Medieval Ashkenaz: Men, Women, and Everyday Religious Observance*. Philadelphia: University of Pennsylvania Press, 2016.

Bea, Augustin. *Die Kirche und das jüdische Volk*. Freiburg: Herder Verlag, 1966.

Becker, Adam H. and Annette Yoshiko Reed. *The Ways That Never Parted: Jews and Christians in Late Antiquity and the Early Middle Ages*. Minneapolis, MN: Fortress Press, 2007.

Bernhardt, Reinhold. *Der Absolutheitsanspruch im Christentum: Von der Aufklärung bis zur pluralistischen Religionstheologie*. Second edition. Gütersloh: Gütersloher Verlagshaus Mohn, 1993.

Bernhardt, Reinhold and Perry Schmidt-Leukel, eds. *Interreligiöse Theologie. Chancen und Probleme*. Zürich: TVZ, 2013.

Blum, Edward and Paul Harvey. *The Color of Christ: The Son of God and the Sage of Race in America*. Chapel Hill: The University of North Carolina Press, 2014.

Bodenheimer, Alfred. *Haut ab! Die Juden in der Beschneidungsdebatte*. Göttingen: Wallstein Verlag, 2012.

Boff, Leonardo. *Introducing Liberation Theology*. Maryknoll, NY: Orbis Books, 1987.

Bonhoeffer, Dietrich. *The Cost of Discipleship*. Translated by Reginald H. Fuller. New York: Macmillan, 1959.

Ethics. New York: Touchstone, 1995.

Nachfolge. Munich: Kaiser, 1937.

Botticini, Maristella and Zvi Eckstein. *The Chosen Few: How Education Shaped Jewish History, 70–1492*. Princeton, NJ: Princeton University Press, 2012.

Boyarin, Daniel. *Border Lines: The Partition of Judaeo-Christianity*. Philadelphia: University of Pennsylvania Press. 2004.

Dying for God: Martyrdom and the Making of Christianity. Stanford, CA: Stanford University Press, 1999.

The Jewish Gospels: The Story of the Jewish Christ. New York: The New Press, 2012.

A Radical Jew: Paul and the Politics of Identity. Berkeley: University of California Press, 1994.

"Semantic Differences; or, 'Judaism'/'Christianity'." In Adam H. Becker and Annette Yoshiko Reed, eds. *The Ways That Never Parted: Jews and Christians in Late Antiquity and the Early Middle Ages*. Minneapolis, MN: Fortress Press, 2007. 65–85.

"Two Powers in Heaven, or the Making of Heresy." In Hindy Najman and Judith H. Newman, eds., *The Idea of Biblical Interpretation: Essays in Honor of James L. Kugel*. Leiden: Brill, 2004. 331–370.

Boys, Mary C. *Redeeming Our Sacred Story: The Death of Jesus and Relations between Jews and Christians*. Mahwah, NJ: Paulist Press, 2013.

Braiterman, Zachary. *(God)After Auschwitz: Tradition and Change in Post-Holocaust Jewish Thought*. Princeton, NJ: Princeton University Press, 1998.

Brock, Rita Nakashima and Rebecca Ann Parker. *Proverbs of Ashes: Violence, Redemptive Suffering and the Search for What Saves Us.* Boston: Beacon Press, 2001.

Brueggemann, Walter. *Theology of the Old Testament: Testimony, Dispute, Advocacy.* Minneapolis, MN: Fortress, 1997.

Buber, Martin. *Eclipse of God: Studies in the Relation between Religion and Philosophy.* New York: Harper & Row, 1957.

Bultmann, Rudolf. "Christ the End of the Law." In Rudolph Bultmann, ed., *Essays: Philosophical and Theological.* New York: Macmillan, 1955. 36–66.

Jesus. Berlin: Deutsche Bibliotek. 1926.

Charlesworth, James H. and Loren L. Johns. *Hillel and Jesus: Comparisons of Two Major Religious Leaders.* Minneapolis, MN: Fortress Press, 1997.

Cohen, Gerson D. *Sefer Ha-Kabbalah of Abraham ibn Daud.* Philadelphia, PA: JPS, 1967.

Cohen, Shaye J. D. *The Beginnings of Jewishness: Boundaries, Varieties, Uncertainties.* Berkeley: University of California Press, 2001.

"A Common Word between Us and You: The Open Letter." *Sophia: The Journal of Traditional Studies* 14:2 (2008/9): 16–38.

Cone, James. *A Black Theology of Liberation.* Philadelphia, PA: Lippincott, 1970/1990.

God of the Oppressed. Maryknoll, NY: Orbis Books, 1975/1997.

Cook, Michael J. "How Credible Is Jewish Scholarship on Jesus?" In Zev Garber, ed., *The Jewish Jesus: Revelation, Reflection, Reclamation.* West Lafayette, IN: Purdue University Press, 2011. 251–270.

Cunningham, Philip A. "Celebrating Judaism as a 'Sacrament of Every Otherness'." In Kristen Colberg and Robert Krieg, eds., *The Theology of Cardinal Walter Kasper: Speaking Truth in Love.* St. Johns, MN: Liturgical Press, 2014. 223–240.

"A Covenantal Christology." *Studies in Christian-Jewish Relations.* 1 (2005–2006): 41–52.

"Reviving the Catholic Observance of the Feast of the Circumcision of Jesus." In Celia Deutsch, Eugene J. Fisher, and A. James Rudin, eds., *Toward the Future: Essays on Catholic-Jewish Relations in Memory of Rabbi Leon Klenicki.* Mahwah, NY: Paulist Press 2013. 129–46.

Seeking Shalom. The Journey to Right Relationship between Catholics and Jews. Grand Rapids, MI: Erdmans, 2015.

"The Sources Behind 'The Gifts and the Calling of God Are Irrevocable' (Rom 11:29): A Reflection on Theological Questions Pertaining to Catholic-Jewish Relations on the Occasion of the 50th Anniversary of Nostra Aetate." (No. 4), Commission of the Holy See for Religious Relations with the Jews, December 10, 2015. *SCJR* 12:1 (2017): 1–19.

Cunningham, Philip A. and Didier Pollefeyt. "The Triune One, the Incarnate Logos, and Israel's Covenantal Life." In Philip A. Cunningham, Joseph Sievers, Mary C. Boys, Hans Hermann Henrix, Jesper Svartvik, eds., *Christ Jesus and the Jewish People Today: New Explorations of Theological Interrelationships.* Grand Rapids, MI and Cambridge: William B. Eerdmans Publishing Company, 2011. 183–201.

Cunningham, Philip A., Joseph Sievers, Mary C. Boys, Hans Hermann Henrix, and Jesper Svartvik, eds., *Christ Jesus and the Jewish People Today: New Explorations of Theological Interrelationships.* Grand Rapids, MI and Cambridge: William B. Eerdmans, 2011.

Diner, Dan. *Cataclysms: A History of the Twentieth Century from Europe's Edge.* Madison: University of Wisconsin Press, 2007.

Gegenläufige Gedächtnisse. Über Geltung und Wirkung des Holocaust. Göttingen: Vandenhoeck & Ruprecht, 2007.

Dorff, Elliot N. and Laurie Zoloth, eds. *Jews and Genes: The Genetic Future in Contemporary Jewish Thought.* Lincoln: University of Nebraska Press, Jewish Publication Society, 2015.

Dunn, James D. G. *Jesus Remembered.* Grand Rapids, MI: Wm. B. Eerdmans Publishing Co., 2003.

Eckardt, A. Roy. *Christianity and the Children of Israel.* New York: King's Crown Press, 1948.

Elder and Younger Brothers. New York: Schocken Books, 1973.

Reclaiming the Jesus of History: Christology Today. Minneapolis, MN: Fortress Press, 1992.

"The Shoah and the Affirmation of the Resurrection of Jesus: A Revisionist Marginal Note." In *Bearing Witness to the Holocaust 1939–1989.* Lewiston, NY: Edwin Mellen Press, 1991. 313–331.

Eckardt, A. Roy. and Alice L. Eckardt. *Long Night's Journey into Day: Life and Faith after the Holocaust.* Detroit: Wayne State University Press, 1982.

Eckardt, Alice. "Leiden – Herausforderung des Glaubens – Herausforderung Gottes." In Reinhold Boschki and Dagmar Mensink, eds. *Kultur allein ist nicht genug: Das Werk von Elie Wiesel – Herausforderung für Religion und Gesellschaft.* Münster, Lit Verlag, 1998. 245–261.

"Suffering, Theology and the Shoah," Steven L. Jacobs, ed., *Contemporary Christian Religious Responses to the Shoah: Studies in the Shoah.* 6 (1993): 34–57.

Erll, Astrid. "Travelling Memory." In Rick Crownshaw, ed., *Transcultural Memory.* London and New York: Routledge, 2014. 9–23, 14.

Eshkenazi, Tamara Cohn, Gary A. Phillips, and David Jobling, eds. *Levinas and Biblical Studies: Society of Biblical Literature. N. 43.* Atlanta, GA: Society of Biblical Studies, 2003.

Fackenheim, Emil. *To Mend the World: Foundations of Post-Holocaust Jewish Thought.* New York: Schocken, 1989.

Falk, Harvey. *Jesus the Pharisee: A New Look at the Jewishness of Jesus.* Eugene, OR: Wipf & Stock Publishers, 2003.

Felder, Cain Hope, ed. *Stony the Road We Trod: African American Biblical Interpretation.* Minneapolis, MN: Fortress Press, 1991.

Fermaglich, Kirsten Lise. *American Dreams and Nazi Nightmares: Early Holocaust Consciousness and Liberal America, 1957–1965.* Waltham, MA: Brandeis University Press, 2006.

Fisch, Menachem. "Judaism, and the Religious Crisis of Modern Science." In J. M. van der Meer and S. Mandelbrote, eds. *Nature & Scripture in the Abrahamic Religions: 1700–Present.* Leiden: Brill, 2008. 525–567.

Rational Rabbis: Science and Talmudic Culture. Bloomington, IA: Indiana University Press, 1997.

Fishman, Sylvia Barack. *The Way into the Varieties of Jewishness.* Woodstock, VT: Jewish Lights Publishing, 2008.

Flusser, David. *Jesus.* Third edition. Jerusalem: Hebrew University Magnes Press, 2001.

Jewish Sources in Early Christianity. New York: Adama Books, 1987.

Ford, David E. *The Future of Christian Theology.* Malden, MA: Wiley-Blackwell, 2011.

Self and Salvation: Being Transformed. Cambridge: Cambridge University Press, 1999.

Theology: A Very Short Introduction. Second edition. Oxford: Oxford University Press, 2013.

Frederikson, Paula. *From Jesus to Christ: The Origin of the New Testament Images of Jesus.* Second edition. New Haven, CT: Yale University Press, 2000 [1988].

Furstenberg, Yair. "Defilement Penetrating the Body: A New Understanding of Contamination in Mark 7,15." *NTS* 54 (2008): 176–200.

Gager, John G. *Reinventing Paul.* Oxford: Oxford University Press, 2002.

"Scholarship as Moral Vision: David Flusser on Jesus, Paul, and the Birth of Christianity." *Jewish Quarterly Review* 95 (2005): 60–73.

Garber, Zev, ed. *The Jewish Jesus: Revelation, Reflection, Reclamation.* West Lafayette, IN: Purdue University Press, 2011.

Gaston, Lloyd. "Legicide and the Problem of the Christian Old Testament: A Plea for a New Hermeneutic of the Apostolic Writings." *Jewish–Christian Relations.* www.jcrelations.net/Legicide.2192.0.html?id=720&L=3&searchText=Gaston&searchFilter=%2A.

Paul and the Torah. Eugene, OR: Wipf & Stock, 1987.

Goldberg, Harvey E., Steven M. Cohen, and Ezra Kopelowitz, eds. *Dynamic Belonging: Contemporary Jewish Collective Identities.* New York: Berghahn Books, 2011.

Goldstein, David B. *Jacob's Legacy: A Genetic View of Jewish History.* New Haven, CT: Yale University Press, 2008.

Graebe, Uwe. *Kontextuelle palästinensische Theologie: Streitbare und umstrittene Beiträge zum ökumenischen und interreligiösen Gespräch.* Erlangen: Erlanger Verlag für Mission und Ökumene, 1999.

Grant, Jacquelyn. *White Women's Christ and Black Women's Jesus: Feminist Christology and Womanist Response.* Atlanta, GA: Scholars Press, 1989.

Greenberg, Irving. "Cloud of Smoke, Pillar of Fire," in Steven T. Katz, Shlomo Biderman and Gershon Greenberg, eds., *Wrestling with God: Jewish Theological Responses During and After the Holocaust.* Oxford: Oxford University Press, 2007. 497–555.

Guenther, Lisa. *The Gift of the Other: Levinas and the Politics of Reproduction.* Albany: State University of New York Press, 2006.

Guitierrez, Gustavo. *A Theology of Liberation: History, Politics, and Salvation.* Maryknoll, NY: Orbis Books, 1973.

Halivni, David Weiss. *Midrash, Mishnah and Gemara: The Jewish Predilection for Justified Law.* Cambridge, MA: Harvard University Press, 1986.

Harnack, Adolf von. *The Gospel of the Alien God.* Eugene, OR: Wipf and Stock, 2007.

Marcion: Das Evangelium vom unbekannten Gott. Leipzig: Hinrichs, 1921.

Harvey, Warren Zev. "Harry Austryn Wolfson on the Jews' reclamation of Jesus." In Neta Stahl, ed., *Jesus among the Jews: Representation and Thought.* New York: Routledge, 2012. 152–158.

Henrix, Hans Hermann. "The Son of God Became Human as a Jew: Implications of the Jewishness of Jesus for Christology." In Philip A. Cunningham, Joseph Sievers, Mary C. Boys, Hans Hermann Henrix, and Jesper Svartvik, eds., *Christ Jesus and the Jewish People Today: New Explorations of Theological Interrelationships.* Grand Rapids, MI and Cambridge: William B. Eerdmans, 2011): 114–143.

Heschel, Susannah. *The Aryan Jesus: Christian Theologians and the Bible.* Princeton, NJ: Princeton University Press, 2008.

Hesslein, Kayko Driedger. *Dual Citizenship: Two-Natures Christologies and the Jewish Jesus.* Bloomsbury: T&T Clark, 2015.

Hoffman, Matthew. *From Rebel to Rabbi: Reclaiming Jesus and the Making of Modern Jewish Culture.* Stanford, CA: Stanford University Press, 2007.

Homolka, Walter. *Jesus Reclaimed: Jewish Perspectives on the Nazarene.* New York and Oxford: Berghahn, 2015.

Jewish Jesus Research and Its Challenge to Christology Today. Leiden, Boston: Brill, 2016.

Honneth, Axel. *The Struggle for Recognition: The moral Grammar of Social Conflicts.* Translated by Joel Anderson, Cambridge, MA: MIT 1996.

Horsely, Richard A. *Bandits, Prophets, and Messiahs: Popular Movements at the Time of Jesus.* Salem, OR: Trinity Press, 1999.

Jacobs, Andrew S. *Christ Circumcised: A Study in Early Christian History and Difference.* Philadelphia: University of Pennsylvania Press, 2012.

"A Jewish Statement on Christians and Christianity." In Tikva Frymer-Kensky, David Novak, Peter Ochs, David Fox Sandmel, and Michael A. Signer, eds., *Christianity in Jewish Terms.* Boulder, CO: Westview Press, 2000.

Johnson, Elizabeth. *Truly Our Sister: A Theology of Mary in the Communion of Saints.* London: Bloomsbury Publishing, 2003.

Kairos, Palestine. "A Word of Faith, Hope, and Love from the Heart of Palestinian Suffering." In Rifat Odeh Kassis, *Kairos for Palestine.* Ramallah: Badayl/Alternatives, 2011. 177–197.

Kansteiner, Wulf. *In Pursuit of German Memory: History, Television, and Politics after Auschwitz.* Athens, OH: Ohio University Press, 2006.

Karnein, Anja. *A Theory of Unborn Life: From Abortion to Genetic Manipulation.* Oxford: Oxford University Press, 2012.

Karp, Jonathan and Adam Sutcliffe, eds. *Philosemitism in History.* New York: Cambridge University Press, 2011.

Katz, Steven T., Gershon Greenberg, and Shlomo Biderman, eds. *Wrestling with God: Jewish Theological Responses during and after the Holocaust*. Oxford: Oxford University Press, 2007.

Kellenbach, Katharina von. *Anti-Judaism in Religious Feminist Writing*. Atlanta, GA: Scholars Press, 1994.

Kendall, Soulen. *The God of Israel and Christian Theology*. Minneapolis, MN: Augsburg Fortress, 1996.

Kepnes, Steven. *The Future of Jewish Theology*. Malden, MA: Wiley-Blackwell, 2013.

Klausner, Joseph. *From Jesus to Paul*. New York: Macmillan, 1943.

Jesus of Nazareth: His Life, Times and Teaching. Translated by Herbert Danby. New York and London: Allen and Unwin, 1925.

Yeshu Ha-Notzri: Zmano, Hayav, ve-Torato. Jerusalem: Shtib, 1922.

Kristeva, Julia. *Hannah Arendt*. New York: Columbia University Press, 2001.

Hannah Arendt: Life Is a Narrative. Toronto: University of Toronto Press, 2001.

Krupp, Michael. *Jesus und die galiläischen Chassidim*. Tübingen: TVT Medien-verlag, 2014.

LaCocque, Andre. *Jesus, the Central Jew: His Times and His People*. Atlanta, GA: SBL Press, 2015.

Langer, Ruth. *Cursing the Christians? A History of the Birkat HaMinim*. Oxford: Oxford University Press, 2011.

Levi, Primo. *The Drowned and the Saved*. New York: Simon & Schuster, 2017.

If This Is a Man. London: Abacus, 1987.

Levinas, Emmanuel. *Difficult Freedom: Essays on Judaism*. Baltimore: John Hopkins University Press, 1990.

Otherwise than Being or Beyond Essence. Pittsburgh: Duquesne University Press, 1998.

"Useless Suffering." In Robert Bernasconi and David Wood, eds., *The Provocation of Levinas: Rethinking the Other*. London and New York: Routledge, 1988. 156–167.

Levine, Amy-Jill. *The Misunderstood Jew: The Church and the Scandal of the Jewish Jesus*. San Francisco: Harper, 2006.

Short Stories by Jesus: The Enigmatic Parables of a Controversial Rabbi. New York: Harper Collins, 2014.

Levine, Amy-Jill. and Marc Zvi Brettler, eds. *The Jewish Annotated New Testament: New Revised Standard Version Bible Translation*, second edition. Oxford: Oxford University Press, 2017.

Littell, Franklin H. *Historical Atlas of Christianity*. New York and London: Continuum, 2001.

Lohfink, Norbert. *The Covenant Never Revoked: Biblical Reflections on Christian–Jewish Dialogue*. New York: Paulist Press, 1991.

Luther, Martin. *"Dass Jesus Christus ein geborner Jude sei," Kritische Gesamtausgabe*, Bd. 11, *Predigten und Schriften, 1523*, 314–336. Weimar: Weimar Böhlau, 1900.

Magid, Shaul. *Hasidism Incarnate: Hasidism, Christianity and the Construction of Modern Judaism*. Stanford, CA: Stanford University Press, 2014.

Margalit, Avishai. *The Ethics of Memory*. Cambridge, MA and London: Harvard University Press, 2002.

Marquardt, Friedrich-Wilhelm. *Das christliche Bekenntnis zu Jesus, dem Juden. Eine Christologie*. Two volumes. Munich: Kaiser, 1990 and 1991.

Eia, wärn wir da – eine theologische Utopie. Gütersloh: Kaiser, 1997.

Von Elend und Heimsuchung der Theologie. Prolegomena zur Dogmatik. Second revised and expanded edition. Munich: Kaiser, 1988 and 1992.

Was dürfen wir hoffen, wenn wir hoffen dürften? Eine Eschatologie. Gütersloh: Chr. Kaiser/Gutersloh Verlaghaus, 1993, 1994, and 1996.

Meier, John P. *A Marginal Jew: Rethinking the Historical Jesus*. Volume 3. *Companions and Competitors*. New York: Yale University Press, 2001.

Meir, Ephraim. *Interreligious Theology: Its Value and Mooring in Modern Jewish Philosophy*. Oldenbourg: De Gruyter, 2015.

Melnick, Jeffrey. *A Right to Sing the Blues: African Americans, Jews and American Popular Song*. Cambridge, MA: Harvard University Press, 2001.

Mendelsohn, Amitai. *Behold the Man: Jesus in Israeli Art*. Jerusalem: Magnes, 2017.

Mendelssohn, Moses. *Jerusalem, or On Religious Power and Judaism*. Translated by Allan Arkush. Hanover, NH: Brandeis University Press, 1983.

Mendes-Flohr, Paul and Jehuda Reinharz, eds. *The Jew in the Modern World: A Documentary History*, third edition. Oxford: Oxford University Press, 2011.

Metz, Johann Baptist. *Memoria Passionis: Ein provozierendes Gedächtnis in pluralistischer Gesellschaft*, second edition. Herder: Freiburg i.Br., 2006.

Zum Begriff der Neuen Politischen Theologie: 1967–1997. Grünewald Verlag: Mainz, 1997.

Metz, Johann Baptist, Johann Reikerstorfer, and Jürgen Werbick. *Gottesrede*. Münster: LIT, 2001.

Meyer, Barbara U. "Die andere Ethik der Erinnerung und die eigenen Erinnerungen: Kritische Überlegungen zu Avishai Margalit." In Inge Hansen-Schaberg and Ulrike Müller, eds., *Ethik der Erinnerung in der Praxis: Zur Vermittlung von Verfolgungs- und Exilerfahrungen*. Wuppertal: Arco Wissenschaft, 2005. 35–49.

"Applying for Otherness." In R. Burggraeve, J. Hansel, M.-A. Lescourret, J.-F. Rey, and J.-M. Salanskis, eds., *Recherches Levinassiennes, Bibliotheque Philosophique du Louvain* 82. Louvain: Peeters, 2012. 437–449.

Christologie im Schatten der Shoah – im Lichte Israels: Studien zu Paul van Buren und Wilhelm-Friedrich Marquardt. Zurich: Theologischer Verlag Zürich, 2004.

"The Dogmatic Significance of Christ Being Jewish." In Philip A. Cunningham, Joseph Sievers, Mary C. Boys, Hans Hermann Henrix, and Jesper Svartvik, eds., *Christ Jesus and the Jewish People Today: New Explorations of Theological Interrelationships*. Grand Rapids, MI: William B. Eerdmans Publishing Company, 2011. 144–156.

"Memory and Moral: The Challenge to Christianity" (Hebrew). In Yotam Benziman, ed., *Memory Games: Concepts of Time and Memory in Jewish Culture*. Jerusalem: Van Leer Institute and Hakibbutz Hameuchad Publishing House, 2008. 153–162.

"Moses – Their Rabbi or Our Rabbi? Lutheran Hermeneutics re-visited" (Hebrew). In Moshe Hallamish, Hanoch Ben-Pazi, and Hannah Kasher, eds., *Moses the Man – Master of the Prophets*. Ramat Gan: Bar Ilan University Press, 2010. 320–329.

"Sfat ben" ["Son Language"]. In Avital Wohlman and Yossef Schwartz, eds., *The Christian Poet of Zion: In Memory of Marcel-Jaques Dubois (1920–2007)*. Jerusalem: Van Leer Institute and Hakibbutz Hameuchad, 2012. 61–68.

"Structures of Violence and the Denigration of Law in Christian Thought." *Studies in Christian–Jewish Relations* (SCJR) 13:1 (2018): 1–21.

"Theodicy and Its Critique in Christian post-Shoah Thought." In Beate Ego, Ute Gause, Ron Margolin, and Dalit Rom-Shiloni, eds., *Theodicy and Protest*. Tübingen: Evangelische Verlagsanstalt, 2018.

"Wahrhaft historisch, wahrhaft jüdisch – Ein Plädoyer für die fortgesetzte wissenschaftliche Suche nach Jesus in den letzten Tagen geboren aus Miriam." In *Begegnungen. Zeitschrift für Kirche und Judentum* 1 (2015): 32–41.

"Walking the Way of the Star: Paul van Buren." In Yehoyada Amir, Joseph Turner, and Martin Brasser, eds., *Faith, Truth and Reason: New Perspectives on Franz Rosenzweig's "Star of Redemption."* Freiburg i.Br.: Karl Alber, 2012. 409–421.

"Was haben Christen heute mit der Beschneidung zu tun?" *Begegnungen. Zeitschrift für Kirche und Judentum* 1 (2013): 14–21.

"Welches Gesetz ist heilig, gerecht und gut und für wen? Christliche Umkehr zum Gesetz." In Andreas Pangritz, ed., *Biblische Radikalitäten. Judentum, Sozialismus und Recht in der Theologie Friedrich-Wilhelm Marquardts*. Würzburg: Ergon Verlag, 2010. 129–140.

Meyer, Michael A. *Jewish Identity in the Modern World*. Seattle & London: University of Washington Press, 1990.

Response to Modernity: A History of the Reform Movement in Judaism. New York: Oxford University Press, 1988.

Moll, Sebastian. *The Arch-Heretic Marcion*. Tübingen: Mohr Siebeck, 2010.

Moller, Hilde Brekke. *The Vermes Quest: The Significance of Geza Vermes for Jesus Research*. London and New York: Bloomsbury T&T Clark, 2017.

Morgenstern, Matthias. *Dass Jesus Christus ein geborener Jude sei und andere Judenschriften. Bearbeitet und kommentiert von Matthias Morgenstern*. Berlin: Berlin University Press, 2019.

Moyn, Samuel. *Origins of the Other. Emmanuel Levinas between Revelation and Ethics*. Ithaca, NY: Cornell University Press, 2005.

Myers, David N. *Re-Inventing the Jewish Past: European Jewish Intellectuals and the Zionist Return to History*. New York: Oxford University Press, 1995.

Nelson, Eric. *The Hebrew Republic: Jewish Sources and the Transformation of European Political Thought*. Cambridge, MA: Harvard University Press, 2010.

Neusner, Jacob. *A Rabbi Talks with Jesus*. Montreal: McGill Queens University Press, 2000.

Nirenberg, David. *Anti-Judaism: The Western Tradition*. New York: W.W. Norton & Company, 2014.

Novak, David. *Zionism and Judaism: A New Theory*. Cambridge: Cambridge University Press, 2015.

Nussbaum, Martha. *Anger and Forgiveness: Resentment, Generosity, Justice*. New York: Oxford University Press, 2016.

    The Fragility of Goodness: Luck and Ethics in Greek Tragedy and Philosophy. Second, revised edition. Cambridge: Cambridge University Press, 2001.

    Upheavals of Thought: The Intelligence of Emotions. New York: Cambridge University Press, 2001.

Ophir, Adi. *Orders of Evils: Toward an Ontology of Morals*. Cambridge, MA: Zone Books, 2005.

Oppenheimer, Aharon. *The 'Am Ha-Aretz: A Study in the Social History of the Jewish People in the Hellenistic-Roman Period*. Translated by I. H. Levine. Leiden: E.J. Brill, 1977.

Oz, Amos. *Judas*. New York: Houghton Mifflin Harcourt, 2016.

Parkes, James. *Jesus, Paul and the Jews*. London: Student Christian Movement Press, 1936.

Pawlikowski, John T. *Christ in the Light of the Jewish–Christian Dialogue*. New York: Paulist Press, 1982.

    "Historical Memory and Christian–Jewish Relations." In Philip A. Cunningham, Joseph Sievers, Mary Boys, Hans Hermann Henrix, and Jesper Svartvik, ed., *Christ Jesus and the Jewish People Today: New Explorations of Theological Interrelationships*. Grand Rapids, MI: Eerdmans, 2011. 14–26.

    "The Historicizing of the Eschatological." In Alan T. Davies, ed., *Antisemitism and the Foundations of Christianity*. New York: Paulist Press, 1979. 151–166.

Petzel, Paul and Norbert Reck, eds., *Erinnern: Erkundungen zu einer theologischen Basiskategorie*. Darmstadt: Wissenschaftliche Buchgesellschaft, 2003.

Raheb, Mitri. *Faith in the Face of Empire: The Bible through Palestinian Eyes*. Maryknoll, NY: Orbis Books, 2014.

Raphael, Melissa. *The Female Face of God in Auschwitz: A Jewish Feminist Theology of the Holocaust*. London and New York: Routledge, 2003.

Reinhartz, Adele and Wayne O. McCready. *Common Judaism: Explorations in Second-Temple Judaism*. Second revised edition. Minneapolis, MN: Fortress Press, 2011.

Riceour, Paul. "Memory and Forgetting." In *Questioning Ethics: Contemporary Debates in Philosophy*. In Richard Kearney and Mark Dooley, eds., London and New York: Routledge, 1999.

Ritschl, Dietrich. *The Logic of Theology*. Philadelphia: Fortress Press, 1987.

    Memory and Hope. An Inquiry Concerning the Presence of Christ. New York: Macmillan 1967.

    "Praising God as Interpreter and Critic of History." in David S. Cunningham, Ralph Del Colle, and Lucas Lamadrid, eds., *Ecumenical Theology in Worship, Doctrine and Life: Essays Presented to Geoffrey Wainright on his Sixtieth Birthday*. Oxford: Oxford University Press, 1999. 69–77.

Rosen-Zvi, Ishay. "Pauline Traditions and the Rabbis: Three Case Studies." *Harvard Theological Review* 110:2 (2017): 169–194.

Rosman, Moshe. *How Jewish Is Jewish History?* Liverpool: Liverpool University Press, 2008.

Ross, Tamar. *Expanding the Palace of Torah: Orthodoxy and Feminism.* Waltham, MA: Brandeis University Press, 2004.

Rothberg, Michael. *Multidirectional Memory: Remembering the Holocaust in the Age of Decolonization.* Stanford, CA: Stanford University Press, 2009.

Rubenstein, Richard L. *After Auschwitz: History, Theology and Contemporary Judaism.* Baltimore: Johns Hopkins University Press, 1992 [1966].

Ruether, Rosemary Radford. *Faith and Fratricide: The Theological Roots of Anti-Semitism.* Eugene, OR: Wipf and Stock, 1997.

Sacks, Jonathan. *The Dignity of Difference: How to Avoid the Clash of Civilizations.* New York: Continuum, 2002.

Safrai, Shmuel. "Jesus and the Hasidim." *Jerusalem Perspectives* 42–44 (1994): 3–22.

Sanders, E. P. *Comparing Judaism and Christianity: Common Judaism, Paul, and the Inner and the Outer in Ancient Religion.* Minneapolis, MN: Fortress Press, 2016.

Jesus and Judaism. London: SCM Press, 1985.

Jewish Law from Jesus to the Mishnah. Minneapolis, MN: Fortress Press, 2016.

Judaism: Practice and Belief, 63BCE–66CE. Minneapolis, MN: Fortress Press, 2016.

Paul, the Law, and the Jewish People. Philadelphia: Fortress Press, 1983.

The Question of Uniqueness in the Teaching of Jesus. London: The University of London Press, 1990.

Schäfer, Peter. *Jesus in the Talmud.* Princeton, NJ: Princeton University Press, 2007.

The Jewish Jesus: How Judaism and Christianity Shaped Each Other. Princeton, NJ and Oxford: Princeton University Press, 2012.

Schiffman, Lawrence, ed. *Texts and Traditions: A Source Reader for the Study of the Second Temple and Rabbinic Judaism.* Hoboken, NJ: Ktav, 1998.

Schmidt-Leukel, Perry. *Religious Pluralism and Interreligious Theology.* Maryknoll, NY: Orbis Books, 2017.

Schoon, Simon. *Onopgeefbar verbonden.* Kampen: Kok, 1998.

Schorsch, Ismar. *From Text to Context: The Turn to History in Modern Judaism.* Hanover, NH: University Press of New England, 1994.

Schües, Christina. *Philosophie des Geborenseins.* Freiburg: Karl Alber, 2008.

Schwartz, Seth. *Imperialism and Jewish Society: 200 B.C.E.–640 C.E.* Princeton, NJ: Princeton University Press, 2001.

Schwartz, Yossef. "Die Entfremdete Nähe: Rosenzweig's Blick auf Islam." In Franz Rosenzweig, *Innerlich bleibt die Welt eine: Ausgewählte Schriften zum Islam.* Ed. by Yossef Schwartz. Berlin: Philo, 2003. 111–147.

Shavit, Zohar and Yaakov Shavit. "Jewish Culture, What Is It? In Search of Jewish Culture." In Mitchel B. Hart and Tony Michels, eds., *The Cambridge History of Judaism: The Modern Period, 1815–Present.* New York: Cambridge University Press, 2017. 677–698.

Signer. Michael "Searching the Scriptures: Jews, Christians, and the Book." In Tikva Frymer-Kensky, David Novak, Peter Ochs, David Fox Sandmel, and

Michael A. Signer, eds., *Christianity in Jewish Terms*. Boulder, Colorado: Westview Press 2000. 85–98.

Smith, Anthony. *The Ethnic Origins of Nations*. Oxford: Blackwell Publishers, 1986.

Soelle, Dorothee. *Suffering*. Philadelphia: Fortress Press, 1975.

Soloveitchik, Joseph B. *Halakhic Man*. Philadelphia: Jewish Publication Society, 1983 [1944].

Spiegel, Shalom. *The Last Trial: On the Legends and Lore of the Command to Abraham to Offer Isaac as a Sacrifice*. New York: Pantheon, 1967.

Stahl, Neta. *Other and Brother: Jesus in the 20th Century Jewish Literary Landscape*. Oxford: Oxford University Press, 2013.

——— ed., *Jesus among the Jews: Representation and Thought*. New York: Routledge, 2012.

Stegemann, Wolfgang. *Jesus und seine Zeit*. Stuttgart: Kohlhammer, 2010.

Stendahl, Krister. "Die nächste Generation in den jüdisch-christlichen Beziehungen." *Kirche und Israel* 1 (1986): 11–15.

Tanner, Norman, ed. *Decrees of the Ecumenical Councils*. Washington, DC: Georgetown University Press, 2017.

Theissen, Gerd and Annette Merz. *The Historical Jesus: A Comprehensive Guide*. Minneapolis, MN: Fortress Press, 1998.

Tilley, Terrence W. "Remembering the Historic Jesus – A New Research Program?" *Theological Studies* 68 (2007): 3–35.

Tillich, Paul. *Systematic Theology*. Vol.2, *Existence and the Christ*. Chicago: University of Chicago Press, 1957.

——— *Systematic Theology. Three Volumes in One*. Chicago: Chicago University Press, 1967.

Trelstad, Marit, ed. *Cross Examinations: Readings on the Meanings of the Cross Today*. Minneapolis, MN: Augsburg Fortress, 2006.

Tyson, Joseph B. "Anti-Judaism in Marcion and His Opponents." *Studies in Christian-Jewish Relations* (SCJR) 1 (2005–2006): 196–208.

Van Buren, Paul M. *A Theology of the Jewish–Christian Reality*, Part I: *Discerning the Way*, 1980, Part II: *A Christian Theology of the People Israel*, 1983, Part III: *Christ in Context*. San Francisco: Harper & Row, 1988.

Vermes, Geza. *The Changing Faces of Jesus*. New York: Viking Compass, 2000.

——— *Christian Beginnings: From Nazareth to Nicaea*. New Haven, CT: Yale University Press, 2014.

——— *Jesus the Jew: A Historian's Reading of the Gospels*. Minneapolis, MN: Fortress Press, 1973.

Walzer, Michael. *Exodus and Revolution*. New York: Basic Books, 1985.

Weber, Elisabeth. *Jüdisches Denken in Frankreich*. Frankfurt: Suhrkamp, 1994.

Weinrich, Michael. *Karl Barth: Leben – Werk – Wirkung*. Göttingen: Vandenhoeck Ruprecht, 2019.

Wengst, Klaus. *Der wirkliche Jesus? Eine Streitschrift über die historisch wenig ergiebige und theologisch sinnlose Suche nach dem "historischen" Jesus*. Stuttgart: Kohlhammer, 2013.

——— *Mirjams Sohn – Gottes Gesalbter: Mit den vier Evangelisten Jesus entdecken*. Munich: Gütersloh, 2016.

Wimpfheimer, Barry Scott. *The Talmud: A Biography*. Princeton, NJ: Princeton University Press, 2018.

Witherington, Ben. *The Jesus Quest: The Third Search for the Jew of Nazareth*. Second edition. Downers Grove, IL: InterVarity Press, 1997.

Wolf, Miroslav, Ghazi bin Muhammad, and Melissa Yarrington, eds. *A Common Word: Muslims and Christians on Loving God and Neighbor*. Grand Rapids, MI: William B. Eerdmans, 2010.

Wolfson, Harry Austryn. "How the Jews Will Reclaim Jesus." Introduction to Joseph Jacobs, *Jesus as Others Saw Him*. New York: Arno Press, 1973.

The Philosophy of the Kalam. Cambridge, MA: Harvard University Press 1976.

Repercussions of the Kalam in Jewish Philosophy. Forward by Isadore Twersky. Cambridge, MA: Harvard University Press, 1979.

Wright, N. T. *Jesus and the Victory of God*. Minneapolis, MN: Fortress Press, 1997.

Yerushalmi, Yosef Hayim. *Zakhor: Jewish History and Jewish Memory*. New York: Schocken Books, 1989.

Young, Brad H. *Meet the Rabbis: Rabbinic Thought and the Teachings of Jesus*. Peabody, MA: Hendrickson, 2007.

Yuval, Israel Jacob. *Two Nations in Your Womb: Perceptions of Jews and Christians in Late Antiquity and the Middle Ages*. Berkeley: University of California Press, 2006.

Zertal, Idith. *Israel's Holocaust and the Politics of Nationhood*. Cambridge: Cambridge University Press, 2010.

Zur Erneuerung des Verhältnisses von Christen und Juden. Handreichung der Evangelischen Kirche im Rheinland. Düsseldorf: Evangelische Kirche im Rheinland, 1980.

Index

206